Contents

ELF ELECTROMAGNETIC FIELDS AND THE RISK OF CANCER

Report of an Advisory Group on Non-ionising Radiation

CHAIRMAN: SIR RICHARD DOLL

This report from the Advisory Group on Non-ionising Radiation reflects understanding and evaluation of the current scientific evidence as presented and referenced in this document.

Advisory Group on Non-ionising Radiation

CHAIRMAN

Sir Richard Doll
Imperial Cancer Research Fund Cancer Studies Unit, Oxford

MEMBERS

Professor C Blakemore
University of Oxford

Professor E H Grant
Microwave Consultants Limited, London

Professor D G Harnden
Wythenshawe Hospital, Manchester

Professor J M Harrington
Institute of Occupational Health, Birmingham

Professor T W Meade
St Bartholomew's and Royal London School of Medicine

Professor A J Swerdlow
Institute of Cancer Research, London

SECRETARIAT

Dr R D Saunders
National Radiological Protection Board, Chilton

OBSERVERS

Dr H Walker
Department of Health, London

ASSESSORS

Dr A F McKinlay
National Radiological Protection Board, Chilton

Dr C R Muirhead
National Radiological Protection Board, Chilton

Dr J W Stather
National Radiological Protection Board, Chilton

CONSULTANT

Mr S G Allen
National Radiological Protection Board, Chilton

1 Introduction

1 Modern industrial development has resulted in people being increasingly exposed to a complex mix of electric and magnetic fields and radiation that cover a wide frequency range. Major sources of exposure to electromagnetic fields (EMFs) arise from electrical power generation, transmission and use in residential and occupational situations, and from telecommunications and broadcasting. In addition, electronic devices for communications, security and process control have proliferated in industrial plants, in offices, homes, cars and in the environment.

2 The National Radiological Protection Board (NRPB) has a statutory responsibility for advising UK government departments on standards of protection for exposure to non-ionising radiation. This covers static and low frequency electric and magnetic fields and radiofrequency radiations (including microwaves), as well as optical radiation (including ultraviolet radiation). The electromagnetic spectrum is shown in Figure 1.1 and the frequency ranges for different sources are summarised in Table 1.1.

3 To provide support for the development of the NRPB advice on non-ionising radiation, the Director set up, in 1990, an Advisory Group on Non-ionising Radiation. The terms of reference of the Advisory Group are:

> **'to review work on the biological effects of non-ionising radiation relevant to human health and to advise on research priorities'**

4 The Advisory Group was reconstituted in 1999 as an independent body and now reports directly to the Board of NRPB. The Advisory Group has to date issued five reports (NRPB, 1992, 1993, 1994a,b, 1995). The first report, on 'Electromagnetic Fields and the Risk of Cancer', was published in March 1992 (NRPB, 1992).

5 That report comprehensively reviewed experimental and epidemiological studies concerned with the effects of exposure to static and time-varying electromagnetic fields. Information was also given on typical levels of exposure in residential environments and in the workplace. The experimental evidence reviewed strongly suggested that these fields do not harm genetic material and so would not normally be expected to initiate cancer. There was, however, a possibility that they might act as tumour promoters; that is, they might increase the growth of potentially malignant cells. The results of experimental studies, when taken together were, however, inconclusive. It could not be concluded that any effect of electromagnetic fields on cells and tissues could be regarded as potentially carcinogenic in humans.

6 The epidemiological studies that were examined related to both residential and occupational exposure. Although some studies had suggested that the incidence of leukaemia may be influenced by magnetic fields, a review of the totality of the evidence indicated that the excess reported could have resulted from selective publication and the inappropriate choice of controls. The only epidemiological finding that was at all notable was the consistency with which the least weak evidence pointed to a possible association between electromagnetic fields and an increased risk of tumours of the brain. This had been reported both in some residential studies in children and in some

occupational studies. As brain tumours in childhood and adult life are different in origin, arising from different types of cell, this evidence was considered to be less impressive than might appear. In the case of residential studies of childhood tumours there were problems with study designs; the positive results may have been artefacts of the method of enquiry. In the case of brain cancer observed in studies of workers involved in electrical occupations, it was impossible to decide whether the risk, if one existed, was due to exposure to electromagnetic fields or to some chemical associated with the work.

7 In the absence of any unambiguous experimental evidence to suggest that exposure to these electromagnetic fields was likely to be carcinogenic, the Advisory Group concluded that the findings of the epidemiological studies that had been reviewed could be regarded only as sufficient to justify formulating hypotheses for testing by further investigation. They provided 'no firm evidence of a carcinogenic hazard' to either children or adults from exposure to normal levels of power frequency electromagnetic fields.

8 The Advisory Group also made a number of recommendations for further work. It stressed that experimental studies would have a significant role to play in resolving uncertainties on the possible association between electromagnetic fields and carcinogenesis. It also supported the need for further epidemiological studies. With regard to occupational exposures it was considered that the immediate need was for improved characterisation of exposures in the workplace and an assessment of the numbers of workers likely to be exposed to different levels and to different extents. The Advisory Group also concluded there was a strong case for carrying out a large-scale epidemiological study of cancer in children, partly because assessments of lifetime exposure can be more readily made in children than in adults.

9 Following publication of the first report of the Advisory Group, several more epidemiological studies were reported relating to residential and occupational exposure to power frequency electromagnetic fields. The Group issued supplementary reports in May 1993 and April 1994 giving its views on these additional studies and on the results of more recent experimental investigations (NRPB, 1993, 1994).

10 With regard to the occupational studies, the Advisory Group concluded (NRPB, 1994) that four occupational studies strengthened the evidence for believing that some groups of workers, where exposure to electromagnetic fields may have been particularly elevated, have an increased risk of leukaemia, but not brain cancer. The results of the studies were, however, neither consistent in the type of leukaemia found to be increased nor consistent in finding a progressive increase in risk with increasing exposure.

11 Three residential studies of childhood cancer conducted in Scandinavia were also reviewed. It was concluded that these more recent studies were well controlled and substantially more informative than those that had previously reported associations with childhood cancer. The studies did not, however, establish that exposure to electromagnetic fields is a cause of cancer but, taken together, suggested that the possibility exists in the case of childhood leukaemia. The number of affected children in the three studies was, however, very small.

12 Experimental studies were also considered by the Advisory Group, but these had so far failed to establish any biological mechanism whereby carcinogenic processes can be influenced by exposure to the low levels of electromagnetic fields to which the majority of the population are exposed.

13 The Advisory Group concluded that 'there is no persuasive biological evidence that ELF electromagnetic fields can influence any of the accepted stages in carcinogenesis. There is no clear basis from which to derive a meaningful assessment of risk nor is there any indication of how any putative risk might vary with exposure' (NRPB, 1994).

14 It is now nine years since the Advisory Group published its first report (NRPB, 1992). Since then much of the experimental work that was being carried out at the time has been completed. A number of substantial occupational and residential epidemiological studies have been published, some of which have taken advantage of improved methods of exposure assessment and of experimental design. In addition, a number of reviews on health effects related to exposure to electromagnetic fields have been issued (ORAU, 1992; NRC, 1997; NIEHS, 1998). The Advisory Group has, therefore, thought it timely to undertake a further comprehensive review of the experimental and epidemiological studies that have been carried out since its first report.

15 This present report is concerned specifically with the possible risk of cancer resulting from exposure to power frequency (extremely low frequency, ELF) electromagnetic fields (50 Hz in the UK). It is not concerned with exposures to high frequencies. A number of studies have suggested associations with disease, such as Alzheimer's disease and neurological disorders. These observations are considered to provide hypotheses that need to be examined by further testing and cannot be evaluated on their own.

16 There is an increasing interest in possible health effects of exposure to high frequency radiations arising from mobile phones and their base stations. The Advisory Group is also keeping under review relevant experimental and epidemiological studies related to exposure to radiofrequencies and will report on them in due course. The Advisory Group notes the publication by the Independent Expert Group on Mobile Phones (IEGMP, 2000) of the report on mobile phones and health.

17 One limitation of the epidemiological studies published prior to the 1992 report was the weakness of the information available on personal exposure. In residential studies, 'wire codes' were commonly used as a surrogate for individual exposure, despite the limitations in the a[illegible]h and the possibility of confounding. In the last nine years considerable advances have been made that now permit substantial improvements in measurements of exposure at work and at home. Chapter 2 reviews methods that have been used for exposure assessment in epidemiological studies and comments on their strengths and weaknesses. It also gives representative information on exposures from various sources, including high voltage transmission and distribution lines, and cables and industrial equipment.

18 Cellular studies have played a vitally important part in the early identification of chemicals and other agents to which humans may be exposed and which have the potential to play a part in the causation of cancer. Chapter 3 of this report reviews the experimental evidence from recent molecular and cellular studies for the ability of ELF electromagnetic fields to act in either an initiating or a promoting capacity. Particular consideration is given to evidence concerning transforming ability, genotoxicity, mutation and DNA damage as indicators of initiation, and tests of promoting activity which include enhanced cellular proliferation, perturbation of the cell cycle, interference in intracellular signalling effects on gene expression and abnormalities in apoptosis (programmed cell death).

19 The evidence from a large number of animal studies of the possible effects of exposure to ELF electromagnetic fields on carcinogenic processes that have been published since the 1992 report is reviewed in Chapter 4. In particular, a number of medium- and long-term studies are considered that have looked for evidence of an effect on tumour incidence in animals exposed only to electromagnetic fields or following the application of known carcinogens and tumour promoters. The major tumour types examined include leukaemias, lymphomas and chemically induced skin and mammary tumours. In addition, the evidence for possible inhibitory effects of power frequency electromagnetic fields on circulating levels of serum melatonin, implicated in the development of mammary and perhaps other tumours, is discussed. Finally, a possible role for electromagnetic field exposure effects on tumour development via compromised immune system function is explored.

20 Many of the exposure assessment techniques considered in Chapter 2 have been applied in recent epidemiological studies on occupational and residential exposure to electric and magnetic fields. Residential studies published since the 1992 report are reviewed in Chapter 5. In particular, it describes four studies published in Scandinavia and case-control studies of childhood cancer carried out in the UK, in North America and in Canada. In the UK, the Childhood Cancer Study has examined a number of possible causes of childhood cancer, including exposure to ionising radiation, potentially hazardous chemicals, infections and electric and magnetic fields. The magnetic field study was carried out in two phases, the second of which included a 48 hour measurement in homes (UKCCS, 1999). In addition, a further study has examined the incidence of childhood cancer as a function of distance from the electrical supply distribution network (UKCCS, 2000). The National Cancer Institute and the Children's Cancer Group studied children diagnosed with acute lymphoblastic leukaemia in 11 states in the USA (Linet *et al*, 1997). The major focus was on exposure to electromagnetic fields, through 24 hour measurements in current and past homes, although wire codes were also assessed for comparison with past studies. Information has also been collected on levels of radon, background radiation and the use of pesticides. A Canadian case–control study of childhood leukaemia considered children diagnosed with the disease between 1990 and 1995 (McBride *et al*, 1999). Exposure assessment included 48 hour personal electromagnetic field measurements, wire coding (proximity to power supply cables) and magnetic field measurements for subjects' residences from conception to the case's diagnosis (or the control's reference date). These residential studies have recently been subject to pooled analyses by Ahlbom *et al* (2000) and Greenland *et al* (2000).

21 Chapter 6 reviews recent epidemiological studies concerned with occupational exposure to electromagnetic fields. Since 1992, there has been a progressive shift from national or regional studies of individuals involved in electrical or electronic trades towards cohort studies of industrial groups in the electricity supply industry, as well as in some industries that are significant users of electricity. Features of recent studies have been attempts to concentrate on large population bases, improvements in the characterisation of exposures in the workplace by the use of personal dosemeters, and efforts to make retrospective exposure assessments.

22 The principal conclusions of the Advisory Group are given in Chapter 7 and recommendations for research in Chapter 8.

REFERENCES

Ahlbom A, Day N, Feychting M, *et al* (2000). A pooled analysis of magnetic fields and childhood leukaemia. *Br J Cancer*, **83**(5), 692–8.

Greenland S, Sheppard A R, Kaune W T, *et al* (2000). A pooled analysis of magnetic fields, wire codes, and childhood leukemia. *Epidemiology*, **11**, 624–34.

IEGMP (2000). Mobile phones and health. Report of the Independent Expert Group on Mobile Phones (Chairman: Sir William Stewart). Chilton, NRPB.

Linet M S, Hatch E E, Kleinerman R A, *et al* (1997). Residential exposure to magnetic fields and acute lymphoblastic leukaemia in children. *New Engl J Med*, **337**, 1–7.

McBride M L, Gallagher R P, Thériault G, *et al* (1999). Power-frequency electric and magnetic fields and the risk of childhood leukaemia in Canada. *Am J Epidemiol*, **149**, 831–42.

NIEHS (1998). Health effects from exposure to power-line frequency electric and magnetic fields. Research Triangle Park, NC, National Institute of Environmental Health Sciences, NIH Publication No. 98-3981.

NRC (1997). Possible health effects of exposure to residential electric and magnetic fields. Washington DC, National Research Council, National Academy Press.

NRPB (1992). Electromagnetic fields and the risk of cancer. Report of an Advisory Group on Non-ionising Radiation. *Doc NRPB*, **3**(1), 1–138.

NRPB (1993). Electromagnetic fields and the risk of cancer. Supplementary report by the Advisory Group on Non-ionising Radiation (May 1993). *Doc NRPB*, **4**(5), 65–9.

NRPB (1994a). Electromagnetic fields and the risk of cancer. Supplementary report by the Advisory Group on Non-ionising Radiation (12 April 1994). *Doc NRPB*, **5**(2), 77–81.

NRPB (1994b). Health effects related to the use of visual display units. Report of an Advisory Group on Non-ionising Radiation. *Doc NRPB*, **5**(2), 1–75.

NRPB (1995). Health effects from ultraviolet radiation. Report of an Advisory Group on Non-ionising Radiation. *Doc NRPB*, **6**(2), 7–190.

ORAU (1992). Health effects of low frequency electric and magnetic fields. Oak Ridge Associated Universities, ORAU 92/F8.

UKCCS (1999). Exposure to power-frequency magnetic fields and the risk of childhood cancer. *Lancet*, **354**, 1925–31.

UKCCS (2000). Childhood cancer and residential proximity to power lines. *Br J Cancer*, **83**, 1573–80.

2 ELF Electric and Magnetic Fields: Sources and Measurements

INTRODUCTION

1 People are exposed to electric and magnetic fields (EMFs) arising from a wide variety of sources which use electrical energy at various frequencies (Allen and Harlen, 1983; Allen *et al*, 1994; Repacholi, 1983).

2 Whilst the term radiation is appropriate at high frequencies, it is preferable to think in terms of the individual electric and magnetic field components at frequencies where there is only a slow variation with time such as 50/60 Hz used for power generation and distribution. The wavelength at 50 Hz is 6000 km – consequently people are exposed to fields from sources at distances very much less than a wavelength where the electric and magnetic field components are dissociated.

3 Electric fields are associated with voltage and the electric field strength has the unit volt per metre ($V m^{-1}$); electric fields do not require current to flow. Magnetic fields are associated with current flow and magnetic field strength has the unit ampere per metre ($A m^{-1}$). Magnetic fields can be described also by the use of the quantity magnetic flux density. The latter depends on the permeability of the medium in which the measurement takes place and has the unit tesla (T).

4 Man-made sources dominate exposure to time-varying fields and radiation. Over that part of the frequency spectrum used for electrical power, man-made fields are many thousands of times greater than natural fields arising from either the Sun or the Earth.

5 Naturally occurring time-varying magnetic fields are associated with changes in ionospheric currents which are most affected by the Sun's activity. Magnetic flux densities of 0.5 μT at frequencies of a few hertz can be generated at times of intense solar activity, but normal daily variations from pulses of less than 0.1 Hz are about 0.03 μT. This may be compared to the Earth's static magnetic flux density which is in the range 30–70 μT and around 50 μT in the UK. Lightning strikes can generate a wide range of frequencies up to the megahertz region, the peak intensity occurring at frequencies of a few kilohertz but under normal circumstances the magnetic flux density decreases from 10^{-5} μT at several hertz to 10^{-8} μT at a few kilohertz. Atmospheric time-varying electric fields up to 1 kHz are less than 0.5 $V m^{-1}$ and decrease with increasing frequency.

6 In practice, the waveform may be a simple sinusoid, such as found in 50 Hz power generation and transmission, or may be complex as, for example, when a circuit is heavily loaded in various industrial processes. In these circumstances the complex waveform indicates the presence of significant harmonics of the fundamental frequency. In addition to the manner in which such fields of mixed frequency interact with people, interpretation of measurement results using instruments which may be frequency dependent needs to be considered.

EXPOSURE ASSESSMENT

Field measurements and dosimetry

7 Many of the effects of exposure can be related to the response to electric fields and currents induced in tissues. Dosimetric concepts have been developed which provide a basis for linking external electric and magnetic fields to the electric field strength, induced current density and the energy absorption rate in tissues (Bernhardt, 1988; Dimbylow, 1987, 1988). The physical quantities and units used to evaluate the interaction between electric and magnetic fields and people are shown in Table 2.1 and commonly used multiples and submultiples in Table 2.2.

8 The magnetic flux density, B, and the magnetic field strength, H, are related by the magnetic permeability of the medium, μ, such that

$$B = \mu H$$

9 For air and most biological materials, the permeability can be taken to be that of free space and

$$1\ \mu\text{T} = 0.8\ \text{A m}^{-1}$$

TABLE 2.1
Quantities and units

Quantity	Symbol	Unit	Symbol
Current density	J	ampere per square metre	A m^{-2}
Conductivity	σ	siemens per metre	S m^{-1}
Electric field strength	E	volt per metre	V m^{-1}
Frequency	F	hertz	Hz
Magnetic field strength	H	ampere per metre	A m^{-1}
Magnetic flux density	B	tesla	T
Permeability	μ	henry per metre	H m^{-1}
Permittivity	ε	farad per metre	F m^{-1}

TABLE 2.2
Commonly used unit multiples and submultiples and their equivalence

Quantity and units	Equivalent multiples and submultiples
Electric field strength	
Volt per metre (V m^{-1})	
Kilovolt per metre (kV m^{-1})	$1\ \text{kV m}^{-1} = 10^3\ \text{V m}^{-1}$
Magnetic flux density	
Tesla (T)	
Millitesla (mT)	$1\ \text{T} = 10^3\ \text{mT} = 10^6\ \mu\text{T} = 10^9\ \text{nT}$
Microtesla (μT)	$1\ \text{mT} = 10^3\ \mu\text{T} = 10^6\ \text{nT}$
Nanotesla (nT)	$1\ \mu\text{T} = 10^3\ \text{nT}$
Magnetic field strength	
Ampere per metre (A m^{-1})	$1\ \text{A m}^{-1} = 10^3\ \text{mA m}^{-1} = 10^6\ \mu\text{A m}^{-1}$
Milliampere per metre (mA m^{-1})	$1\ \text{mA m}^{-1} = 10^3\ \mu\text{A m}^{-1}$
Microampere per metre ($\mu\text{A m}^{-1}$)	
Current density	
Ampere per square metre (A m^{-2})	$1\ \text{A m}^{-2} = 10^3\ \text{mA m}^{-2}$
Milliampere per square metre (mA m^{-2})	$1\ \text{mA m}^{-2} = 10^3\ \mu\text{A m}^{-2}$
Microampere per square metre ($\mu\text{A m}^{-2}$)	

10 An older unit frequently seen in the literature is the gauss, G.

$$10^4\,\mathrm{G} = 1\,\mathrm{T}$$

and

$$10\,\mathrm{mG} = 1\,\mu\mathrm{T}$$

Induced current densities from electric fields

11 At the frequencies used for power distribution, electric field strengths inside tissue are about a million times smaller than the external field strength. At 50 Hz, for every kilovolt per metre of external field strength vertically aligned with a standing person, a current is induced in the body which is proportional to the surface area of the body and for an average adult the short-circuit current is about 14 μA. Current densities, which depend upon the conductivity of the body tissues, range from about 80 $\mu\mathrm{A\,m^{-2}}$ to 1.7 $\mathrm{mA\,m^{-2}}$ in the head and trunk when averaged over 1 $\mathrm{cm^2}$. For central nervous system tissues the maximum current density is about 210 $\mu\mathrm{A\,m^{-2}}$ (Dimbylow, 2000).

Induced current densities from magnetic fields

12 Magnetic fields induce circulating current loops in the body, the current density depending upon the radius of the loop and the conductivity of the tissues. For example, at a frequency of 50 Hz, a 1 μT uniform horizontal magnetic field incident on tissue of conductivity 0.2 $\mathrm{S\,m^{-1}}$ will induce a current density of 6.3 $\mu\mathrm{A\,m^{-2}}$ in the surface tissues of a 20 cm radius object.

13 The internal quantities such as electric field strength and current density are not easily measurable. The consequence is that exposure assessments are generally carried out with reference to external field quantities and whilst protection guidelines are founded on fundamental restrictions on current and current density, they are supported by a framework of external field strength values.

14 Exposure assessment may be achieved by calculation, the use of some form of surrogate for exposure, reference to similar exposure, or measurement.

15 Calculation usually involves simplifying assumptions that may not always accurately reflect the reality of exposure although relatively realistic models of people have been developed to examine the way in which ELF magnetic fields couple to the body. Specific exposure situations have been analysed using a finite element mesh comprising tetrahedral segments modelled to represent a 1.8 m tall male (Baraton and Hutzler, 1996). Three examples that have been modelled include a standing man, a person engaged in live line working and a person using a hair dryer. In a uniform magnetic field of 1.25 μT, peak current densities of about 10 $\mu\mathrm{A\,m^{-2}}$ have been computed for the standing man. For a man carrying out live line working astride a conductor, a 1 A current can induce a peak current density of about 7 $\mu\mathrm{A\,m^{-2}}$. A hair dryer that creates a magnetic flux density of 23.5 μT close to the skin of the head induces current densities of about 130 $\mu\mathrm{A\,m^{-2}}$ in the outer part of the brain.

16 More detailed models of a standing man formed from magnetic resonance images of the body have been successfully used to predict current densities in 2 mm cube cells of the body using the finite-difference time-domain computational method. At 50 Hz a uniform magnetic flux density of 1 μT directed from front to back of the body has been calculated to induce a maximum current density of 3.6 $\mu\mathrm{A\,m^{-2}}$ in central nervous system tissues when averaged over 1 $\mathrm{cm^2}$ (Dimbylow, 1998).

17 In many situations the definitive way of evaluating exposure with respect to guidelines is to use appropriate instrumentation to carry out measurements. In some

circumstances it is possible to measure directly the magnitude of induced currents which flow to ground. Generally, however, the most practical approach is to measure the external electric or magnetic field strengths.

Instrumentation and methods

Electric fields

18 Measuring the induced current flowing between two electrically insulated halves of a metallic shell, which is generally spherical or rectangular in shape, is the most common method of electric field strength measurement. Amplifiers mounted within the probe body provide a self-contained instrument with either in-built metering or remote metering using fibre-optic coupled readout stations to minimise field perturbation. It is normally the root mean square (RMS) value of the electric field strength that is recorded when the separated halves of the probe are aligned with the electric field component. Calibration of such instruments can be achieved using parallel plate systems to set up a uniform field to an accuracy of about 1%, although the perturbation caused by inserting the instrument in the field should be taken into account. In practice, it is unlikely that measurement uncertainty will be better than 10% given the perturbation arising from people and objects in the field. People close to the instruments can materially affect the local field distribution and, as a consequence, the instrument reading, the magnitude depending upon the local field conditions. The proximity effect of the person carrying out measurements is likely to be less than 5% for distances greater than 1.5 m from the instrument. Electric field sensors suitable for carrying out environmental measurements have been designed to utilise existing data logging devices to provide a record over extended periods by sampling every few seconds. Such equipment has been utilised in the UK Childhood Cancer Study (UKCCS, 1999). Sensors have been developed to simultaneously record orthogonal components of electric field strength over a 10 cm cube.

Magnetic fields

19 Magnetic field strength measurements are made using coils, which are designed to shield against the effect of any electric field component. The rate of change of magnetic flux through the area intercepted by the coil produces an induced electromotive force from which the magnetic flux density can be ascertained by using an appropriate voltmeter. Instruments have been designed with orthogonal loops to provide independence of field orientation and, in contrast to electric field strength measurements, field perturbation causes minimal problems for measurements in practice. Accurate calibration of magnetic field strength instruments can be achieved by using Helmholtz coils which can be designed to provide a uniform magnetic field over the volume occupied by the measuring instrument.

Personal dosemeters

Magnetic fields

20 In recent years there has been considerable effort placed in the development of ELF magnetic field personal dosemeters which are suited to epidemiological studies of both adults and children. The devices are designed to log the magnetic field exposure of the wearer and one instrument has incorporated a facility for responding to electric fields. Instruments are available which can measure orthogonal magnetic field

components including harmonics up to 800 Hz and the electric field strength at the surface of the body. The fields can be sampled at intervals from about one second and the information can be logged continuously over several days dependent upon the sampling rate. Measurements can be made in either the broadband (fundamental plus harmonic) or harmonic mode which filters out the fundamental frequency component. Subtraction of the harmonic from broadband components can be used to obtain the fundamental but with some loss of precision where there are rapid changes in exposure levels over the necessary sampling period. When downloaded on to a personal computer the data can be analysed using comprehensive statistical software packages.

21 Instruments developed for evaluating exposures in homes and general work environments may be limited in specific occupational circumstances where industrial processes or equipment may give rise to relatively high level, complex fields with high harmonic content. In such circumstances it is necessary to utilise dosemeters which are of sufficient dynamic range and frequency response to record meaningfully the exposure of people working in those environments. Analysis of the effects of complex fields on the function of personal dosemeters is a prerequisite to accurate exposure assessment (Chadwick, 1997).

22 A variety of instruments are used to evaluate exposure. In some cases, short-term (spot) measurement instruments are used to characterise environmental levels from which exposure can be inferred using occupancy factors. Some personal dosemeters record only the time-weighted average, others assign exposures within specified amplitude ranges, whilst the more sophisticated instruments permit a detailed time-dependent breakdown of exposure.

23 Such instruments have been used in epidemiological studies to evaluate the exposure of the wearer over time or to carry out spot measurements that serve as surrogates of exposure. For example, the use of spot measurements of duration ranging from 3 minutes to 48 hours has provided the measurement contribution to the exposure assessment framework for the UKCCS (1999). An intercomparison of personal exposure measurements on more than 100 children, with a spot measurement protocol including adjustment for annual power line load at home and at school, has provided the basis for validation. Diurnal and seasonal effects can be evaluated by suitable planning of repeat one-week exposure assessment periods over the year.

24 Interest in a number of parameters that have been postulated to have significance with regard to possible interaction mechanisms has led to the development of specific research instruments. Parameters such as field strength, intermittency, harmonic content, induced current, polarisation and the relative orientation of the alternating field (AC) to the Earth's static (DC) magnetic field have been measured.

Electric fields

25 Some measurements have been made of personal exposure to electric fields of workers in the electricity industry. The use of such instruments and interpretation of the measurements requires care in that the measurement is of the perturbed field and is therefore dependent on the individual wearing the dosemeter and the location and design of the instrument. Calibration of such equipment and the response in different environments is therefore more problematical than dosemeters used for magnetic field exposure.

EXPOSURE TO ELF FIELDS

26 People are exposed to fields arising from the transmission, distribution and use of electricity at 50 Hz in the UK and Western Europe. The ubiquitous nature of power frequency electric and magnetic fields is one of the reasons why it is important to consider exposures both at work and at home. From an epidemiological standpoint, various groups may be the focus of particular interest because of their proximity to specific sources of exposure such as local power lines and substations or because of their use of electrical appliances. These sources are not necessarily the dominant contributors to their time-weighted average exposure if the latter is indeed the parameter of interest for such studies. Various other metrics that reflect aspects of the intermittent and transient characteristics of the fields have been proposed.

Residential exposure

Background exposure

27 Away from overhead lines, fields in homes arise from currents flowing in the distribution circuits, conducting pipework and the ground, and from the use of appliances (Swanson and Renew, 1994).

28 Under conditions where the load current drawn by a particular house exactly matches the current returning via the neutral conductor, there is cancellation of the magnetic fields generated, particularly where the conductors are close together. In practice, this rarely occurs due to return currents deviating from the associated neutral cable. This can arise from currents returning via interconnected neutral cables or due to protective multiple earthing which requires bonding the neutral to various service pipes such as gas and water. This diversion of current from the neutral associated with a particular phase cable, results in unbalanced currents – hence a net current which gives rise to a residual magnetic field. It is these fields that form the general background level in UK homes.

29 In the UK remote from power lines, the background levels in most homes range from about 0.01 to 0.2 μT and very few exceed 0.3 μT. From a review of 27 residential studies (Swanson and Kaune, 1999) that included 14 in North America and 5 from the UK, a comparison of average magnetic flux densities away from appliances indicated that the higher levels in the USA resulted in a USA/UK ratio that ranged from 1.5 to 1.9. This can be explained in terms of the different operating characteristics and wiring practices used in the two countries. The geometric mean background field for the UK was estimated to be in the range 36–39 nT.

Fields from appliances

30 The highest magnetic flux densities to which most people are exposed arise close to domestic appliances that incorporate motors, transformers, and heaters. The flux density changes rapidly with distance from appliances and at 1 m distance the flux density will be of the same order as the background levels, eg 0.01–0.3 μT. At 3 cm distance, magnetic flux densities may be several hundred microtesla from devices such as hair dryers and can openers, although there can be wide variations in fields at the same distance from similar appliances.

31 In considering exposure to power frequency magnetic fields, motorised household appliances can be divided into three main groups, as follows:

(a) small appliances such as hair dryers, electric shavers, electric drills and saws, can openers and food mixers which can be used close to the body,
(b) larger high power appliances such as vacuum cleaners that tend to be operated further from the body,
(c) large fixed position appliances such as refrigerators, dish washers and washing machines whose motors may be at some distance from the closest position of normal approach.

32 Examples of magnetic flux densities from UK appliances (Preece *et al*, 1997) are given in Table 2.3, although it should be noted that some of the measurements are based on a small number of examples.

33 The magnetic fields from appliances decrease rapidly with distance varying between the inverse cube and inverse square with distance. Examples of the rate of change of magnetic flux density with distance from the surface of the appliance are shown in Figure 2.1, which illustrates the effect of the magnetic field source being further from the surface in the case of the larger appliance.

34 Exposure to most household appliances is intermittent, whereas exposure to magnetic fields from electric over-blankets can be prolonged. The magnetic flux density for a 1 cm blanket/body separation has been measured in the range 2–3 μT and in the range 0.05–0.45 μT for the head (Florig and Hoburg, 1990).

FIGURE 2.1
Magnetic flux densities close to the surface of household appliances

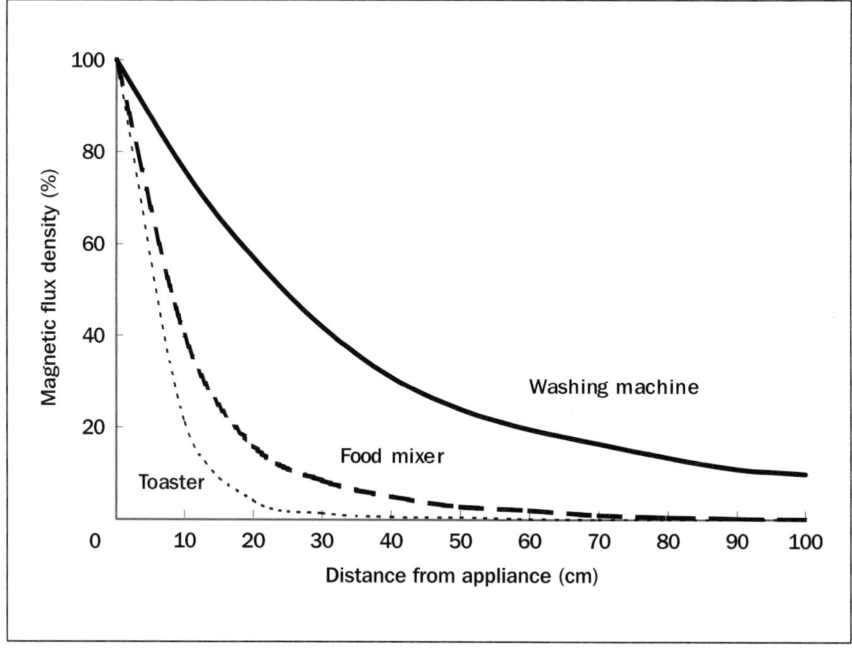

TABLE 2.3 UK appliance magnetic flux density (μT) (Preece et al. 1997)

		Magnetic flux density at specified distance from appliance (μT)					
Appliance	Number	0.05 m	SD*	0.5 m	SD*	1 m	SD*
Electric shavers	1	164.75	-	0.84	-	0.12	-
Can openers	3	145.7	106.23	1.33	1.33	0.2	0.21
Hand blenders	8	76.75	87.09	0.97	1.05	0.15	0.16
Fish tank pumps	6	75.58	64.74	0.32	0.09	0.05	0.01
Food mixers	6	69.91	69.91	0.69	0.69	0.11	0.11
Central heating pumps	21	61.09	59.58	0.51	0.47	0.1	0.1
Extractor fans	9	45.18	107.96	0.5	0.93	0.08	0.14
Vacuum cleaners	42	39.53	74.58	0.78	0.74	0.16	0.12
Electric showers	12	30.82	35.04	0.44	0.75	0.11	0.25
Microwave cookers	34	27.25	16.74	1.66	0.36	0.37	0.14
Electric knives	5	27.03	13.88	0.12	0.05	0.02	0.01
Hair dryers	39	17.44	15.56	0.12	0.1	0.02	0.02
Food processors	10	12.84	12.84	0.23	0.23	0.04	0.04
Washing machines	34	7.73	7.03	0.96	0.56	0.27	0.14
Dish washers	13	5.93	4.99	0.8	0.46	0.23	0.13
Cooker hoods	9	4.77	2.53	0.26	0.1	0.06	0.02
Tumble dryers	7	3.93	5.45	0.34	0.42	0.1	0.1
Fan heaters	3	3.64	1.41	0.22	0.18	0.06	0.06
Liquidisers	2	3.28	1.19	0.29	0.35	0.09	0.12
Coffee mills	1	2.47	-	0.28	-	0.07	-
Tape players	1	2	-	0.24	-	0.06	-
Hi-fi systems	30	1.56	4.29	0.08	0.14	0.02	0.03
Coffee makers	2	0.57	0.03	0.06	0.07	0.02	0.02
Bottle sterilisers	42	0.57	0.52	0.06	0.05	0.02	0.02
Freezers	13	0.42	0.87	0.04	0.02	0.01	0.01
Video (VCR)	2	0.41	0.17	0.01	0.005	0.005	0.005
Fridge/freezers	23	0.21	0.14	0.05	0.03	0.02	0.01

*Standard deviation.

Underfloor heating

35 Underfloor heating consists of an arrangement of cables embedded in, typically, a concrete matrix. The magnetic flux density at floor level generated by the cable array will depend on the configuration of the cables, the depth of material overlying them and the current flowing in the cables. Some underfloor heating systems are switched on only at night and make use of cheap off-peak electricity, relying upon the heat capacity of the floor to provide warmth during the day.

36 Magnetic flux densities of up to 1.25 μT at floor level are typical, falling to 0.5 to 0.7 μT at 1 m above the floor.

Personal exposure measurements

37 Merchant *et al* (1994a) have summarised the fields encountered at home by 214 electricity supply industry staff wearing personal dosemeters. The geometric-mean time-weighted average magnetic flux densities were affected by the type of dwelling: flats 0.109 μT, semi-detached 0.06 μT, terraced 0.056 μT and detached 0.043 μT. Whilst it was shown that the high voltage lines of 132 kV and above were dominant influences on exposure at distances within 100 m from the lines, there was no significant difference for supplies from 415 V to 66 kV.

38 Preece *et al* (1996) in a study of 50 houses in Avon measured a 24-hour mean of three main occupancy rooms of 0.044 ± 0.06 μT. Personal dosemeters, worn over the same period by mothers participating in a longitudinal study of pregnancy and childhood, recorded 0.067 ± 0.08 μT.

Long-term changes in exposure

39 Measurements made to assess exposure to magnetic fields are a relatively recent development and in large-scale population studies the measurement approach is constrained by resources and tends to be of restricted duration.

40 It is of interest to examine the long-term trends in exposure over time as a result of changes in the way electricity is transmitted and distributed and as a consequence of changes in the number and use of electrical appliances.

41 In the UK, the issue has been considered in detail (Swanson, 1996) over the 40-year period from 1949 to 1989. The factors influencing the change in population exposure have been determined to be due principally to the increased background fields in residences as a reflection of domestic demand and the increased use of appliances. The contribution to exposure from individual source components is considered for particular subgroups of the population. Taken overall, the increase in the population exposure from 1949 to 1989 is estimated to be at least a factor of 4.5. In Figure 2.2 the solid line (a) is that obtained from domestic demand data and the dotted line (b) is that calculated by Swanson. The decrease in demand in the mid- to late-1970s was the consequence of the oil crisis, resulting in increased costs to the consumer.

Wire coding

42 In the UK, electricity is distributed to the majority of homes via underground cables. This is not so in the USA. In American studies a system of coding the conductors or wires supplying current for transmission or distribution has been used as a surrogate for magnetic field exposure.

43 A summary of the tiered system of wire coding is exemplified in Figure 2.3, where VHCC = very high current configuration, OHCC = ordinary high current configuration, OLCC = ordinary low current configuration, and VLCC = very low current configuration.

44 The underlying principle of wire coding is that the thickness of conductors, the number of conductors, and the number of circuits reflect the magnitude of the current carried. This in turn reflects the magnitude of the magnetic flux density in nearby homes. Hence a house may be categorised as shown on the basis of its distance from a particular current carrying source. Differentiation of the categories by measurement of magnetic fields has suggested that only the VHCC and OHCC homes can be readily identified. A modified three-tier wire-coding system has been proposed (Kaune, 1994) and is reported to increase precision and accuracy of magnetic field prediction over the original coding system.

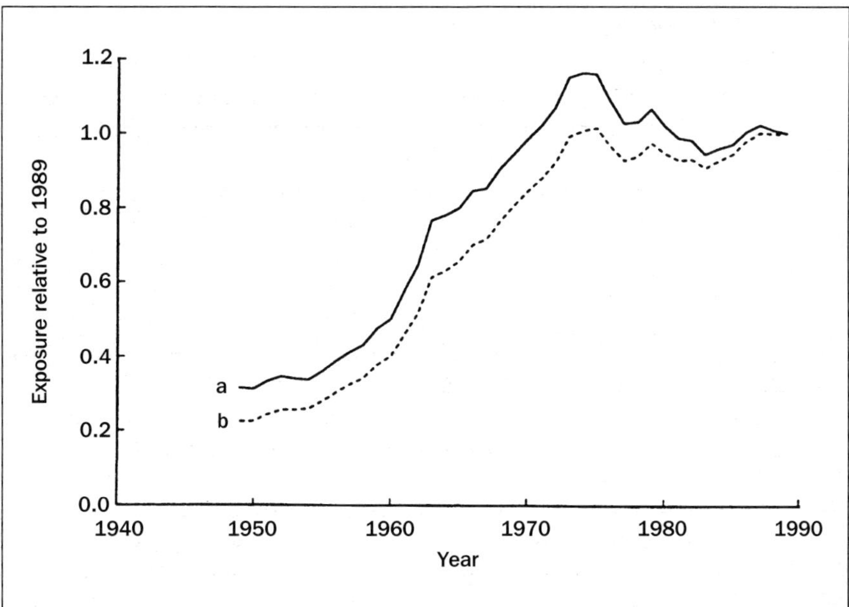

FIGURE 2.2 Trends in population exposure (England and Wales) 1949–89 (Swanson, 1996)

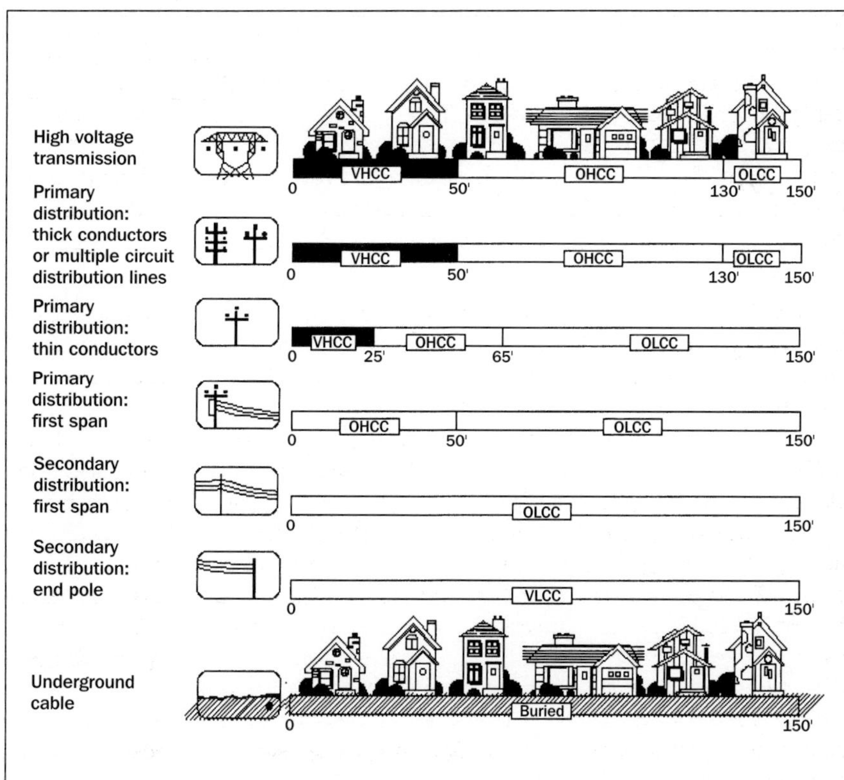

FIGURE 2.3 USA wire code system (Ebi, 1999) (measurements given in feet)

Other public exposure

Transmission lines

45 In the UK, high voltage transmission of power by National Grid plc is carried out at 132, 275 and 400 kV. Electricity from the regional electricity companies is distributed at high voltages from 11 to 132 kV and to homes at 415 V.

46 High voltage power lines give rise to the highest electric field strengths that are likely to be encountered by people. The maximum electric field strength immediately under the highest voltage transmission line of 400 kV in the UK is about 11 kV m^{-1} at the minimum clearance of 7.6 m, although, in general, people will be exposed to fields well below this level. At 25 m lateral displacement from the mid-span position the field strength is about 1 kV m^{-1}. Table 2.4 illustrates the field strength directly beneath, and at 25 m lateral displacement from, 400, 275 and 132 kV lines.

47 Figure 2.4 illustrates the variation of electric field strength with distance from the centreline of typical high voltage transmission lines where the phases of a two-circuit system have been transposed.

48 Objects such as trees and other electrically grounded objects will introduce screening effects and will substantially reduce the electric field strength in their vicinity. Buildings provide considerable attenuation also and the external electric field strength arising from a transmission line will be reduced by a factor of between 10 and 1000, depending upon the characteristics of the building and the local electric field. Electric

TABLE 2.4 Electric field strengths near power lines

	Electric field strength (kV m^{-1})		
	Power line (kV)		
Location	400	275	132
Maximum at ground level for minimum conductor clearance	11	6	2
25 m lateral displacement from centreline	1	0.2	0.05

FIGURE 2.4 Electric fields from high voltage overhead lines

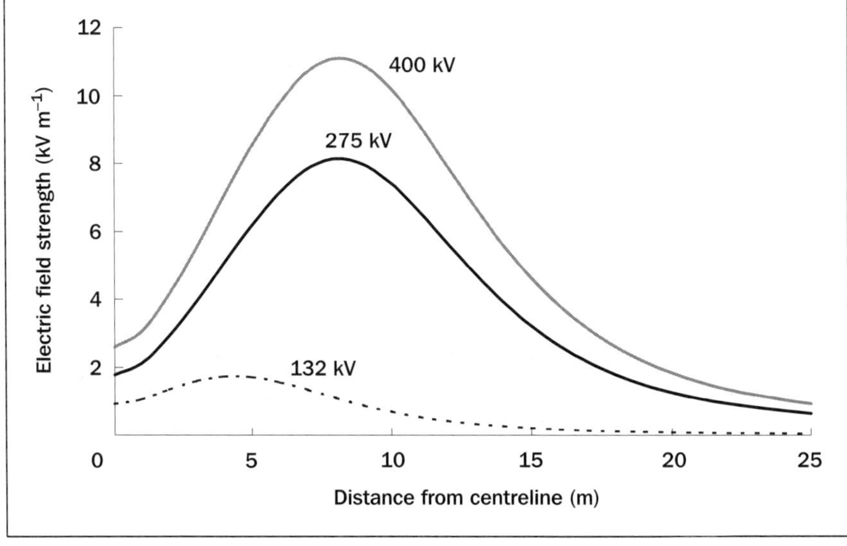

field exposures within buildings will be due predominantly to fields arising from proximity to internal wiring and appliances.

49 Electric field strengths of several kilovolts per metre may be encountered close to high voltage lines. In the home and in buildings where the supply voltage is reduced to 240 V, electric field strengths in the centre of rooms are generally in the range 1–20 V m^{-1}, and close to domestic appliances and cables this may increase to a few hundred volts per metre.

50 In addition to the direct exposure of people to electric fields, indirect effects have been considered arising from changes in the concentration and deposition of particulates in the presence of an alternating (AC) field and due to changes in the static or DC electric field resulting from the generation of corona ions (Fews *et al*, 1999a,b; Swanson and Kaune, 1999). Detailed consideration has been given to the magnitude of these electric fields, and the physical aspects of their effect on airborne particles (Fews *et al*, 1996b; Swanson and Jeffers, 1999). Fews *et al* (1999a,b) suggested that, in proximity to overhead power lines, these interactions will result in increased human exposure to radon decay products, notably ^{218}Po and ^{214}Po, and other environmental pollutants through increased deposition on body surfaces. The physical principles for enhanced aerosol deposition in large electric fields are well understood. However, it has not been demonstrated that any such enhanced deposition will increase human exposure in a way that will result in adverse health effects to the general public.

51 In contrast to electric fields where the highest exposures are likely to be experienced close to high voltage transmission lines, the highest magnetic flux densities are more likely to be in the vicinity of equipment that is carrying large currents. A theoretical worst-case calculation of magnetic flux density beneath the highest voltage transmission line in the UK is 100 μT. Typical maximum magnetic flux densities likely to be encountered beneath high voltage lines are summarised in Table 2.5, although under most normal operating conditions, the levels will be considerably lower and in the case of 400 kV lines often less than 10 μT.

52 Figure 2.5 shows the variation of magnetic flux density with distance from transmission lines carrying a high winter load current for similar operating criteria of phase orientation and percentage loading. The currents carried per circuit are 2, 1 and 0.35 kA for the 400, 275 and 132 kV lines, respectively.

Overhead lines and underground cables

53 The high visibility of overhead power lines has resulted in most concern being associated with exposure to fields generated by such lines. For a single wire conductor carrying electric current, the magnetic field strength will increase with the current carried and decrease with the inverse of the distance from the conductor. In practice, electricity carried by the National Grid is generally transmitted using three separate phases seen as the three conductor bundles vertically spaced by about 7–10 m on the arms of one side of metal pylons. Often pylons carry two circuits, one on each set of arms. As a result of the spatial arrangement of the different phases for each circuit, fields decrease more rapidly than from a single current carrying conductor, usually as inverse square to inverse cube with distance. To prevent flashover hazards, 400 kV lines require a minimum ground clearance of 7.6 m and this restricts the distance of approach to overhead lines.

TABLE 2.5 Magnetic flux densities near power lines

Location	Magnetic flux density (μT) Power line (kV) 400	275	132
Maximum at ground level directly beneath power line	40	22	7
25 m lateral displacement from centreline	8	4	0.5

FIGURE 2.5 Magnetic fields from high voltage overhead lines

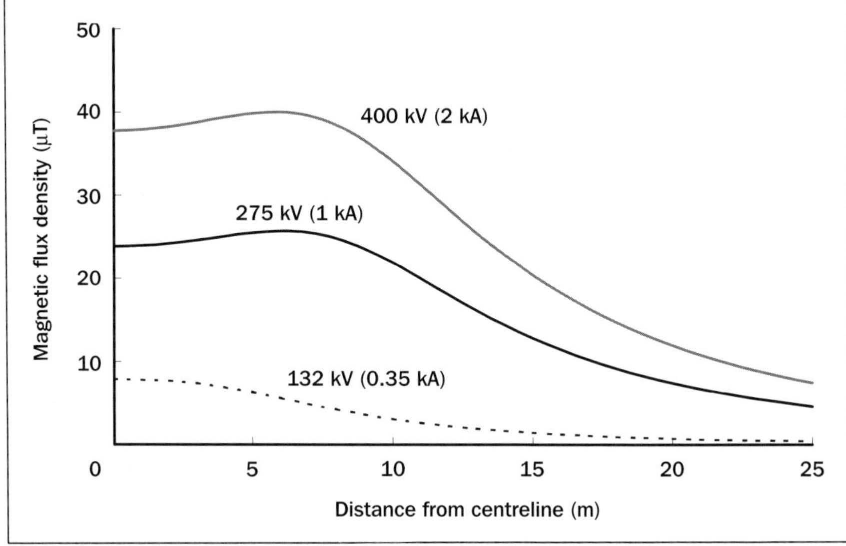

54 About 300 km or 4% of the high voltage grid system is buried beneath ground (Swanson and Renew, 1994). The cables are individually insulated and placed very much closer together than overhead conductors. As a result of the close physical spacing of the phase conductors, field cancellation occurs over much shorter distances than the widely spaced overhead lines. The result is that, due to screening, electric fields from buried cables are negligible at ground level and, due to cable spacing, magnetic fields decrease more rapidly with distance than from overhead lines. Field cancellation means that at distances of a few metres the field strength would be less than that arising from the equivalent current carrying overhead lines. However, it is possible to approach much closer to underground cables that are buried often at a depth of about 1 m; consequently for conductors carrying similar current to an overhead line the magnetic field encountered may be higher at accessible positions close to the cable. The variation of magnetic flux density with distance is shown in Figure 2.6 at a height of 1 m above ground level for 400 kV lines and cables carrying a 2 kA current.

Local area substations

55 Local area substations normally comprise three principal components, namely switch gear, a transformer and a low voltage board. The switch gear is to isolate parts of the system in the event of a fault or for maintenance, the transformer is used to step-down the 11 kV voltage to 415 V and the feed pillar or low voltage board is used to switch or disconnect the low voltage feeder cables.

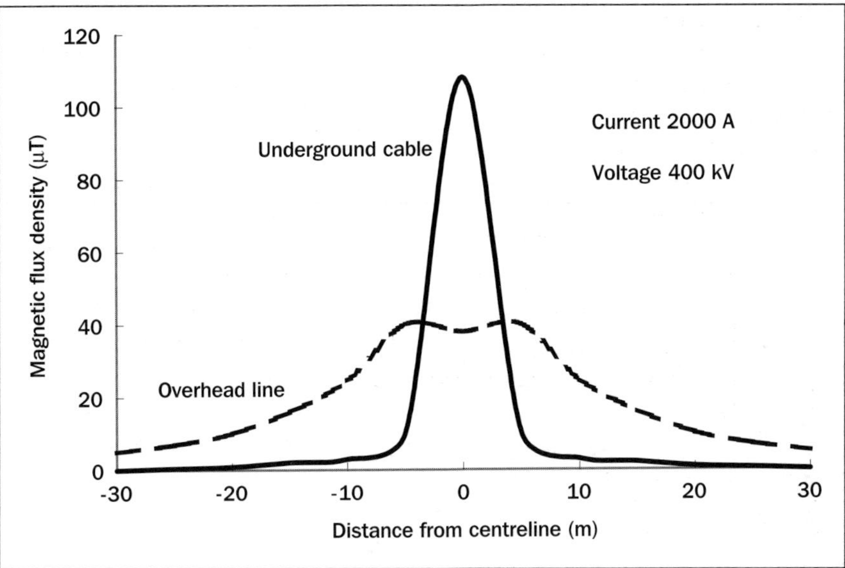

FIGURE 2.6
Magnetic fields from overhead lines and underground cables

Magnetic fields

56 Power cables and lines are a major source of high magnetic flux densities at substations and a dominant source of high fields beyond their vicinity. In a survey of 25 suburban substations transforming 11 kV to 415 V (Renew *et al*, 1990), mean magnetic fields at 0.5 m above ground level within 1 m of the enclosures were about 1.9 μT. These decreased to about half this magnitude in an average distance of 1.3 m, becoming indistinguishable from the background due to other domestic sources within 5 m. An NRPB survey of 27 substations in the South Oxfordshire region (Maslanyj, 1996) revealed an overall mean magnetic flux density of 1.1 μT at 1 m above ground level adjacent to enclosure walls, with individual substation mean flux densities ranging from 0.1 to 6.6 μT. Magnetic flux densities of 2–10 μT were encountered opposite the 415 V feed pillars where separation of phase resulted in less efficient field cancellation. Magnetic flux densities less than 1 and 0.5 μT were measured opposite transformers and switching units, respectively. Magnetic fields decayed rapidly with increasing distance, *r*, from the substations, with falloff rates proportional to $1/r^2$ in the vicinity of the feed pillar and $1/r$ in other areas. Ignoring power lines and cables, the magnetic fields associated with the substations were indistinguishable from typical background levels in the home at distances in the range 5–10 m. Repeat measurements established that magnetic flux densities could double during peak load periods. Beneath overhead connecting lines and above underground cables associated with the substations, magnetic flux densities of 0.4 and 0.05–0.8 μT, respectively, were measured at 1 m above ground level.

Electric fields

57 In 11 kV to 415 V substations, the metallic casing around components of the substation and the insulation on power cables all tend to shield electric fields, and the electric field strengths at the boundaries are likely to be no more than a few volts per metre. Close to the boundary fence of a major high voltage 132 kV substation on an industrial site, maximum electric field strengths of 200 V m^{-1} have been measured, falling to 10 V m^{-1} at 5 m.

Occupational exposure

58 All industries and workplaces involving exposure to electric and magnetic fields arise due to the use of electricity; however, there are particular occupations where higher levels of exposure may be anticipated due to the presence of relatively high voltages or currents. In some industries the characterisation of exposure has been examined in some depth, particularly for workers in the electricity transmission and distribution industry. In others, the issue has still to be addressed. The use of personal dosemeters has provided the basis of exposure assessment through extended wearing of such dosemeters or enabled exposure categories to be defined for particular types of job. Paragraphs 59–101 provide an overview of the exposure of people at work as determined by either personal dosemeters or spot measurements using environmental monitoring equipment.

Electricity generation, transmission and distribution

59 Tables 2.4 and 2.5 summarised the electric field strengths and magnetic flux densities close to power lines, although it is likely that some transmission and distribution workers are exposed transiently to fields greater than those indicated.

60 Stuchly (1986) reported measurements of magnetic flux densities of up to 12 mT in a German generating station. Bowman *et al* (1988) measured magnetic flux densities of up to 7.2 μT for transmission station staff, up to 5.4 μT for distribution substation staff, up to 11.8 μT for generating station staff, and up to 91 μT for transmission line staff.

61 Exposure assessments of power industry staff have employed integrating dosemeters to estimate mean exposure. Renew *et al* (1990) reported individual mean exposures in the range 65 nT to 8.4 μT for 75 workers on operational sites. Deadman *et al* (1988) reported time-weighted average electric and magnetic field exposures for a range of power industry workers. The highest mean magnetic flux density of 18.48 μT and the highest recorded electric field strength of 1.756 kV m^{-1} were both recorded on dosemeters worn by apparatus electricians. Table 2.6 summarises the range of daily time-weighted exposures obtained by Deadman *et al*.

62 Merchant *et al* (1994b) summarised the relative contribution of various activities to weekly exposures of staff employed in the electricity supply industry. The percentage mean exposure arising from the various activities is summarised in Table 2.7, the integrated weekly exposure for all categories being 42 μT hours.

63 The exposures at work for 214 staff by site and job description are summarised in Table 2.8 which provides the time-weighted average values of the geometric mean, arithmetic mean, the 5th percentile (P5) and the 95th percentile (P95) values.

64 On the basis of the time-weighted geometric mean, office workers at transmission sites experienced higher fields (0.48 μT) than headquarters staff (0.18 μT). The exposure of power station electrical workers (0.46 μT) was higher than that of mechanical workers (0.25 μT). Transmission substation attendants experienced the highest magnetic flux densities of 1.16 μT.

65 A study of occupational exposure of 2066 electric utility workers in Canada and France (Thériault *et al*, 1994) using personal dosemeters for periods between 5 and 102 weeks provided data for a wide range of jobs in generation, transmission and distribution, and other areas of activity. The arithmetic mean exposure for workers in the hydroelectric, nuclear and thermoelectric stations ranged from 0.13–5.39 μT. For transmission workers the range was 0.31–1.79 μT, for substation workers 0.43–2.36 μT, for distribution workers 0.09–1.87 μT, and for meter readers/installers 0.15–0.42 μT. Blue- and white-collar workers ranged from 0.13–0.50 μT.

Occupation	Mean electric field strength (V m^{-1})	Mean magnetic flux density (μT)
Distribution linemen	Up to 416	0.03–4.57
Apparatus electricians	7.4–1756	0.77–18.48
Transmission linemen	7.3–1430	0.15–3.51
Splicers	4.1–15.7	0.20–17.12
Apparatus mechanics	Up to 6.8	0.03–5.17
Generating station assistant operators	Up to 16.8	0.18–1.72

TABLE 2.6 Range of daily time-weighted average exposures of power industry workers to 60 Hz electric fields and magnetic flux densities

Activity	% contribution
Asleep	13.3
Awake at home	15.2
Out	3.8
Travel	2.9
At work	64.8

TABLE 2.7 Contribution to total exposure by activity category

	Number of people	P5 (μT)	Geometric mean (μT)	Arithmetic mean (μT)	P95 (μT)
Office workers					
Headquarters	36	0.07	0.18	0.22	0.57
Distribution	11	0.04	0.12	0.14	0.27
Power stations	8	0.10	0.23	0.27	0.61
Transmission	7	0.08	0.48	0.68	1.40
Shop staff					
Shops	9	0.11	0.23	0.25	0.47
Power station staff					
Electrical	38	0.07	0.46	1.05	3.54
Mechanical	12	0.06	0.25	0.35	1.47
Transmission staff					
Substation attendants	6	0.46	1.16	1.36	2.44
Fitters and foremen	20	0.10	0.88	1.22	4.53
Engineers	14	0.22	0.72	1.62	8.34
Linemen	11	0.08	0.70	0.88	1.93
Distribution staff					
Fitters and foremen	7	0.14	0.48	0.64	1.39
Engineers	10	0.04	0.28	0.40	1.06
Lines and cables	18	0.03	0.20	0.28	1.01
Domestic	7	0.06	0.17	0.21	0.43

TABLE 2.8 Exposures at work by site and job description

66 Guenel *et al* (1993) used personal dosemeters to devise a job exposure matrix based on 184 workers over 776 days in thermoelectric power plants of Electricité de France. A similar exercise was carried out for 113 electrical utility workers over a period of 483 days. Place of work appeared to be the most important determinant of magnetic field exposure. Exposures were log-normally distributed with geometric means of 0.21 μT for power plant workers and 0.09 μT for office workers. Plant and type of plant were more important determinants of exposure than job title. The study found more heterogeneity for magnetic fields than for electric fields.

67 A thorough evaluation of exposure indices was described by Kromhout *et al* (1995) in their review of 2842 full shift measurements obtained using personal dosemeters for the study by Savitz and Loomis (1995) of five electrical utilities in the USA. Average exposures ranged from 0.11 to 1.5 μT and were found to be greater in urban than in rural sites, with day-to-day variation greater within than between worker groups. Using five groups based on estimated exposure, occupational category, company, occupational category and company, and measured exposure, the variation in real measurements was high. The authors then added the additional information of job title. The 'optimal' grouping for average exposure levels of 0.12, 0.21, 0.39, 0.62 and 1.27 μT showed considerable overlap. The difficulties in establishing reliable exposure estimates were illustrated by Kromhout and Loomis (1996) who pointed out that linesmen, relay technicians and splicers with ten years seniority received exposures that were 20%–35% lower than for workers with less than one year. This was in contrast to technical workers and substation attendants whose exposure increased by 50%–60% for those with ten years seniority.

68 Armstrong *et al* (1994) examined the exposure of electrical utility workers in a Canada–France study to high frequency transient fields using a channel of the personal dosemeter to register the time spent exposed to high frequency radiofrequency fields above 200 $V m^{-1}$. A potential problem identified was that of possible electromagnetic interference arising from effects due to radiofrequency fields from hand-held and vehicle-mounted radios. Electromagnetic compatibility of instrumentation is an important consideration where other sources of electromagnetic fields are present.

Arc and spot welding

69 In arc welding, metal parts are fused together by the energy of a plasma arc struck between two electrodes or between one electrode and the metal to be welded. A power frequency current usually produces the arc but higher frequencies may be used in addition to strike or to maintain the arc.

70 A feature of arc welding is that the welding cable, which can carry currents of hundreds of amps, can touch the body of the operator. Stuchly and Lecuyer (1989) have surveyed magnetic fields from a range of arc welders and have determined separately the exposure at 10 cm from the head, chest, waist, gonads, hands and legs. Whilst it is possible to have hand exposures in excess of 1 mT, exposures to the trunk are typically several hundred microtesla. Once the arc has been struck, these welders operate at comparatively low voltages and this is reflected in the measured electric field strengths of up to a few tens of volts per metre.

71 Bowman *et al* (1988) have measured operator exposures of up to 90 μT for a tungsten-inert-gas (TIG) welder. NRPB measurements on a TIG welder indicate magnetic flux densities of up to 100 μT close to the power supply, 1 mT at the surface of the welding cable and at the surface of the power supply, and 100–200 μT at the operator position.

72 NRPB has examined exposure to magnetic fields from a tin-plate flow melter, a projection welder and an experimental spot welder (Allen *et al.* 1994). The operation of the flow melter involved passing a large 100 Hz current through a piece of tin-plated steel until the tin melted and flowed off the steel. The electric field strength at the operator position, 30 cm from the plate, was found to be less than 1 V m^{-1} and the magnetic flux density to be 418 μT. The projection welder was a conventional 50 Hz seam welder, which gave rise to a magnetic flux density of 1278 μT at 35 cm.

Induction furnaces

73 Measurements on induction furnaces and heaters operating in the frequency range from 50 Hz to 10 kHz have been reported on by Lovsund *et al* (1982) and are summarised in Table 2.9. The fields vary rapidly with distance from the coils and the highest magnetic flux densities arise within a few centimetres of the coils and do not reflect whole-body exposure.

74 The exposure of induction heater operators is characterised by short excursions at relatively high levels as the induction coils are approached. Personal dosemeters have been used to assess the exposure of the operators of 50 Hz billet heaters, and 150 and 250 Hz induction furnaces (Chadwick, 1997). The frequency response of the dosemeters has to be sufficiently broadband to encompass the harmonics present and a capability of assessing harmonic content is a prerequisite to exposure assessment.

75 Billet heater measurements indicated a mean magnetic flux density of 12 μT with a standard deviation of 40.5 μT and a maximum of 514 μT. The mean exposure for the 150 and 250 Hz furnaces ranged from 0.47 to 14 μT and the maxima from 26.7 to 716 μT.

Type of machine	Number	Frequency band	Magnetic flux density (μT): measured ranges
Ladle furnace in conjunction with 1.6 Hz magnetic stirrer, measurements made at 0.5 to 1 m from furnace	1	1.6 Hz, 50 Hz	200–10 000
Induction furnace			
at 0.6–0.9 m	2	50 Hz	100–900
at 0.8–2.0 m	5	600 Hz	100–900
Channel furnace, at 0.6–3.0 m	3	50 Hz	100–400
Induction heater, at 0.1–1.0 m	5	50 Hz - 10 kHz	1 000–60 000

TABLE 2.9 Swedish study of magnetic fields from induction furnaces (Lovsund et al. 1982)

Occupations using motorised equipment

76 There is inevitably overlap between appliances used at work and those used at home, electric drills and other equipment with motors being commonplace in both locations. Whilst the fields from such equipment may be similar, the manner and degree to which similar equipment may be used at home and at work may differ considerably. Sobel *et al* (1995) have investigated the exposure of dressmakers, seamstresses and tailors using sewing machines. The measurements of magnetic flux density at representative anatomical positions on four industrial and two domestic machines resulted in an average value of 1.93 μT.

77 This does not provide any indication of the way in which exposure changes with distance from the appliance. The magnetic fields close to appliances containing motors or transformers will decrease very rapidly with distance, approximately as the inverse cube of the distance. Thus magnetic flux densities which may be high close to sources are rarely above the general levels caused by distribution of electricity at distances in excess of about 1 m. In countries such as the USA where the mains voltage is lower and the current used is therefore higher than in the UK for similar power devices, the magnetic flux densities will be higher. Measurements made on appliances in the USA are therefore descriptive of the manner in which fields decay but do not necessarily reflect the magnitude of magnetic flux density from equipment used with a 240 V supply.

78 Although the magnetic flux density close to electric motors can be quite large, it tends to exhibit great spatial variation. Magnetic flux densities of up to 2 mT have been reported at 3 cm from small motors in domestic appliance (Gauger, 1995), but at a distance of 1 m the magnetic flux densities are likely to have fallen to a few hundred nanotesla. NRPB has made measurements close to a few motors (Allen *et al*, 1994). A magnetic flux density of 1 mT at 1 cm from a 1 kW water pump reduced to 4 μT at 40 cm. The magnetic flux density at the casing of an 18 kW motor was 100 μT, but at the nearest possible whole-body exposure position of 20 cm the magnetic flux density was 8 μT. A 7.5 kW motor again gave rise to a magnetic flux density of 100 μT at the case, reducing to 10 μT at 20 cm.

79 Owing to the rapid spatial change of magnetic flux density in the vicinity of appliances as exemplified in Figure 2.1, it is difficult to use environmental (spot) measurements to assess exposure where approach to the appliance is close. In such circumstances the use of personal dosemeters may also be problematical without detailed investigation as a dosemeter sited at one position of the body may not reflect exposure overall.

Miscellaneous

80 There are several occupations in which workers may undergo incidental exposures to ELF electric and magnetic fields to a greater or lesser degree. Bowman *et al* (1988) have investigated the exposures associated with various classes of job and some of their results are summarised in Table 2.10. The data are banded together as exposures in the ELF band and no further frequency discrimination is made.

81 Floderus *et al* (1993) have investigated 1015 sets of measurements in the workplace using EMDEX-100 and EMDEX-C personal dosemeters. This is a noteworthy study in that it covered 169 different jobs with the dosemeters worn for a mean duration of 6.8 hours. The distribution of all one second sampling period results for all 1015 measurements is shown in Figure 2.7, the most common measurement being 0.05 μT and measurements above 1 μT being rare. Railway workers were identified as having high levels of exposure.

82 Abdollahzadeh *et al* (1995) have carried out measurements on a total of 192 semiconductor industry fabrication room workers using primarily AMEX-3D instruments which provide a time-weighted average value of exposure. The results were obtained over a period of a shift and for two companies repeat results were obtained at approximately a one-year interval. The time-weighted average exposures ranged from 0.17 ± 0.06 μT for etching process workers to 1.24 ± 0.38 μT for furnace workers. Consistent results for particular processes were obtained over the one-year period.

Job class	Maximum magnetic flux density (μT)	Maximum electric field strength ($V\ m^{-1}$)
Electricians	10.3	4.2
Electronics – assemblers		
Sputtering	4.3	5.5
Soldering	0.16	8.7
Microelectronics	0.006	3
Projectionists	4.5	2
Fork-lift operators	125	0.2
Electronics – engineers and technicians		
Laser laboratory	20.2	8
Calibration laboratory	0.07	4
Office	0.02	1
Radio and TV repairers	2.6	110
Secretaries, non-VDU users	0.4	5

TABLE 2.10 Miscellaneous occupational ELF exposures

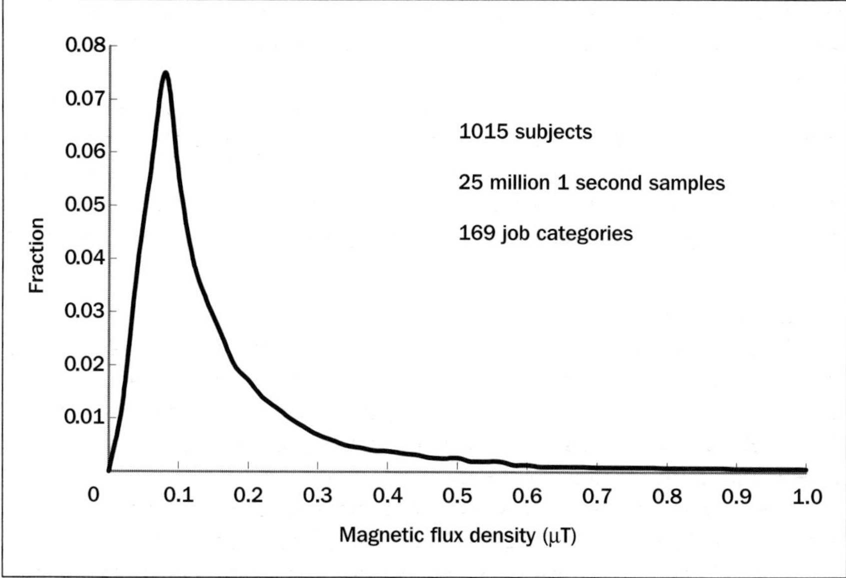

FIGURE 2.7 Distribution of all occupational magnetic field samples (Floderus, 1993)

83 Tape erasers use an alternating (usually power frequency) magnetic field to remove data stored on magnetic media. They can be divided broadly into two types according to size: desktop (or larger) and hand-held. Measurements on a 70 kg desktop model have shown magnetic flux densities at the surface of the case to be 500 μT and, at 15 cm, 170 μT. It is possible that much greater exposures of the hands may occur for larger unshielded erasers. NRPB has measured magnetic flux densities of 1 mT at the handle of a hand-held bulk tape eraser and 7 μT at the surface of the case. The exposure to the trunk of an operator during normal use of the hand-held tape eraser was estimated to be 100 μT (Allen *et al*, 1994).

84 Breysse *et al* (1994) reported on exposure assessments for telephone lineworkers using personal dosemeters. The 238 full shift sample procedure found that the cable splicing technicians had the highest mean and median exposure of 0.4 and 0.3 μT, respectively, followed by central office technicians with mean and median exposures of 0.25 and 0.22 μT, respectively. If work breaks and driving periods were excluded, the cable splicers mean and median exposure rose to 0.64 and 0.53 μT, respectively, which suggested to the researchers that this group should be treated separately in any future studies.

85 Barroetavena *et al* (1994) used environmental field strength meters to characterise exposure in the paper and pulp industry. Electric field strengths appeared to differ little from the general population, but magnetic flux densities exceeded 0.3 μT for more than four hours per day in about half of the workers considered. There were, however, wide variations between workers with exposures ranging between 0.01 and 70 μT, with the highest value for workers near a plant with the highest electricity consumption.

86 Philips *et al* (1995) used magnetic field dosemeters to assess both spot and personal exposure (40–800 Hz) of health care workers working in a research hospital. Spot measurements varied between 0.08 and 6.5 μT, whereas time-weighted average exposures ranged from 0.12 to 1.04 μT with peak excursions to 10.37 μT. The authors suggested that summary indices such as time-weighted averages, means and medians were insufficient to characterise the highly variable exposure.

Electrified transport

87 Worldwide, there is a considerable variation in the way in which electricity is utilised in the provision of public transportation. From the standpoint of exposure to electric and magnetic fields the operating characteristics are important as power is supplied as DC or at alternating frequencies up to those used for power distribution. Many European countries such as Germany, Austria, Switzerland, Sweden and Norway have quasi-DC systems that operate at $16^2/_3$ Hz. Irrespective of the nature of the supply current, most of these systems use a DC traction motor, rectification being carried out either on-board or prior to supply. On-board rectification is single phase and so a smoothing inductor is required, a major source of static and 100 Hz magnetic fields. Even for systems that are supplied with nominal DC there is little smoothing at the rectification stage because three- or six-phase rectification is used, resulting in a significant alternating component in the 'static' magnetic fields.

88 With the exception of three airport 'people movers', all the major electrified transport systems in the UK are conventional 'steel wheel on steel rail' railways (Chadwick and Lowes, 1998). The majority of British mainline electric services use an overhead 50 Hz supply but all the other conventional rail systems are supplied with DC. Of these DC systems, all except trams and the majority of the Light Rapid Transit systems, have their electricity supplied by a third rail.

89 Older DC traction engines use rheostatic current control but newer stock uses a chopped supply. Line filter inductors are used to reduce audiofrequency interference on the DC supply. It is apparent that the major sources of magnetic fields on trains are smoothing and line filter inductors and not the motors themselves, which are designed to minimise flux leakage.

London Underground

90 This is a DC 600 V system, in which there is one extra rail to supply current at +400 V and one at −200 V to act as a return.

91 Measurements at floor level in the passenger compartments of a tube gauge train gave static magnetic flux densities of 0.1 to 2.0 mT. At floor level in the driver's cab, the magnetic flux density was 0.2 mT. At a height of 1 m, all measured magnetic flux densities were at or below 0.2 mT.

92 Alternating fields on both standard and experimental trains have been investigated and magnetic flux densities of the order of 20 μT have been measured, arising from the traction components and on board smoothing inductors.

Overground third rail systems in the UK

93 This system, in which power is supplied at 750 V DC *via* a third rail, is used for example on mainline and suburban trains to the south of London, and for Merseyrail. The current return is *via* the running rails. All the traction and control circuitry, AC or DC, is mounted under the steel floor between the bogies. Suburban or commuter trains consist of one or more electric multiple units (EMUs). Each EMU comprises two to four cars that include one or two motor-cars which pick up power from traction motors on the bogies. The driver's cars are not usually motor-cars and even, if they are, the driver is further from the source of the fields than the passengers.

94 In passenger cars, magnetic flux densities in the range 16–64 μT have been recorded at table height in 750 V DC EMUs. Outside the train, on the platform of the station, magnetic flux densities of 16–48 μT have been measured. Measurements made in a train with a variable frequency AC induction motor indicate that magnetic flux densities 150 mm above the smoothing inductor, again the greatest source of exposure, would be up to 1 mT. This would be a DC field with AC modulation.

British overhead wire systems

95 The majority of British mainline electric trains and many suburban services have an overhead 25 kV, 50 Hz supply. Broadly, two types of trains are used, both featuring on-board rectification. On fast intercity routes, an electric locomotive pulls or pushes a formation of coaches. Traction power is confined to the individual locomotive.

96 Similar EMUs to those used for suburban trains have given rise to magnetic flux densities of up to 15 mT at floor level above an air cooled inductor, although this has been reduced to 1 mT in later types. These fields have 100 Hz modulation with the static and time-varying components being of similar magnitude.

97 Trains hauled by electric locomotives differ from EMUs in that the traction circuitry, including the smoothing inductors, is in a separate car from the passengers. The cabs are made of glass-reinforced plastic but there is a steel bulkhead between the cab and the equipment compartment.

98 Under power, static magnetic flux densities of up to 27 μT have been measured at 1.4 m above the floor in the driver's cab. In the walkway through the equipment car the magnetic flux densities were up to 2 mT. At 0.5 m above the floor, the maximum static magnetic flux density in the equipment car was found to be 3 mT and the maximum magnetic flux density at 100 Hz was 2.5 mT.

99 There is a lack of exposure data for passengers travelling on electrified transport in the UK. NRPB has made power frequency field measurements aboard an intercity

Bowman J D, Garabant D H, Sobel E, *et al* (1988). Exposures to extremely low frequency (ELF) electromagnetic fields in occupations with elevated leukaemia rates. *Appl Indust Hyg*, **3**(5), 189–94.

Breysse P N, Matanoski G M, Elliott E A, *et al* (1994). 60 hertz magnetic field exposure assessment for an investigation of leukaemia in telephone lineworkers. *Am J Indust Med*, **26**, 681–91.

Chadwick P J (1997). Investigation of the suitability of EMDEX magnetic field dosemeters for assessment of the exposure to induction heating workers. Sudbury, HSE Books, Report 128/1997.

Chadwick P and Lowes F (1998). Magnetic fields on British trains. *Ann Occup Hyg*, **42**(5), 331–5.

Deadman J E, Camus M, Armstrong B G, *et al* (1988). Occupational and residential 60 Hz electromagnetic fields and high-frequency electric transients: exposure assessment using a new dosimeter. *J Indust Hyg Assoc*, **49**, 409.

Dimbylow P J (1987). Finite difference calculations of current densities in a homogeneous model of a man exposed to extremely low frequency electric fields. *Bioelectromagnetics*, **8**, 355–75.

Dimbylow P J (1988). The calculation of induced currents and absorbed power in a realistic, heterogeneous model of the lower leg for applied fields from 60 Hz to 30 MHz. *Phys Med Biol*, **33**(12), 1453–68.

Dimbylow P J (1998). Induced current densities from low-frequency magnetic fields in a 2 mm resolution, anatomically realistic model of the body. *Phys Med Biol*, **43**, 221–30.

Dimbylow P J (2000). Current densities in a 2 mm resolution anatomically realistic model of the body induced by low frequency electric fields. *Phys Med Biol*, **45**, 1013–22.

Ebi K L (1999). Developments in the generation and interpretation of wire codes. *Radiat Prot Dosim*, **83**(1–2), 71–8.

Fews A P, Henshaw D L, Keitch P A, *et al* (1999a). Increased exposure to pollutant aerosols under high voltage power lines. *Int J Radiat Biol*, **75**(12), 1505–21.

Fews A P, Henshaw D L, Wilding R J, *et al* (1999b). Corona ions from powerlines and increased exposure to pollutant aerosols. *Int J Radiat Biol*, **75**(12), 1523–31.

Floderus B, Persson T, Stenlund C, *et al* (1993). Occupational exposure to electromagnetic fields in relation to leukemia and brain tumors: a case-control study in Sweden. *Cancer Causes Control*, **4**, 465–76.

Florig H K and Hoburg J F (1990). Power frequency magnetic fields from electric blankets. *Health Phys*, **58**(4), 493.

Gauger J R (1985). Household appliance magnetic field survey. *IEE Trans Power Appar Syst*, **PAS-104**(9), 2436.

Guenel P, Nicolau J, Imbernon G, *et al* (1993). Design of a job exposure matrix on electric and magnetic fields: selection of an efficient job classification for workers in thermo-electric power production plants. *Int J Epidemiol*, **22** (Supplement 2), S16–S21.

Kaune W T (1994). Simplification of the Wertheimer-Leeper wire code. *Bioelectromagnetics*, **15**, 275–82.

Kromhout H and Loomis D (1996). Influence of seniority on occupational exposures to magnetic fields. *Am J Indust Med*, **29**, 570.

Kromhout H, Loomis D P, Mihlaw G J, *et al* (1995). Assessment and grouping of occupational magnetic field exposure in five electric utility companies. *Scand J Work Environ Health*, **21**, 43–50.

Lovsund P, Oberg P A and Nilsson S E (1982). ELF magnetic fields in electrosteel and welding industries. *Radio Sci*, **17**(5S), 35S–38S.

Merchant C J, Renew D C and Swanson J (1994a). Exposures to power-frequency magnetic fields in the home. *J Radiol Prot*, **14**(1), 77–87.

Merchant C J, Renew D C and Swanson J (1994b). Origins and magnitudes of exposure to power-frequency magnetic fields in the UK. Paris, Cigré, August-September.

Maslanyj M P (1996). Power-frequency electromagnetic fields associated with local area substations. Chilton, NRPB-M751.

Philips K L, Morandi M T, Oehme D, *et al* (1995). Occupational exposure to low frequency magnetic fields in health care facilities. *Am Indust Hyg Assoc J*, **56**, 677–85.

Preece A W, Grainger P, Golding J, *et al* (1996). Domestic magnetic field exposures in Avon. *Phys Med Biol*, **41**, 71–81.

Preece A W, Kaune W, Grainger P, *et al* (1997). Magnetic fields from domestic appliances in the UK. *Phys Med Biol*, **42**, 67–76.

Renew D C, Male J C and Maddock B J (1990). Power-frequency magnetic fields: measurement and exposure assessment. Paris, Cigré, pp 36–105.

Repacholi M H (1983). Sources and applications of radiofrequency (RF) and microwave energy. IN *Biological Effects and Dosimetry of Non-ionizing Radiation, Radiofrequency and Microwave Energies* (M Grandolfo *et al*, Eds). New York, Plenum Press.

Savitz D A and Loomis D P (1995). Magnetic field exposure in relation to leukaemia and brain cancer mortality among electrical utility workers. *Am J Epidemiol*, **141**, 123–34.

Sobel E, Davanipour Z, Sulkava R, *et al* (1995). Occupations with exposures to electromagnetic fields: a possible risk factor for Alzheimer's disease. *Am J Epidemiol*, **142**(5), 515–24.

Stuchly M A (1986). Human exposures to static and time-varying magnetic fields. *Health Phys*, **51**(2), 215–25.

Stuchly M A and Lecuyer D W (1989). Exposure to electromagnetic fields in arc welding. *Health Phys*, **56**(3), 297.

Swanson J (1996). Long-term variation in the exposure of the population of England and Wales to power-frequency magnetic fields. *J Radiol Prot*, **16**(4), 287–301.

Swanson J and Jeffers D (1999). Possible mechanisms by which electric fields from power lines might affect airborne particles harmful to health. *J Radiol Prot*, **19**(3), 213–29.

Swanson J and Kaune W T (1999). Comparison of residential power-frequency magnetic fields away from appliances in different countries. *Bioelectromagnetics*, **20**, 244–54.

Swanson J and Renew D C (1994). Power-frequency fields and people. *Engineering Science and Education Journal*, April.

Thériault G, Goldberg M, Miller A B, *et al* (1994). Cancer risks associated with occupational exposure to magnetic fields among electricity utility workers in Ontario and Quebec, Canada and France: 1970–1989. *Am J Epidemiol*, **139**(6), 550–72.

Tynes T, Jynge H and Vistnes A I (1994). Leukemia and brain tumors in Norwegian railway workers, a nested case-control study. *Am J Epidemiol*, **139**(7), 645–53.

UKCCS (1999). Exposure to power-frequency magnetic fields and the risk of childhood cancer. *Lancet*, **354**, 1925–31.

3 Recent Cellular Studies Relevant to Carcinogenesis

INTRODUCTION

1 Since the earlier Advisory Group report on electromagnetic fields and the risk of cancer was published in 1992 (NRPB, 1992), a great many papers have been published describing cellular studies aimed at demonstrating whether or not electric or magnetic fields are capable of bringing about biological effects which could be relevant to the causation of cancer. This chapter, therefore, is not intended as a comprehensive review. It will address specific issues which have received most attention, giving some examples, and will include conclusions reached by other reviewers, notably those reached in the report of a Working Group of the National Institute of Environmental Health Sciences on the assessment of health effects from exposure to power line frequency electric and magnetic fields (NIEHS, 1998).

2 Most of the studies that have been carried out do not attempt to demonstrate a direct transformation of normal cells into cancer cells. They aim to identify effects on normal cellular processes which, when they malfunction, would contribute to the development of cancer. Demonstration that an external agent is capable of inducing a biological response does not necessarily mean that this will result in a damaging consequence. Such alterations may be of considerable scientific interest but caution must be exercised before concluding that they will lead to pathological changes such as cancer.

3 It follows, therefore, that studies at the cellular level can neither prove nor disprove conclusively that any particular agent has the capacity to cause cancer. However, a whole range of cellular tests has been used for many years to identify interactions between specific cells and environmental agencies, which suggests that the environmental factor has the potential to play a part in the causation of cancer. These tests have played a vitally important part in the identification, at an early stage, of compounds such as medicines, herbicides or food additives, to which the population will be exposed and which do have such potential. As they are relatively inexpensive and rapid, they are often used as prescreens to identify materials which are suitable for entry into long-term testing on animals or in human studies. Nevertheless, on their own they can be powerful indicators of carcinogenic potential.

4 It is now widely agreed that cancer is initiated by alterations in the genetic structure of the cell, although some non-genotoxic carcinogens have been recognised. After initiation, the cell may progress to full malignancy without any apparent further external stimulus (after treatment with the so-called complete carcinogens) but more often further events are required, which may be further genomic alterations or other cellular events such as a stimulus to divide or the absence of signals required for differentiation. An agent that will cause this further progression towards malignancy is often termed a *promoting agent*. This is by analogy with the classic animal experiments that identified agents as either initiating agents which caused cancer directly or promoting agents which did not themselves have the ability to initiate but which would enhance the

effects of initiators, eg by causing subminimal doses of initiators to become fully effective. Although the analogy may not always be appropriate for agencies other than chemicals, it is convenient to consider the carcinogenic potential of ELF electromagnetic fields as either 'initiating' or 'promoting'.

5 Initiators are usually identified by one of two properties:

(a) transforming ability, ie altering normal cells into cells that have the characteristics of cancer cells,
(b) genotoxicity, the ability to cause genetic alterations that may be recognised by a variety of tests such as mutagenicity, chromosome damage, or direct damage to DNA.

6 Tests for promoting activity include enhancement of cellular proliferation, perturbation of the cell cycle, interference in intracellular signalling, inappropriate gene expression or abnormalities of the programmed cell death mechanism (apoptosis).

7 It should be borne in mind that the development of cancer may be the result of interaction between two or more different agencies. It is essential, therefore, to formally consider the possibility that exposure to electromagnetic fields could influence the activity of other carcinogenic agents.

8 While demonstration of activity at the cellular level would not necessarily prove that exposure to electromagnetic fields causes cancer, it would be an indication that they have that potential and that more sophisticated tests on animals would be justified. This would also provide support for further epidemiological studies which is the only way in which formal proof can be obtained.

INITIATION

9 In its earlier report the Advisory Group concluded that exposure to electromagnetic fields was not genotoxic (NRPB, 1992). This is supported by comprehensive reviews by Murphy *et al* (1993) and McCann *et al* (1993). Lacy-Hulbert *et al* (1998), who confined their review to fields below 1 mT, also concluded that at these field strengths there was no evidence of mutagenicity. However, the NIEHS report (1998), while agreeing that exposures at flux densities below 0.1 mT did not have an effect, concluded that exposure in the range of 0.2–400 mT increased the mutation rate after x-ray or gamma-ray initiation (the minimum being about 1000 times greater than the flux densities likely to be encountered in the home).

Transformation

10 There are remarkably few studies which attempt to show transforming activity by ELF electromagnetic fields. Jacobson-Kram *et al* (1997) using pulsed fields, of the types used clinically to stimulate bone and tissue growth, failed to find any effect in a standard BALB/3T3 cell transformation assay in repeat assays at both clinical and supraclinical doses. Balcer-Kubiczek *et al* (1996) also failed to find any effect of 24 hour, 200 μT continuous magnetic field exposure in two standard transformation systems (Syrian hamster embryo cells and C3H/10T½ fibroblasts). Post treatment with a chemical promoting agent TPA also failed to show any significant effect. The ability to grow in soft agar is taken as one measure of transformation and, in such an assay using P^+ JB6 mouse epidermal cells which are unusually sensitive to promoting effects, Saffer *et al* (1997) failed to find any effect of 60 Hz magnetic fields at a range of flux densities up to 1.1 mT. Furthermore, the enhancement of transformation in these cells by the promoting agent TPA was not influenced by the magnetic fields.

11 West *et al* (1994) did, however, report an increase in anchorage independent growth when 5B6 cells were exposed to a 60 Hz, 1.1 mT field. Cain *et al* (1993a,b) used a model in which focus formation by transformed mouse cells was inhibited by the presence of normal fibroblasts. Addition of the tumour promoter PMA permits expression of the transformed foci. In their first study they found that exposure to a 60 Hz, 100 μT field for 1 hour per day for 29 days significantly enhanced focus formation in the presence of low concentrations of PMA. There was, however, considerable variability in the results and they even reported suppression of focus formation by 60 Hz fields of 1–200 μT.

12 Cellular immortalisation is one feature of cellular transformation. Gamble *et al* (1999), using a very sensitive Syrian hamster dermal cell system, failed to find any effect on the frequency of cellular immortalisation following exposure to a range of electromagnetic fields from 10 to 1000 μT at 50 Hz for 60 hours. Moreover, there was no enhancement of the immortalisation induced by ionising radiation following exposure to such ELF electromagnetic fields. Thus, there is no convincing evidence that cellular transformation can be affected by ELF electromagnetic fields even in conjunction with promoting or initiating agents. Indeed Miyakoshi *et al* (2000a) reported a suppression of x-ray induced cellular transformation by exposure to an ELF electromagnetic field. C3H/10T½ mouse cells were exposed to 5, 50, or 400 mT at 60 Hz for 24 hours or to 3 Gy x-irradiation followed by the same electromagnetic field exposure. No difference was detected between sham-exposed cells and those exposed to ELF electromagnetic fields alone. Exposure to x-rays alone showed an increase in transformants and the presence of the tumour promotor TPA increased transformation frequency still further. In neither case did the ELF electromagnetic field exposure increase the rate of transformation. There was some tendency for transformation to decline with increasing field density. When the cells were exposed to a 5 mT field for 6 weeks after 3 Gy irradiation there was a highly significant suppression of transformation frequency. The authors suggested that the effect may have been due to activation of protein kinase C (PKC) by the electromagnetic field.

Genotoxicity

13 In order for any type of radiation to cause genetic change the deposition of energy in the DNA must be sufficient to bring about changes in the chemical structures. This is quite clear for both ionising radiation and ultraviolet radiation. It appears that electromagnetic fields do not have the necessary energy deposition to directly cause DNA damage. If such ELF electromagnetic fields are to be considered to be genotoxic it is necessary to suggest an indirect mechanism. Two such mechanisms have been postulated. First, the radical pair mechanism suggests that an appropriate field could prolong by a very small amount the separation of free radicals and thus make naturally occurring free radicals available to interact with DNA. Second, the induction of electric fields within tissue could possibly disrupt cellular processes and thus indirectly cause genetic changes. Both effects are likely to have minimal biological effect. A more plausible hypothesis is that exposure to electromagnetic fields will alter in some way the action of known carcinogenic agents and therefore particular attention should be paid to tests which examine synergy between ELF electromagnetic fields and other agencies.

Mutation

14 The classic test for mutation used in many prescreens is the Ames Test, which identifies mutants in especially sensitive strains of bacteria. Nafziger *et al* (1993) found no effect on mutation frequency of 50 Hz fields up to 10 μT. Similarly, Tabrah *et al* (1994) found no effect of ELF electromagnetic fields alone (60 Hz and up to 200 μT) but did find an increase in azide-induced mutations in the Ames Test after 48 hours in such a field. Jacobson-Kram *et al* (1997) found no evidence of mutagenicity in an Ames Test with either electric or electromagnetic pulsed fields. Using a rat embryo fibroblast cell line which carries an *E coli* lac 1 gene (known as Big Blue®), Suri *et al* (1996) determined mutant frequencies in cells exposed to a magnetic field of 60 Hz, 3 mT either after or concurrently with one of two well-documented carcinogenic agents: N-methylnitosourea (MNU) or 2-methyl-1,4-naphthoquinone (menadione). In no case was any enhancement of mutation frequency observed. This seems particularly important since Suri *et al* were quite specifically attempting to discriminate between a carcinogen which is believed to act through a free radical mechanism (methadione) and MNU which does not.

15 Using a mutation test in *Drosophila melanogaster*, Koana *et al* (1997) found a statistically significant enhancement of somatic recombination in larvae exposed to an exceptionally strong static field of 5 T for 24 hours as compared to the unexposed control. This effect was suppressed by the addition of vitamin E and the authors postulated a free radical mechanism affecting the lifetime of spontaneously produced free radicals. Miyakoshi *et al* (1996a, 1997) reported increased mutation at the hypoxanthine-guanine phophoribosyl transferase (hprt) gene locus in cultured human MeWo cells, particularly during the S-phase of synchronously growing cells exposed to a high density (400 mT, 50 Hz) low frequency magnetic field. They further reported that such induced mutations could be suppressed by the action of a wild type *p53* gene (Miyakoshi *et al*, 1998). This suggests a DNA replication error and/or disturbance of mismatch repair but it is unlikely that such a field would be encountered outside a specialised laboratory facility.

16 Recently, evidence has emerged suggesting that exposure to ELF electromagnetic fields may increase the yield of mutations following prior exposure to ionising radiation. Following exposure to 3 Gy of x-rays a slight increase in mutation was observed when CHO cells were subsequently exposed to ELF electromagnetic fields (60 Hz, 5 mT) (Miyakoshi *et al*, 1999). Similarly, Walleczek *et al* (1999) found a dose-related increase in mutation frequency when cells pre-exposed to 2 Gy of gamma-irradiation were then placed in a 60 Hz field ranging from 0.47 to 0.7 mT. Both studies are potentially very important but in each case there are methodological uncertainties. The Walleczek *et al* study presented the results as mutants per 10^5 surviving cells. The number of mutants in excess of the control level was quite small (1.8-fold overall) and there was substantial variability between replicate experiments. The time allowed for the expression of induced mutations allowed for ten population doublings and could have introduced further uncertainty where small numbers of mutants were involved. It was interesting, nevertheless, that there was an excess of mutants in the cultures exposed to ELF electromagnetic fields in seven out of nine replicates. In the Miyakoshi *et al* study the magnetic field was applied to the cells for a period of up to six weeks following x-ray exposure. This permitted the re-emergence of spontaneous mutants, and the large number of subcultures necessary to maintain the exponentially growing cultures introduced further variability. The consistency of the excess in the cultures exposed to ELF electromagnetic fields at different time points and in three separate experiments was, however, of considerable interest.

17 These results are not, however, supported by a study by Ansari and Hei (2000) using a different cell system. Cells of a human-hamster hybrid cell line, A_1, were exposed to either gamma-irradiation (1.5 and 3 Gy) or a chemical carcinogen, N-methyl-N^1-nitro-N-nitrosguanidine (MNNG), followed by a short (24 hour) or long (7 day) electromagnetic field exposure (60 Hz, 100 μT). Electromagnetic field exposure alone was non-toxic and non-mutagenic. Both gamma-irradiation and MNNG exposure reduced survival and gave substantial yields of mutants but this effect was not enhanced by the subsequent electromagnetic field exposure.

18 The possibility that ELF electromagnetic fields could potentiate the effects of known mutagenic agents is worthy of further study. The use of higher doses of ionising radiation could increase the sensitivity. The use of a lower dose rate for the ionising radiation together with concomitant exposure to ELF electromagnetic fields could explore possible effects on repair of DNA damage.

19 Thus there is some support for a role of ELF electromagnetic fields of high flux density in the induction of mutations by indirect means, via a free radical mechanism or the enhancement of other agents.

20 It should be noted, however, that in studies on large numbers of mice exposed to both gamma-radiation and ELF electromagnetic fields Babbitt *et al* (2000) found no evidence for the initiation of lymphomas but the data did suggest that tumour development may be promoted by exposure to an electromagnetic field. This effect is not, however, statistically significant and is considered in more detail in Chapter 4.

21 *DNA damage* can be measured in a number of ways. The most direct is the single cell electrophoresis assay, also known as the 'comet' assay, which measures the migration of DNA away from the nucleus following exposure to a damaging agent. Using such an assay Lai and Singh (1997) studied the brain cells of rats exposed *in vivo* to different intensities (flux densities of 0.1, 0.25 and 0.5 mT) of a 60 Hz magnetic field for 2 hours. Increased single strand breaks (alkaline conditions) were detected at all flux densities, while increased double strand breaks (neutral conditions) were detected only at the higher levels as compared with unexposed controls.

22 Fairbairn and O'Neil (1994), however, failed to find any effect of a 50 Hz, 5 mT field on a variety of human cells using the comet assay. Exposure to the ELF electromagnetic field did not alter the frequency of breaks induced by H_2O_2. Cantoni *et al* (1995) exposed cultured mammalian cells to 50 Hz electric (0.2–20 kV m^{-1}), magnetic (0.2–200 μT) or combined fields and found that these did not affect the rate of repair of DNA single strand breaks or double strand breaks which had been induced chemically. In a later paper, Cantoni *et al* (1996) measured repair of DNA single strand breaks in three different cultured mammalian cell lines following exposure to three different carcinogens, methyl methane sulphonate (MMS), chromate and 254 nm ultraviolet radiation. In no case did exposure to electric or magnetic or combined fields (as in the previous study) show any effect on DNA repair. Again, a negative result following the use of a treatment which combines both electromagnetic fields and known carcinogens is considered to be particularly significant. Jacobson-Kram *et al* (1997) also reported a failure to find any effect of electromagnetic fields on DNA damage as measured by an unscheduled DNA synthesis test, confirming the earlier findings of Fiorani *et al* (1992).

Chromosomal aberrations

23 Several authors use chromosomal damage as a measure of mutagenic potential. In their wide-ranging study Jacobson-Kram *et al* (1997) reported no effect of either electric or magnetic fields on a direct assay of chromosomal aberrations in CHO cells. While Nordenson *et al* (1994) found an increase in chromosomal aberrations after intermittent exposure of human amniotic cells to a 50 Hz, 30 μT field over a period of 72 hours, Galt *et al* (1995) failed to find an effect in a similar 50 Hz field. Antonopoulos *et al* (1995) found no effect on the frequency of sister chromatid exchanges (SCEs) in human lymphocytes after exposure to an electromagnetic field (50 Hz, 5 mT). They noted that while they had no evidence of an initiating effect, their studies on cell stimulation/cell division did suggest a promoting effect. Yaguchi *et al* (1999) reported a significant elevation of SCEs when cultured mouse m5S cells were exposed to an electromagnetic field (60 Hz, 400 mT). The effect was small, approximately a 25% increase over control levels. Fields of lower strength had no effect. When the cells were exposed to mitomycin C, a well-known inducer of SCEs, as well as to the electromagnetic field there was an apparent additive effect, suggesting that there was no interaction between the two agents.

24 A rapid surrogate for chromosomal damage is the micronucleus test which enables very large numbers of non-dividing cells to be examined for micronuclei which are the remnants of broken chromosomes that have failed to be included in the cell nuclei following cell division. Scarfi *et al* (1994) found no effect on micronucleus formation in human peripheral lymphocytes following exposure to a pulsed 50 Hz, 2.5 mT field over a period of 72 hours. Similarly, Paile *et al* (1995) found no increase in micronuclei after exposure to a 50 Hz sinusoidal magnetic field. Lagroye and Poncy (1997) used a combination of ionising radiation exposure (2 and 6 Gy gamma rays) followed by a 24 hour exposure to a complex magnetic field, but found no increase in micronuclei in the exposed rat tracheal epithelial cells. They did, however, notice an increase in binucleated cells with micronuclei following exposure to 6 Gy and to an ELF electromagnetic field and suggested that this could enhance subsequent genomic alterations.

25 Simko *et al* (1998) suggested that different cell lines may respond differently to ELF electromagnetic field exposure. They found a statistically significant increase in micronucleus frequency after 48 and 72 hours continuous exposure to a 50 Hz, 0.8 mT and 1.0 mT field of a human squamous cell carcinoma cell line (SCLII) but no effect on AFC, a human amniotic fluid cell line. They interpreted this to mean that the ELF electromagnetic field could be a promoter rather than an initiator. The work of Lai and Singh (1997) could suggest the operation of an indirect free radical mechanism. The two possible mechanisms of a free radical effect of low frequency fields, namely, germinate recombination and radical recombination, could change the yields of free radicals at

best by a factor of two (Brocklehurst and McLauchlin, 1996). Since there are many cellular defence mechanisms against free radicals such a mechanism would be expected to operate only if there were inherent defects in the repair systems. The results of Lai and Singh should therefore be considered with some caution.

26 There is therefore only limited support for the notion that ELF electromagnetic fields on their own are genotoxic. The work of Miyakoshi *et al* (1999) and of Walleczek *et al* (1999) does, however, suggest that ELF electromagnetic fields may enhance the effects of ionising radiation. The NIEHS report concludes that 'multiple self consistent reports demonstrate a dose dependent effect on a process or end point commonly considered to be associated with carcinogenesis' (NIEHS, 1998). Any future studies could, therefore, most profitably be focused on determining whether concurrent or subsequent exposure to an ELF electromagnetic field enhances the genotoxic effect of known mutagens and carcinogens.

PROMOTION OR ALTERATION OF CELLULAR PROCESSES WHICH COULD AFFECT THE MECHANISMS LEADING TO CANCER

27 While in many cancers secondary genetic changes are very important in causing progression towards full malignancy, these changes often exert their effect by affecting specific cellular processes in an inappropriate way or at an inappropriate time. For example, if an intracellular signalling mechanism, which normally follows receipt of an external stimulus, malfunctions by, say, sending out a signal without an external stimulus, this could lead to a cascade of events resulting in inappropriate gene transcription. If the gene(s) is(are) involved in the control of cell division then this could contribute to the development of cancer. Thus 'promotion' may simply be the abnormal expression of a normal cellular function.

Apoptosis

28 Cells require a series of external stimuli to carry out their normal functions. In many cases, the absence of these external signals leads to a process of programmed cell death or apoptosis. Similarly, apoptosis may be triggered if a cell is damaged in such a way that repair is unlikely to restore normal function. Many cancer cells have lost the ability to undergo apoptosis and therefore they may fail to die when damaged or where their normal functions are impaired. Narita *et al* (1997) and Hisamitsu (1997) both found that exposure of the human leukaemic cell line HL60 to a field of 50 Hz at 45 mT for a minimum of 1 hour induced an increase in apoptotic cells but the effect was not observed in human peripheral blood lymphocytes. They ruled out temperature increases. However, it should be noted that this extremely high field is approximately three orders of magnitude greater than would be encountered under high voltage transmission lines. They suggested that an induction current produced by the ELF electromagnetic field may have been one mediator of apoptosis in HL60 cells. Reipert *et al* (1997), using the mouse haemopoetic progenitor cell line FDCP-mix (A4), found no alteration in the frequency of apoptosis following exposure to a variety of different low frequency magnetic fields at 50 Hz and 6 μT, 1 mT and 2 mT for varying periods up to 7 days. Blumenthal *et al* (1997) exposed rat tendon fibroblasts and rat bone marrow cells to a variety of AC and/or DC magnetic fields. The AC fields were at 60 Hz and 1000 Hz and up to 0.25 mT. Several conditions resulted in detachment of the cells from the substratum or in failure to attach. This was accompanied by an increase in apoptosis. Simko *et al* (1998) found an increased frequency of apoptosis in transformed cells but not in normal human cells following exposure to a 50 Hz field around 1.0 mT. These results, although contradictory, seem to indicate a possible increase in apoptosis in some cell types under some conditions and further studies would be of value. However, induction of apoptosis is unlikely to contribute to the progression of cancer – on the contrary it is loss of the ability to undergo apoptosis that is associated with some cancer cells.

Cell proliferation

29 Stimulation of cellular proliferation is often considered to be a major factor in tumour progression and there have been a number of studies which seek to determine whether electromagnetic fields influence cell division and hence cell proliferation. The Advisory Group report (NRPB, 1992) found that evidence for a direct effect on cell proliferation was equivocal. The situation is not clarified by recent studies.

Direct effects on proliferation

30 Although the majority of cell proliferation studies failed to find an effect, there are a number of reports of positive effects. In two studies Schimmelpfeng and Dertinger (1993, 1997) reported cell cycle effects which resulted in a small increase in several measures of proliferation. The effect was found in both SV40 transformed 3T3 mouse cells and human leukaemic HL60 cells in a 2 mT, 50 Hz magnetic field. They concluded that the effects on cell growth were due to an induced electric field expressed only above a threshold of between 4 and 8 $mV_{pk}\,m^{-1}$. A small increase in incorporation of ^{3}H-thymidine into TE85 human osteosarcoma cells following exposure to a 10–16 Hz, 10 $\mu V\,m^{-1}$ field for 30 minutes was reported by Fitzsimmons *et al* (1992), indicating a stimulation of DNA synthesis and hence growth of the cells. Sauer *et al* (1997) studied a system in which prostate tumour cells were grown in culture as aggregates known as spheroids. After exposure to a single DC pulse of 5000 $V\,m^{-1}$ for 60 seconds they found that the volume doubling time was reduced to 1–2 days as compared to 4–5 days for control samples. Six days after the pulse, the necrotic core which occurs in all spheroids was reduced in diameter and the active external rim was increased in thickness on average from 60 $\pm$ 6 μm to 107 $\pm$ 11 μm.

31 In a second report of stimulation of cell cycle activity in multicellular tumour spheroids the same group, Wartenburg *et al* (1997), suggested that the stimulation caused by a single DC electric field pulse was due to the production of reactive oxygen species which in turn mediated Ca^{2+} release from intracellular stores.

32 Having failed to find any effect on sister chromatid exchanges, Antonopoulos *et al* (1995) reported a stimulation of the cell cycle in dividing human peripheral blood lymphocytes in the presence of an electromagnetic field of 50 Hz and 5 mT and concluded that the field had no initiating effects but probably did have promoting effects.

33 Two particularly interesting studies failed to find any proliferation stimulating effect of ELF electromagnetic fields but did observe stimulation of differentiation. In a study prompted by the observation that ELF electromagnetic fields of various kinds can alter

osteogenesis *in vivo*, Landry *et al* (1997) examined the effect of exposure for 1-3 days to a 10 μT, 60 Hz field on periosteal proliferation and differentiation in normal rat tibia or tibia 1–14 days after a surgical injury. The ELF electromagnetic fields had no effect on the normal tissues. Following injury, there was an increase in the number of mature osteoblasts but apparently no effect on proliferation, suggesting that the ELF electromagnetic field promoted differentiation rather than cell division. Hisenkamp *et al* (1997) examined the effects of a low frequency pulsed electric current on cultured human skin keratinocytes. They found that the balance between proliferation and differentiation was significantly modified in favour in differentiation in the electrically treated samples as compared to non-exposed controls. However, Macleod and Collazo (2000) found a negative effect on differentiation using an osteoblast-like mouse cell line (MC-3T3) which showed entry into a more differentiated state by a rise in alkaline phosphatase. After exposure to a 30 Hz, 1.8 mT field, this activity was progressively suppressed. The authors suggested that this represented an inhibition of differentiation by exposure to the ELF electromagnetic field.

34 In contrast to these studies, there is a substantial number of reports of failure to identify any effect of exposure to electromagnetic fields. Indeed, in one study, Nindl *et al* (1997) reported a significant inhibition of DNA synthesis in Jurkat (E6.1) cells exposed to a 1.8 mT bone healing electromagnetic field and to fields of 0.1 mT and 40 μT at 60 Hz. The inhibition of cells grown in conditioned media can be up to 60%.

35 Cridland *et al* (1996) found no effect on the rate of cell proliferation as measured by DNA synthesis in HF19 normal human fibroblasts using a 20 μT to 20 mT, 50 Hz field for up to 30 hours. More recently, however, Cridland *et al* (1999) did find an effect of ELF electromagnetic field exposure on the rate of cell cycle progression by normal human fibroblast. They observed a small but significant increase in the length of G1 following exposure to 20 and 200 μT, 50 Hz fields. Curiously, no effect was found at higher flux densities of 2 and 20 mT. The authors suggested that this inverted dose-response relationship could be explained by a free radical mechanism. They also argued that this result was not incompatible with their previous studies since a small change in one part of the cycle may not change the overall rate of cell proliferation. Reipert *et al* (1996) failed to find any effect on cell numbers or on colony forming efficiency of the mouse haemopoetic progenitor cells FDCP-mix A4. These results are similar to the earlier studies of Fiorani *et al* (1992) who found no change in cell number following exposure of K562 myeloid leukaemia cells to a field of 50 Hz, 0.2–200 μT and those of Phillips and McChesney (1991) who found no increase in ^{3}H-thymidine uptake in CCRF-CEM human lymphoblastoid cells following exposure to a field of 72 Hz pulsed 3.5 mT for 30 minutes to 24 hours. It must be concluded, therefore, that the evidence for stimulation of cell division by electromagnetic fields is still equivocal.

36 A major problem in assessing this kind of work is that each group of workers uses a different cell system, a different ELF electromagnetic field exposure and one of a wide range of different measures of proliferation. What is required is careful duplication of those studies that claim a positive effect. More weight could be put on effects demonstrated to be reproducible by other workers. So far, no positive studies have been corroborated but this does not mean they are all wrong – it may be that no one has attempted to reproduce them.

Indirect effects by release of inhibition

37 One special case of stimulation of proliferation arises originally from the work of Liburdy *et al* (1993) who used the oestrogen receptor positive (ER^+) human breast cancer cell line MCF7. In this system, proliferation is blocked by the addition of physiological concentrations (1 nM) of melatonin. When these cells were simultaneously exposed to a 60 Hz, 1.2 μT magnetic field the inhibition caused by melatonin was removed and the cells renewed proliferation. The magnetic field alone did not affect growth in any way. It was suggested that the ELF electromagnetic field disrupted either the ligand/receptor interaction or the subsequent signalling pathway. Liburdy *et al* found no effect at 0.2 μT and suggested a threshold between 0.2 and 1.2 μT. A similar effect of a 60 Hz field was reported by Harland and Liburdy (1995, 1997) and Liburdy and Levine (1998) but using tamoxifen rather than melatonin to bring about the initial inhibition. The effect has been reported in other cell lines, namely a second breast cancer cell line, T47B (Harland *et al*, 1998) and a human glioma cell line, 5F757 (Afzal and Liburdy, 1998). Most of these studies come from Liburdy's group but Blackman *et al* (1998) have also reported replication of these effects. The effects, however, are small (10%–20% growth over 7 days) and the NIEHS report (1998) suggested that the 'nature of the experimental design raises serious concerns about the robustness of the effect' (see the footnote on page 56).

Altered intracellular signalling

38 Stimulation of cells to divide normally comes from the application of stimuli originating externally to the cell. Any evidence that electromagnetic fields can influence the processes of intracellular signalling is therefore relevant to any consideration of the carcinogenic potential of such fields. It is now accepted that in cell free systems, ELF electromagnetic fields can influence chemical and enzymic reactions (see, for example, Hamilton *et al*, 1988; Batchelor *et al*, 1993). Lacy Hulbert *et al* (1998) concluded that there were 'clear, reproducible effects of magnetic fields on biochemical systems with a firm theoretical basis' and that 'these provide a plausible approach to investigating biological effect of low-strength magnetic fields'. It remains to be determined, however, whether these effects influence biological systems *in vivo* and whether they occur at field strengths relevant to environmental exposure.

Calcium flux – non-resonant time-varying fields

39 A number of cell signalling pathways produce transient increases in the intracellular concentration of free Ca^{2+}, initially by stimulating release from intracellular stores, and subsequently by influx across the cell membrane from the extracellular fluid. Several studies have sought to investigate the possibility that electromagnetic fields act to stimulate calcium ion movements, and thereby influence signalling pathways.

40 Exposure of Jurkat human lymphoblastic T-cells to a 50 Hz, 100 μT magnetic field has been reported to elicit an increase in intracellular free Ca^{2+} concentration which was similar in magnitude to that induced by stimulation with an anti-CD3 antibody (Lindström *et al*, 1993) and confirmed using magnetic fields with various frequencies and flux densities (Lindström *et al*, 1995a,b). They found the response at 150 μT over a frequency range from 5 to 100 Hz with a broad peak at 50 Hz. There was no effect below 40 μT and a plateau at 150 μT. However, a specific attempt to replicate these results by Wey *et al* (2000) failed to find any effect. Preliminary reports from other

groups using fluorescent indicators to monitor intracellular ion concentrations in Jurkat cells have indicated that the response to a 60 Hz, 2 mT magnetic field (inducing an electric field of 1.8 mV m^{-1} in the medium) may be dependent on the biological status of the cells (Walleczek *et al*, 1994). This observation is in agreement with previous findings from the same authors on the Con-A-induced calcium response of rat thymic lymphocytes exposed to 3 Hz pulsed magnetic fields (Walleczek and Budinger, 1992); significant effects on Ca^{2+} influx were observed at peak flux densities of 6.5 and 28 mT, and appeared to be dependent on field strength. The report by Galvanovskis *et al* (1996) also suggested that the experimental conditions were crucial in determining whether or not the observed effects were due to the electromagnetic fields. They found that the poly-L-lysine, which is used in many of these studies to cause the Jurkat cells to adhere to the substratum, could itself cause fluctuations in intracellular calcium. They found that when the intracellular calcium concentration was low and non-oscillating, no effect of magnetic field could be detected. However, a 50 Hz, 100 mT field caused significant changes in cells exhibiting prolonged calcium oscillations.

Calcium flux – resonant fields

41 It has been reported that $^{45}Ca^{2+}$ uptake was increased following exposure of a variety of lymphocytic cells to combined static and time-varying magnetic fields 'tuned' to resonant conditions (Lyle *et al*, 1991), although these studies examined the dependence on resonance, for example, by 'detuning' the fields. Furthermore, two other studies found that exposure of either human (Prasad *et al*, 1991) or mouse (Coulton and Barker, 1993) lymphocytes to resonant fields did not affect $^{45}Ca^{2+}$ uptake or intracellular free Ca^{2+} concentration, respectively. In a further study Lyle *et al* (1997) found no effect of a 60 Hz, 0.15 mT field on intracellular signalling in Jurkat E6 human leukaemia cells. They studied the intracellular calcium sensitive fluorescent dye fluo-3 under both optimal growth conditions and sub-optimal conditions of lowered temperature, lowered external calcium and lowered CD3 stimulation.

42 These studies on Jurkat cells are of importance since the various groups are using similar test systems. Agreement is not complete, but there is nevertheless a possibility that calcium ion concentration can be affected by exposure to an electromagnetic field under carefully defined conditions, taking into consideration in particular the biological state of the cells and the precise field conditions used (see the footnote on page 56).

Other effects on signalling

43 Another measure of intracellular signalling is the impact of specific stimuli on the activity of phosphatidyl inositol 3-kinase (PI3 kinase). Clejan *et al* (1995) reported a decrease in erythropoetin stimulated PI3 kinase in the human haemopoetic cell line (TFI), to lower than basal levels in the presence of a pulsed electromagnetic field. Translocation of the regulatory sub-unit of PI3 kinase to the membrane was also inhibited. Phospholipase C was activated as reflected by increases in diacylglycerol and inositol triphosphate. It was suggested that these effects were associated with antiproliferative effects of the ELF electromagnetic field. Santoro *et al* (1997) also concluded that electric and magnetic fields may have interfered with the initiation of the signal cascade pathways. Using a human lymphoid cell line (RAJI) they found multiple effects following exposure for 72 hours to a 50 Hz sinusoidal magnetic field at a density of 2 mT. They found a decrease in membrane fluidity, a reorganisation of cytoskeletal components, a loss of microvilli, a redistribution of actin and interference with protein phosphorylation. However, Miller *et al* (1999) found no effect of ELF electromagnetic field exposure (60 Hz, 0.1 to 1.0 mT) on the signalling pathways controlling the expression of the transcription factors NF-kB or AP-1.

44 There is an interesting report by Ucken *et al* (1995) on the SRC family kinase LYN. Activity of the proto-oncogene-encoded kinase was stimulated in B-lymphoid cells by exposure to a field of 60 Hz, 100 μT. The effect was substantial, rapid and appeared to affect expression of other genes in this signalling pathway. These studies were extended in a later paper by the same group (Dibirdik *et al*, 1998). Using DT40 lymphoma B cells it was found that exposure to a 60 Hz, 0.1 mT field resulted in a tyrosine kinase dependent activation of phospholipase Cγ2 (PLCγ2) leading to an increased inositol phospholipid turnover. Using a variety of gene transfer techniques the authors concluded that electromagnetic field induced PLCγ2 activation was mediated by LYN-regulated stimulation of SYK which acted downstream of LYN kinase but upstream of PLCγ2. These experiments appear to have been rigorously executed and clearly need to be confirmed by other groups. It is a weakness of this field that such an important study has not yet been repeated. Khadir *et al* (1999) reported an increased production of superoxide anion O_2^- and β-glucuronidase by human neutrophils which had been primed by a sub-optimal stimulating dose of phorbolmyristate acetate (PMA) after exposure to a field at 60 Hz and 22 mT. They interpreted this to be an effect mediated by stimulation of a signalling pathway by the exposure to the ELF electromagnetic field.

45 It has already been noted that Blumenthal *et al* (1997) found an increase in apoptosis associated with cellular detachment following alterations in cytoskeletal structure after ELF electromagnetic field exposure. Overall, therefore, there is accumulating evidence that electromagnetic fields can influence early signalling pathways. The results from Ucken's group (see above) appear to be of particular interest.

Effects on general gene expression

46 A considerable number of studies have been carried out of the effects of ELF electromagnetic fields on gene expression, assayed mostly via an analysis of RNA synthesis. Early reports of increased RNA synthesis from several chromosomes in cultured *Sciara coprophilia* salivary glands exposed to a variety of ELF electromagnetic fields (see Goodman and Henderson, 1991) have been extended (Goodman *et al*, 1992a) to include an analysis of transcription from the right arm of chromosome 3 in a similar preparation to *Drosophila melanogaster*. Exposure to a 72 Hz pulsed magnetic field at a flux density of 3.5 mT has been reported to induce a short-term increase in the synthesis of both total and messenger RNA (mRNA) in CCRF-CEM lymphoblastoid cells (Phillips and McChesney, 1991). Exposure of HL60 cells to a 1 mT, 60 Hz sinusoidal magnetic field was reported to produce a temporally similar, although quantitatively smaller, increase in total RNA synthesis which was dependent on the magnitude of the induced electric field (Greene *et al*, 1991). Balcer-Kubiczek *et al* (1998), however, found no evidence of differential expression of any of a very large number of genes screened using a two-gel c-DNA screening method in human leukaemia HL60 cells exposed to a 60 Hz, 2 mT magnetic field. In contrast, exposure of the same cells to 5 Gy of x-rays showed differential expression in approximately 1% of the random pool of c-DNAs.

Effects on specific gene expression

47 The biological significance of the reported short-term increases in gross transcription is difficult to assess. Clear and unequivocal evidence for effects on the transcription of specific genes, particularly those known to be important for regulating cellular behaviour, would be of far greater importance. Unfortunately the evidence for this is much less convincing. In particular, the absence of internal loading controls renders some of the data extremely difficult to interpret. Furthermore, the earlier published studies have mostly been based on dot-blots rather than more analytical assays such as Northern blots or RNAase protection assays, and examples of raw data have rarely been shown. Even where the evidence for magnetic field effects on gene expression appears to be reliable, the magnitude of the response tends to be small and should be viewed in the context of the response to other agents. For example, in cultured fibroblasts, c-*myc* expression can be induced about 20-fold by serum (Campisi *et al*, 1984), 40-fold by platelet-derived growth factor, 15-fold by fibroblast growth factor and 10-fold by the chemical tumour promoter 12-0-tetradecanoylphorbol-13-acetate (TPA) (Kelly *et al*, 1983). Similarly, treatment of B-lymphocytes with the mitogen lipopolysaccharide results in a 20-fold induction of c-*myc* expression, whilst treatment of T-lymphocytes with Con A elicits a 10-fold induction (Kelly *et al*, 1983). For the proto-oncogenes c-*fos* (Shah *et al*, 1993) and c-*jun* (Stein *et al*, 1992), inductions of up to 200-fold have been reported following treatment with serum and ultraviolet radiation, respectively. Thus the biological significance of much smaller inductions by ELF electromagnetic fields must be questionable but is nevertheless worthy of reporting here.

48 It has been reported that exposure of HL60 human lymphocytic cells to either pulsed (1.5–72 Hz, 0.38–19 mT peak) or sinusoidal (5–150 Hz, 0.57–570 mT rms) magnetic fields increased accumulation of transcripts from the B-actin, histone H2B, c-*myc*, c-*src*, and B-tubulin genes (Goodman *et al*, 1989, 1992b, 1994; Wei *et al*, 1990; Goodman and Henderson, 1991; Gold *et al*, 1994); one gene, α-globin, did not respond to magnetic fields, but expression of this gene is normally cell-type specific anyway. Exposure to a 5.7 μT rms, 60 Hz sinusoidal magnetic field has also been reported to induce expression of the heat shock protein gene, *hsp70*, in HL60 cells (Goodman *et al*, 1994). In general, these data suggest the existence of frequency, time and field strength windows for magnetic field effects on transcription. Moreover, the results for histone are puzzling since the expression of histones is normally tightly regulated within the cell cycle, whilst the reported increase in accumulation of mRNA from the proto-oncogene c-*myc* may have little significance since the c-*myc* gene in these cells is abnormally regulated following a gene amplification event. Induction of stress proteins (Sps) by ELF electromagnetic fields has also been reported by Pipkin *et al* (1999). They found that Sp70 and Sp27 were induced by exposure to a 1 mT, 60 Hz field but after a 0.1 mT field exposure. Sp90 was not induced but was found to be phosphorylated after exposure to a 1 mT, 60 Hz field. However, Miyakoshi *et al* (2000b) found that an ELF electromagnetic field at 50 mT and 60 Hz suppressed the expression of heat-induced heat shock protein 70 (hsp70) in a human leukaemia cell line. The effect was not observed at 5 or 0.5 mT. One of the most interesting examples of stimulation of specific gene expression comes from the studies of Junkersdorf *et al* (2000) on the nematode *Caenorhabditis elegans*. They used two different systems. In one, an extrachromosomal element contained a reporter

lacZ gene under the control of a heat shock protein 16 (hsp16) promotor (pPCZ1). In the other a stably integrated lacZ reporter gene was under the control of an hsp70 promotor (pD2047). These tiny animals were exposed to an ELF electromagnetic field at 50 Hz and 1–150 μT at a range of temperatures. The effect on gene expression was measured by β-galactosidase activity. In both strains of *C elegans* it was possible to define an optimum elevated temperature at which a field of 100 μT enhanced the expression of the reporter gene. In strain pPCZ1 expression was elevated almost five-fold at 29 °C and 100 μT, whilst in strain pD2047 expression was elevated on average by about three-fold at 30 °C and 100 μT, although there was considerable variability between experiments.

49 There is some support for magnetic field effects on the expression of c-*myc*, and other regulatory genes, from work in other laboratories. For example, exposure of CEM-CM3 T lymphoblastoid cells to a 100 μT, 60 Hz magnetic field for up to 2 hours resulted in transient changes in the expression of the c-*myc*, c-*fos*, c-*jun*, and protein kinase C (PKC) genes (Phillips *et al*, 1992). In this study the principal approach was to assess the rate of transcription directly using nuclear runoff assays rather than indirectly by estimating the accumulation of transcripts, a parameter which may be influenced by other processes. Slot-blot analysis of cytoplasmic RNA from the same cells indicated that accumulation gave a reasonable estimate of transcription. In general, exposure was reported to increase transcription from the c-*fos*, c-*myc*, and PKC genes, whilst the effect on expression of c-*jun* was variable and dependent on cell density. Time course data indicated that these responses were all observed within an hour, whilst longer exposure was reported to inhibit expression of PKC. It should be noted, however, that in the absence of appropriate internal loading controls it is difficult to reliably assess such small responses (generally around two-fold). Jahreis *et al* (1998) attempted to replicate these results using the same cells and failed to find any effect of a 60 Hz magnetic field at 0.1 mT on the expression of c-*jun*, c-*fos*, or c-*myc*. Using a different system, Loberg *et al* (1999) also failed to find any effect of magnetic field exposure on a c-*myc* expression. Two different human breast epithelial cell lines were exposed to a range of flux densities from 10 to 1000 μT at 60 Hz for varying periods up to 24 hours. There was no significant effect on basal levels of c-*myc* transcripts in either model and no effect on alterations in *c-myc* expression induced by the tumour promoter TPA. Expression of a number of other cancer-associated genes was also unaffected by exposure to these fields.

50 The activation of a gene in response to earlier signalling events occurs as a result of changes in the interaction of protein transcription factors with regulatory elements in the promoter region of the gene. There may be several such elements in the promoters of genes which are responsive to a number of signalling pathways (activated by different stimuli), and identification of the element conferring responsiveness to a particular stimulus may be helpful in elucidating the pathway through which the signal is transduced. It has been reported that a magnetic field responsive element resides between positions –353 and –1257 upstream of the c-*myc* PI initiation site (Lin *et al*, 1994). The element was identified by deletion analysis of the human c-*myc* promoter fused to a chloramphenicol acetyl transferase (CAT) reporter gene, and mediated transcriptional activation in HeLa cells exposed to 60 Hz magnetic fields at 8 μT. However, 900 base pairs is a relatively large fragment of DNA, and there therefore remains considerable scope for defining the location of the element more precisely. Moreover, it should be noted that the CAT activity appeared to be extremely low for all the constructs, suggesting that they were all essentially unresponsive under the conditions tested.

51 In contrast to those discussed above, other studies have failed to find consistent effects on proto-oncogene expression. For example, Parker and Winters (1992) examined transcription in a variety of human and mouse cell lines exposed to 0.1 mT, 60 Hz magnetic fields and found no evidence for increased accumulation of mRNA from the proto-oncogenes c-*fos*, c-*myc*, c-*raf* and c-*ras*; there was also no effect on transcription from hsp70 or, in the case of cells infected with either mouse mammary tumour virus or murine sarcoma virus, viral genes. It should be noted, however, that in addition to suffering many of the methodological flaws criticised above, the minimum exposure time would have been too long to detect transient effects. Desjobert *et al* (1995) also failed to detect any increase in c-*myc* transcripts in either HL60 cells or EBV transformed human lymphoblastic cells following exposure to a 50 Hz field at either 10 or 1 mT.

52 In another study, it was found that exposure of HL60 cells to a 1 mT, 60 Hz field for up to 90 minutes did not affect the accumulation of either c-*myc* or β-actin transcripts; the steady state level of the 28 S ribosomal RNA was also unaffected (Greene *et al*, 1993). Using a unique assay involving pulse labelling of cellular RNA in combination with a nuclease protection step, it was also shown that the transcription rates for c-*myc* and β-actin were unaffected by exposure. There did, however, appear to be an effect on synthesis of the 45 S precursor ribosomal RNA, although this appeared to be associated with a concomitant reduction in the half-life of the 45 S fraction and its mature products the 18 S and 28 S RNAs.

53 A number of studies, which appear to have been carefully designed and performed, have not detected any effect of exposure to magnetic fields. In one study attempting to replicate some of the earlier work of Goodman, Henderson and co-workers (Goodman and Henderson, 1991; Goodman *et al*, 1992b, 1994) but using an improved experimental design, accumulation of c-*myc* RNA was reported as not affected by exposure of HL60 cells to 60 Hz magnetic fields at 1 and 10 μT (Lacy-Hulbert *et al*, 1995a). In particular, the latter experiments were carried out 'blind' and the authors utilised quantitative Northern blot analysis of the mRNA transcripts, normalised to either the housekeeping gene GAPDH or total RNA as internal controls, an improved cell handling protocol and an improved exposure system. In another careful and extensive study, based on the ribonuclease protection assay of mRNA transcripts normalised to β-2-microglobulin, neither c-*myc* nor β-actin appeared to be affected by exposure of either HL60 or Daudi cells to 60 Hz fields at flux densities from 8 μT to 1 mT (Saffer and Thurston, 1995a). Both groups of authors (Lacy-Hulbert *et al*, 1995b; Saffer and Thurston, 1995b) implicated the use of poor experimental techniques in the earlier positive reports of increase c-*myc* expression in HL60 cells. A further preliminary report has indicated that exposure to 50 Hz magnetic fields at either 6 μT or 2 mT did not affect the interleukin-3 induced expression of c-*fos*, c-*jun* or *jun*-B in FDCP-mix human haemopoietic stem cells (Reipert *et al*, 1994).

54 More recent results are also contradictory. Positive results were reported by Lagroye and Poncy (1998) who found increased expression of c-*jun* and c-*fos* in primary

Cantoni O, Sestili P, Fiorani M, *et al* (1995). The effect of 50 Hz sinusoidal electric and/or magnetic fields on the rate of repair of DNA single/double strand breaks in oxidatively injured cells. *Biochem Mol Biol Int*, **37**, 681–9.

Cantoni O, Sestili P, Fiorani M, *et al* (1996). Effect of 50 Hz sinusoidal electric and/or magnetic fields on the rate of DNA single strand breaks in cultured mammalian cells exposed to three different carcinogens: methylmethane sulphonate, chromate and 254 nm UV radiation. *Biochem Mol Biol Int*, **38**, 527–33.

Clejan S, Dotson R S, Ide C F, *et al* (1995). Co-ordinated effects of electromagnetic field exposure on erythropoietin-induced activities of phosphatidylinositol-phospholipase C and phosphatidylinositol 3-kinase. *Cell Biochem Biophys*, **27**, 203.

Coulton L A and Barker A T (1993). Magnetic fields and intracellular calcium: effects on lymphocytes exposed to conditions of 'cyclotron' resonance. *Phys Med Biol*, **38**, 347–60.

Cress L W, Owen R D and Desta A B (1999). Ornithine decarboxylase activity in L929 cells following exposure to 60 Hz magnetic fields. *Carcinogenesis*, **20**, 1025–30.

Cridland N A, Cragg T A, Haylock R G E *et al* (1996). Effects of 50 Hz magnetic field exposure on the rate of DNA synthesis by normal human fibroblasts. *Int J Radiat Biol*, **69**, 503–11.

Cridland N A, Haylock R G E and Saunders R D (1999). 50 Hz magnetic field exposure alters onset of S-phase in normal human fibroblast. *Bioelectromagnetics*, **20**, 446–52.

Dees C, Garrett S, Henley D, *et al* (1996). Effects of 60 Hz fields, estradiol and xenoestrogens on human breast cancer cells. *Radiat Res*, **146**, 444–52.

Desjobert H, Hillion J, Adolphe M, *et al* (1995). Effects of 50 Hz magnetic fields on c-myc transcript levels in nonsynchronized and synchronised human cells. *Bioelectromagnetics*, **16**, 277–83.

Dibirdik I, Kristupaitis D, Kurosaki T, *et al* (1998). Stimulation of Src family protein-tyrosine kinases as a proximal and mandatory step for SYK kinase-dependent phospholipase cγ2 activation in lymphoma B cells exposed to low energy electromagnetic fields. *J Biol Chem*, **273**, 4035–9.

Fairbairn D W and O'Neill K L (1994). The effect of electromagnetic exposure on the formation of DNA single strand breaks in human cells. *Cell Mol Biol*, **40**, 561–7.

Fiorani M, Cantoni O, Sestili P, *et al* (1992). Electric and/or magnetic field effects on DNA structure and function in cultured human cells. *Mutat Res*, **282**, 25–9.

Fitzsimmons R J, Strong D D, Mohan S, *et al* (1992). Low amplitude, low frequency electric field-stimulated bone cell proliferation may in part be mediated by increased IGF II release. *J Cell Physiol*, **150**, 84–9.

Fitzsimmons R J, Ryaby J T, Magee F P, *et al* (1995). IGF II receptor number is increased in TE85 osteosarcoma cells by combined magnetic fields. *J Bone Min Res*, **10**, 812–9.

Galt S, Wahlstrom J, Hamnerius Y, *et al* (1995). Study of effects of 50 Hz magnetic field on chromosome aberrations and the growth related enzyme ODC in human amniotic cells. *Bioelectrochem Bioenerget*, **36**, 1–8.

Galvanovskis J, Sandblom J, Bergqvist B, *et al* (1996). The influence of 50 Hz magnetic field on cytoplasmic Ca^{2+} oscillation in human leukaemia cells. *Sci Total Environ*, **180**, 19–33.

Gamble S C, Wolff H and Arrand J E (1999). Syrian hamster dermal cell immortalisation is not enhanced by power line frequency electromagnetic field exposure. *Br J Cancer*, **81**, 377–80.

Gold S, Goodman R and Shirley-Henderson A (1994). Exposure of Simian Virus-40-transformed human cells to magnetic fields results in increased levels of T-antigen mRNA and protein. *Bioelectromagnetics*, **15**, 329–36.

Goodman R and Henderson A S (1991). Transcription and translation in cells exposed to extremely low frequency electromagnetic fields. *Bioelectrochem Bioenerget*, **25**, 335–55.

Goodman R, Blank M, Lin H, *et al* (1994). Increased levels of hsp70 transcripts induced when cells are exposed to low frequency electromagnetic fields. *Bioelectrochem Bioenerget*, **33**, 115–20.

Goodman R, Weisbrot D, Uluc A, *et al* (1992a). Transcription in *Drosophila melanogaster* salivary gland cells is altered following exposure to low-frequency electromagnetic fields: analysis of chromosome 3R. *Bioelectromagnetics*, **13**, 111–18.

Goodman R, Wei L-X, Bumann J, *et al* (1992b). Exposure to electric and magnetic (EM) fields increases transcripts in HL-60 cells: does adaptation to EM fields occur? *Bioelectrochem Bioenerget*, **29**, 185–92.

Goodman R, Wei L-X, Xu J-C, *et al* (1989). Exposure of human cells to low-frequency electromagnetic fields results in quantitative changes in transcripts. *Biochim Biophys Acta*, **1009**, 216–20.

Greene J J, Skowronski W J, Mullins M, *et al* (1991). Delineation of electric and magnetic field effects of extremely low frequency electromagnetic radiation on transcription. *Biochem Biophys Res Comm*, **174**, 742–9.

Greene J J, Pearson S L, Skowronski W J, *et al* (1993). Gene-specific modulation of RNA synthesis and degradation by extremely low frequency electromagnetic fields. *Cell Mol Biol*, **39**, 261–8.

Grimaldi S, Pasquali E, Barbatano L, *et al* (1997). Epstein Barr virus genome in latently infected human lymphoid cells. *J Environ Pathol Toxicol Oncol*, **16**, 205–7.

Hamilton C A, Hewitt J P and McLauchlan K A (1988). High resolution studies of the effects of magnetic fields on chemical reactions. *Mol Phys*, **65**, 423–38.

Harland J D and Liburdy R P (1995). 60 Hz ELF inhibition of melatonin and tamoxifen action of MCF-7 cells: EVB field components. IN Abstracts, 17th Annual Meeting of the Bioelectromagnetics Society, June 1995, Boston MA, p 16.

Harland J D and Liburdy R P (1997). Environmental magnetic fields inhibit the antiproliferative action of tamoxifen and melatonin in a human breast cancer cell line. *Bioelectromagnetics*, **18**, 555–62.

Harland J D, Levine G A and Liburdy R P (1998). Differential inhibition of tamoxifen's oncostatic functions in a human breast cancer cell line by a 12 mG (1.2 μT) magnetic field. IN *Electricity and Magnetism in Biology and Medicine* (F Bersani, Ed). Bologna, Italy, Plenum Press.

Harrison G H, Balcer-Kubiczek E K, Shi Z-M, *et al* (1997). Kinetics of gene expression following exposure to 60 Hz, 2 mT magnetic field in three human cell lines. *Bioelectrochem Bioenerget*, **43**, 1–6.

Hisamitsu T, Narita K, Kasahara T, *et al* (1997). Induction of apoptosis in human leukaemic cells by magnetic fields. *Japan J Physiol*, **47**, 307–10.

Hisenkamp M, Jercinovic A, de Graef C, *et al* (1997). Effects of low frequency pulsed electrical current on keratinocytes *in vitro*. *Bioelectromagnetics*, **18**, 250–4.

Jacobson-Kram D, Tepper J, Kuo P, *et al* (1997). Evaluation of potential genotoxicity of pulsed electric and electromagnetic fields used for bone growth stimulation. *Mutat Res*, **388**, 45–7.

Jarheis G P, Johnson P G, Zhao Y L, *et al* (1998). Absence of 60 Hz, 0.1 mT magnetic field-induced changes in oncogene transcription rates or levels in CEM-CM3 cells. *Biochem Biophys Acta*, **1443**, 334–42.

Junkersdorf B, Bauer H and Gutzeit H O (2000). Electromagnetic fields enhance the stress response at elevated temperatures in the nematode *Caenorhabdites elegans*. *Bioelectromagnetics*, **21**, 100–106.

Kelly K, Cochran B H, Stiles C D, *et al* (1983). Cell-specific regulation of the c-*myc* gene by lymphocyte mitogens and platelet-derived growth factor. *Cell*, **35**, 603–10.

Khadir R, Morgan J L and Murray J J (1999). Effects of 60 Hz magnetic field exposure on polymorphonuclear leukocyte activation. *Biochem Biophys Acta*, **1472**, 359–67.

Koana T, Okada M O, Ikehata M, *et al* (1997). Increase in the mitotic recombination frequency in *Drosphila melanogaster* by magnetic field exposure and its suppression by vitamin E supplement. *Mutat Res*, **373**, 55–60.

Lacy-Hulbert A, Wilkins R C, Hesketh T R, *et al* (1995a). No effect of 60 Hz electromagnetic fields on myc or beta-actin expression in human leukaemia cells. *Radiat Res*, **144**, 9–17.

Lacy-Hulbert A, Wilkins R C, Hesketh T R, *et al* (1995b). Cancer risk and electromagnetic fields. *Nature*, **375**, 23.

Lacy-Hulbert A, Metcalfe J C and Hesketh R (1998). Biological responses to electromagnetic fields. *FASEB J*, **12**, 395–420.

Lagroye I and Poncy J L (1997). The effect of 50 Hz electromagnetic fields on the formation of micronuclei in rodent cell lines exposed to gamma irradiation. *Int J Radiat Biol*, **72**, 249–54 (1997).

Lagroye I and Poncy J L (1998). Influence of 50 Hz magnetic fields and ionising radiation on c-jun and c-fos oncoproteins. *Bioelectromagnetics*, **19**, 112–6.

Lai H and Singh N P (1997). Acute exposure to a 60 Hz magnetic field increases DNA strand breaks in rat brain cells. *Bioelectromagnetics*, **18**, 156–65.

Landry P S, Sadasivan K K, Marino A A, *et al* (1990). Electromagnetic fields can affect osteogenesis by increasing the rate of differentation. *Clin Orthopaed*, **338**, 262–70.

Liburdy R P, Sloma T R, Sokolic R, *et al* (1993). ELF magnetic fields, breast cancer and melatonin: 60 Hz fields block melatonin's oncostatic action on ER^+ breast cancer cell proliferation. *J Pineal Res*, **14**, 89–97.

Liburdy R P and Levine G A (1998). Magnetic fields and formation of organised structures in normal human mammary cells. IN BEMS Annual Meeting.

Lin H, Goodman R and Shirley-Henderson A (1994). Specific region of the c-myc promoter is responsive to electric and magnetic fields. *J Cell Biochem*, **54**, 281–8.

Lindström E, Lindström P, Berglund A, *et al* (1993). Intracellular calcium oscillations induced in a T-cell line by a weak 50 Hz magnetic field. *J Cell Physiol*, **156**, 395–8.

Lindström E, Lindström P, Berglund A, *et al* (1995a). Intracellular calcium oscillation in a T-cell line after exposure to extremely low frequency magnetic fields with variable frequencies and flux densities. *Bioelectromagnetics*, **16**, 41–7.

Lindström E, Berglund A, Hansson Mild K, *et al* (1995b). CD45 phosphatase in Jurkat cells is necessary for response to applied ELF magnetic fields. *FEBS Lett*, **370**, 118–22.

Litovitz T A, Krause D and Mullins J M (1991). Effects of coherence time of the applied magnetic field on ornithine decarbonylase activity. *Biochem Biophys Res Comm*, **178**, 862–5.

Loberg L I, Gauger J R, Buthod J L, *et al* (1999). Gene expression in human breast epithelial cells exposed to 60 Hz magnetic fields. *Carcinogenesis*, **20**, 1633–6.

Lyle D B, Wang X, Ayotte R D, *et al* (1991). Calcium uptake by leukaemic and normal T-lymphocytes exposed to low frequency magnetic fields. *Bioelectromagnetics*, **12**, 145–56.

Lyle D B, Fuchs T A, Casamento J P, *et al* (1997). Intracellular calcium signalling by Jurkat T-lymphocytes exposed to a 60 Hz magnetic field. *Bioelectromagnetics*, **18**, 439–45.

McCann J, Dietrich F, Rafferty C, *et al* (1993). A critical review of the genotoxic potential of electric and magnetic fields. *Mutat Res*, **297**, 61–95.

Mcleod K J and Collazo L (2000). Suppression of a differentiation response in Mc-3T3-E1 osteoblast-like cells by sustained, low level, 30 Hz magnetic field exposure. *Radiat Res*, **153**, 706–14.

Miller S C, Haberer J, Venkatachalam U, *et al* (1999). NF-kB or AP-1 dependent reporter gene expression is not altered in human cells exposed to power line frequency magnetic fields. *Radiat Res*, **151**, 310–18.

Miyakoshi J, Yamagishi N, Ohtsu S, *et al* (1996a). Increase in hypoxanthine-guanine phosphoribosyl transferase gene mutations by exposure to high density 50 Hz magnetic fields. *Mutat Res*, **349**, 109–14.

Miyakoshi J, Ohtsu S, Shibata T, *et al* (1996b). Exposure to magnetic field (5 mT at 60 Hz) does not affect cell growth or c-myc expression. *J Radiat Res*, **37**, 185–91.

Miyakoshi J, Kitagawa K and Takebe H (1997). Mutation induction by high density 50 Hz magnetic fields in human MeWo cells exposed in the DNA synthesis phase. *Int J Radiat Biol*, **71**, 75–9.

Miyakoshi J, Mori Y, Yamagishi N, *et al* (1998). Suppression of high density magnetic field (400 mT at 50 Hz) induced mutations by wild type p53 expression in human osteosarcoma cells. *Biochem Biophys Res Comm*, **243**, 57–84.

Miyakoshi J, Koji Y, Wakasa T, *et al* (1999). Long term exposure to a magnetic field (5 mT at 60 Hz) increases X ray induced mutations. *J Radiat Res*, **40**, 13–21.

Miyakoshi J, Yoshida M, Yaguchi H, *et al* (2000a). Exposure to extremely low frequency magnetic fields suppresses x-ray induced transformation in mouse C3H 10T½ cells. *Biochem Biophys Res Comm*, **271**, 323–7.

Miyakoshi J, Mori Y, Yaguchi H, *et al* (2000b). Suppression of heat-induced hsp70 by simultaneous exposure to 50 mT magnetic field. *Life Sci*, **66**, 1187–96.

Murphy J C, Kadan D A, Warren J, *et al* (1993). Power frequency electric and magnetic fields: a review of genetic toxicology. *Mutat Res*, **296**, 221–40.

Nafziger J, Desjobert H, Benamar B, *et al* (1993). DNA mutation and 50 Hz electromagnetic fields. *Biochem Bioenerget*, **30**, 133–41.

Narita K, Hanakawa K, Kasahara T, *et al* (1997). Induction of apoptotic death in human leukaemia cell, line HL-60 by extremely low frequency electric magnetic fields: analysis of possible mechanisms *in vitro*. *In Vivo*, **11**, 329–35.

NIEHS (1998). Health effects from exposure to power-line frequency electric and magnetic fields. Research Triangle Park, NC, National Institute of Environmental Health Sciences, NIH Publication No. 98-3981.

Nindl G, Swez J A, Miller J M, *et al* (1997). Growth stage dependent effects of electromagnetic fields on DNA synthesis in Jurkat cells. *FEBS Lett*, **414**, 501–6.

Nordenson I, Hansson Mild K, Andersson G, *et al* (1994). Chromosomal aberrations in human amniotic cells after intermittent exposure to 50 Hz magnetic fields. *Bioelectromagnetics*, **15**, 293–301.

NRPB (1992). Electromagnetic fields and the risk of cancer. Report of an Advisory Group on Non-ionising Radiation. *Doc NRPB*, **3**(1), 1–138.

Paile W, Jokela K, Koivistoinen A, *et al* (1995). Effects of 50 Hz sinusoidal magnetic fields and spark discharges on human lymphocytes *in vitro*. *Bioelectrochem Bioenerget*, **36**, 15–22.

Parker J E and Winters W (1992). Expression of gene specific RNA in cultured cells exposed to rotating 60 Hz magnetic fields. *Biochem Cell Biol*, **70**, 237–41.

Phillips K L, Haggren W, Thomas W J, *et al* (1992). Magnetic field-induced changes in specific gene transcription. *Biochem Biophys Acta*, **1132**, 140–44.

Phillips J L and McChesney L (1991). Effect of 72 Hz pulsed magnetic field exposure on macromolecular synthesis in CCRF-CEM cells. *Cancer Biochem Biophys*, **12**, 1–7.

Pipkin J L, Hinson W G, Young J F, *et al* (1999). Induction of stress proteins by electromagnetic fields in cultured HL60 cells. *Bioelectromagnetics*, **20**, 347–57.

Prasad A V, Miller M W, Carstensen E L, *et al* (1991). Failure to reproduce increased calcium uptake in human lymphocyte at purported cyclotron resonance exposure conditions. *Radiat Environ Biophys*, **30**, 305–20.

Reipert B M, Allan D, Dale R E, *et al* (1994). Interaction of low frequency, low intensity electromagnetic fields with haemopoetic stem cells. IN Abstracts, 16th Annual Meeting of the Bioelectromagnetics Society, Copenhagen, June 1994.

Reipert B M, Allan D and Dexter T M (1996). Exposure to extremely low frequency magnetic fields has no effect on growth rate or clonogenic potential of multipotential haemopoetic progenitor cells. *Growth Factors*, **13**, 205–17.

Reipert B M, Allan D, Reipert S, *et al* (1997). Apoptosis in haemopoetic progenitor cells exposed to extremely low frequency magnetic fields. *Life Sci*, **61**, 1571–82.

Saffer J D and Thurston S J (1995a). Cancer risk and electromagnetic fields. *Nature*, **375**, 22.

Saffer J D and Thurston S J (1995b). Short exposures to 60 Hz magnetic fields do not alter myc expression in HL60 or Daudi cells. *Radiat Res*, **144**, 18–25.

Saffer J D, Chen G, Colborn N H, *et al* (1997). Power frequency magnetic fields do not contribute to transformation of JB6 cells. *Carcinogenesis*, **18**, 1365–70.

Santoro N, Lisi A, Pozzi D, *et al* (1997). Effects of extremely low frequency (ELF) magnetic field exposure on morphological and biophysical properties of human lymphoid cell line (Raji). *Biochem Biophys Acta*, **1357**, 281–90.

Sauer H, Hescheler J, Reis D, *et al* (1997). DC electrical field-induced c-fos expression and growth stimulation in multicellular prostate spheroids. *Br J Cancer*, **75**, 1481–8.

Scarfi M R, Hoi M B, Zeni O, *et al* (1994). Lack of chromosomal aberration and micronuclear induction in human lymphocytes exposed to pulsed magnetic fields. *Mutat Res*, **306**, 129–33.

Schimmelpfeng J and Dertinger H (1993). The action of 50 Hz magnetic and electric fields upon cell proliferation and cyclic AMP content of cultured mammalian cells. *Bioelectrochem Bioenerget*, **30**, 143–50.

Schimmelpfeng J and Dertinger H (1997). Action of a 50 Hz magnetic field on proliferation of cells in culture. *Bioelectromagnetics*, **18**, 177–83.

Shah G, Ghosh R, Amtad P A, *et al* (1993). Mechanism of induction of c-fos by ultraviolet B (290–320 nm) in mouse JB6 epidermal cells. *Cancer Res*, **53**, 38–45.

Simko M, Kriehuber R, Weiss D G, *et al* (1998). Effects of 50 Hz EMF exposure on micronucleus formation and apoptosis in transformed and non-transformed human cell lines. *Bioelectromagnetics*, **19**, 85–91.

Stein B, Angel P, van Damm H, *et al* (1992). Ultraviolet-radiation induced c-jun gene transcription: two AP-1 like binding sites mediate the response. *Photochem Photobiol*, **55**, 409–15.

Suri A, de Boer J, Kusser W, *et al* (1996). A 3 mT, 60 Hz magnetic field is neither mutagenic nor co-mutagenic in the presence of menadione and MNU in a transgenic rat cell line. *Mutat Res*, **372**, 23–31.

Tabrah F L, Hower H F, Batkin S, *et al* (1994). Enhanced mutagenic effect of a 60 Hz time-varying magnetic field on numbers of azide induced TA100 revertant colonies. *Bioelectromagnetics*, **15**, 85–93.

Tuinstra R, Greenebaum B and Goodman E M (1997). Effects of magnetic fields on cell-free transcription in *E coli* and *HeLa* extracts. *Bioelectrochem Bioenerget*, **43**, 7–12.

Uckun F M, Kurosaki T, Jin J, *et al* (1995). Exposure of B-lineage lymphoid cells to low energy electromagnetic fields stimulates LYN kinase. *J Biol Chem*, **270**, 27666–70.

Walleczek J and Budinger T F (1992). Pulsed magnetic field effects on calcium signalling in lymphocytes: dependence on cell status and field intensity. *FEBS Lett*, **314**, 351–5.

Walleczek J, Killoran P L and Adey W R (1994). 60 Hz magnetic field effects on Ca^{2+} (Mn^{2+}) influx in human Jurkat T-cells: strict dependency on cell state. IN Abstracts, 16th Annual Meeting of the Bioelectromagnetics Society, Copenhagen, June 1994, p 76.

Walleczek J, Shiu E and Hahn G M (1999). Increase in radiation-induced HRPT gene mutation frequency after nonthermal exposure to non-ionising 60 Hz electromagnetic fields. *Radiat Res*, **151**, 489–99.

Wartenburg M, Hescheler J and Sauer H (1997). Electrical fields enhance growth of cancer spherioids by reactive oxygen species and intra cellular Ca^{2+}. *Am J Physiol*, **272**, R1677–83.

Wei L-X, Goodman R and Henderson A (1990). Changes in levels of c-*myc* and histone H2B following exposure of cells to low-frequency sinusoidal electromagnetic fields: evidence for a window effect. *Bioelectromagnetics*, **11**, 269–72.

West R W, Hinson W G, Lyle D B, *et al* (1994). Enhancement of anchorage-independent growth in JB6 cells exposed to 60 Hz magnetic fields. *Bioelectrochem Bioenerg*, **34**, 39–43.

Wey H E, Conover D P, Mathias P, *et al* (2000). 50-hertz magnetic fields and calcium transients in Jurkat cells: results of a research and public information dissemination (RAPID) program study. *Environ Health Perspect*, **108**, 135–40.

Yaguchi H, Yoshida M, Ejima V, *et al* (1999). Effect of high-density extremely low frequency magnetic field on sister chromated exchanges in mouse m5S cells. *Mutat Res*, **440**, 189–94.

4 Recent Animal and Volunteer Studies Relevant to Carcinogenesis

INTRODUCTION

1 This chapter reviews the data from animal studies for effects of exposure to ELF (mostly power frequency) electromagnetic fields on carcinogenic processes, concentrating on evidence published since the earlier Advisory Group report (NRPB, 1992). Good, recently published reviews of these studies include those by Boorman *et al* (2000a,b) and McCann *et al* (2000). The process of carcinogenesis is sometimes divided into two principal stages – initiation, which is the induction of stable changes in the genetic information carried in the DNA, and promotion, which is the application of a further stimulus to the initiated cell which can lead to neoplastic conversion and then progression to a fully developed malignancy. Once the potential for full malignancy has been established in a primary tumour, the progression of the disease may be influenced by other factors such as apoptosis, immune surveillance and hormonal dependency. A number of studies of tumour promotion have been carried out using animal carcinogenesis models, but the direct effects of ELF electromagnetic fields on tumour progression, taken here to mean the growth and increased malignancy of the tumour, have been less extensively studied. However, the possibility that these fields could influence the progression of breast cancer via induced changes in the circulating levels of melatonin or affect tumour surveillance via changes in immune responsiveness, has been extensively investigated and is also discussed.

2 Animal studies are frequently used in the evaluation of suspected human carcinogens. Extrapolation of this information to humans, however, cannot be expected *a priori* to be straightforward since there are obvious differences, for example in lifetime, physiology, metabolism, the proliferative capacity of different tissues, DNA repair capacity and many other variables. In addition, many inbred strains of animals are particularly susceptible to various cancers. However, at a molecular level, there are many similarities between carcinogenic processes in animals and humans; animal studies have been very useful in helping unravel the sequence of genetic events in the development of a number of human cancers (Balmain and Harris, 2000). The sensitivity of animal studies for testing human chemical carcinogens has been examined by Wilbourn *et al* (1986). These authors analysed the responses of experimental animals to 30 known and 14 suspected human carcinogens as evaluated within the IARC Monographs series. The results indicated that most (84%) of these known or suspected human carcinogens also have carcinogenic activity in animals. The authors noted that, for all those exposures in the study for which there is sufficient evidence of carcinogenicity in both humans and experimental animals, there is a target organ in common between humans and at least one animal species. Mammary tumours in rats and leukaemia or lymphoma in mice have been widely used as models of the equivalent human cancers (see, for example, Pattengale and Taylor, 1983; Russo and Russo, 1996). With some human cancers, however, such as malignant melanoma, spontaneous brain tumours and the most common form of childhood leukaemia, acute lymphoblastic leukaemia, there are as yet no natural animal models. Transgenic models of these diseases may prove of value in future studies.

IN VIVO STUDIES OF MUTAGENESIS

3 Early stages in the process of carcinogenesis comprise damage to cellular DNA (an agent causing such damage is said to be genotoxic), and the conversion of this damage, probably by misrepair, to specific gene or chromosomal mutations (stable changes in the DNA sequence and possibly chromosome structure or number) in appropriate target cells. Many known carcinogens, such as ultraviolet radiation, ionising radiation and certain chemicals, are genotoxic and mutagenic, and tests of genotoxicity and mutagenicity are thought to form an essential part of any assessment of potential carcinogenicity. However, comprehensive reviews by Murphy *et al* (1993) and McCann *et al* (1993) suggested that exposure to ELF electromagnetic fields was not genotoxic. Similar conclusions were reached by the Advisory Group (NRPB, 1992). Studies of genotoxicity are described in Chapter 3. Tests of mutagenicity in mammals exposed to power frequency electromagnetic fields have centred around an assessment of the frequency of dominant lethal mutations in exposed and unexposed animals. These mutations, which may reflect increased levels of chromosomal aberration frequency and other lethal mutations, result in the prenatal death of any ensuing offspring. Two studies found no evidence of increased dominant lethal mutations in the germ cells of male mice following exposure to power frequency electric fields (Kowalczuk and Saunders, 1990) or magnetic fields (Kowalczuk *et al*, 1995). According to IARC (1980), however, this assay is not sensitive for the detection of weak mutagens.

Summary

4 There is no convincing evidence *in vivo* published since the earlier Advisory Group report (NRPB, 1992) that ELF electric or magnetic fields are mutagenic. However, few *in vivo* studies have been carried out; the majority of studies have been carried out using cultured cells (see Chapter 3).

ANIMAL TUMOUR STUDIES

5 A number of studies of the effects of electromagnetic field exposure on spontaneous tumour incidence have been carried out. However, in the absence of clear genotoxicity, most studies have looked for a promotional effect of electromagnetic field exposure after the application of a known carcinogen. In its previous report on electromagnetic fields and cancer (NRPB, 1992), the Advisory Group concluded that the biological data had yet to reveal consistent evidence for any promotional or co-carcinogenic effects. Since that report was published, a number of studies have been carried out of possible promotional effects. Possible co-promotional effects have also been investigated using two-stage initiation/promotion protocols in conjunction with electromagnetic field exposure. In addition, electromagnetic field effects on tumour progression have been examined in several studies which have looked for changes in the growth of transplanted tumours.

Spontaneous tumour incidence

6 A number of studies have looked at the effect of electromagnetic field exposure alone on spontaneous or background tumour incidence; such studies are potentially capable of revealing whether electromagnetic fields could act as a complete carcinogen or serve to increase the incidence of spontaneous tumours. Often, inbred strains of

mice and rats are for genetic reasons particularly prone to certain cancers and some studies have examined electromagnetic field effects on the incidence of these particular tumours. In addition, transgenic animals are being increasingly used to investigate neoplasia. Other studies have examined the effect of exposure on the background incidence of all the different tumours that occur in that particular strain of animal. Sometimes these studies were incorporated into the design of a promotion/co-promotion study. The recent evidence is summarised in Table 4.1.

Leukaemia/lymphoma

7 Lymphoma and leukaemia are neoplasias of white blood cells (leukocytes) of the immune system. Neoplastic lymphocytic proliferation in the mouse may occur as a lymphoma (involving primarily lymph nodes and splenic white pulp) and/or as a leukaemia (involving primarily bone marrow, peripheral blood and splenic blood) but this distinction can be, at times, rather difficult and somewhat arbitrary (Pattengale, 1990). Each author's own designation of leukaemia or lymphoma is used in this chapter. As indicated above, there is no natural animal model of childhood acute lymphoblastic leukaemia. In particular, although some phenotypic similarities have been suggested (see, for example, Pattengale, 1994), the age-dependent appearance of murine thymic lymphomas does not recapitulate that of childhood acute lymphoblastic leukaemia and its indirect mechanism of induction has no known human counterpart (Fry and Carnes, 1989; UNSCEAR, 1993; Hoyes *et al*, 2000). There are various transgenic mouse models of leukaemia which develop a disease having some similarities to childhood acute lymphoblastic leukaemia; for example, *BCR/ABL* p190 mice (Griffiths *et al*, 1992), an Eμ-*BCL-2* mouse (Gibbons *et al*, 1999), mice incorporating the *pim-1* transgene (Verbeel *et al*, 1991; Kroese *et al*, 1997) and a *TEL-JAK2* mouse model (Carron *et al*, 2000). However, they are all artificial constructs (a novel transgene is expressed in all cells of target tissues) and it is arguable whether they represent ideal models of the disease. Nevertheless, valuable information may still be derived from the use of transgenic animals. Two completed studies (McCormick *et al*, 1998; Harris *et al*, 1998) have used the Eμ-*pim-1* transgenic model referred to above (see Table 4.1 and paragraph 11, and Table 4.2 and paragraph 31). Other transgenic mouse models may also prove useful in future studies.

8 One study (Bellossi *et al*, 1991) found no effect of electromagnetic field exposure over five successive generations to 12 Hz or 460 Hz magnetic fields on the incidence of leukaemia in AKR mice which normally develop high levels (more than 90% lifetime incidence) of lymphoblastic leukaemia. Full details of the experimental protocol and statistical analysis were not given, diminishing the value of the study. However, it was reported that were no statistically significant effects of exposure on survival time, spleen weight and thymus weight (leukaemia in AKR mice is associated with thymic hyperplasia).

9 In contrast to these negative data, albeit from limited observations, Fam and Mikhail (1996) found a high incidence of lymphoma in CFW mice, reported to have a low background incidence of this disease, exposed over three successive generations to an intense (25 mT) 'travelling*' power frequency magnetic field. Control animals,

*A travelling field is described by Fam and Mikhail (1993) as a basic principle of operation of linear synchronous motors used, for example, in the propulsion of 'magnetic' trains.

TABLE 4.1 Animal cancer studies – spontaneous tumours

Animal model	Exposure	Response	Comment	Authors
Leukaemia/lymphoma				
Leukaemia-prone female AKR mice for five generations	12 Hz or 460 Hz, pulsed 6 mT, 1 h per week until death	No effect on survival time, spleen and thymus weight	Experiment procedures not completely described	Bellossi (1991)
Male and female CFW mice over three generations	60 Hz, 25 mT 'travelling' field; continuous exposure	Highly significant increase in lymphoma incidence in 3rd generation	Uncertainties in experimental set up and design; lack of age-matched controls in 2nd generation	Fam and Mikhail (1993, 1996)
Eμ-*pim-1* transgenic mice prone to two types of lymphoma	50 Hz, 1, 100 or 1000 μT continuous or 1000 μT intermittent for 18 months	No effect on thymic lymphoblastic or on non-lymphoblastic lymphoma	Increase in positive control group	Harris *et al* (1998)
Heterozygous TSG-*Trp53* knockout mice prone to low incidence of lymphoma	60 Hz, 1 mT continuous for 18.5 h per day for 23 weeks	No significant effect on lymphoma incidence	Small numbers of mice; low incidence of tumours	McCormick *et al* (1998)
Mammary tumours				
Mammary tumours in female rats (strain unknown)	50 Hz, 20 μT 0.5 or 3 h per day for 2 years	Increased incidence	Increase in positive control group; experimental procedures not adequately described	Beniashvili *et al* (1991)
All tumours				
Male and female B6C3F1 mice	60 Hz, 2, 200 μT or 1 mT continuous or 1 mT intermittent for 2 years	No effect on the incidence of most tumours; slight overall reduction in female mice exposed at higher 'doses'	–	McCormick *et al* (1999), NTP (1999a)
Male and female F344 rats	50 Hz, 500 μT or 5 mT for 2 years	No effect on the incidence of most tumours	Increased subcutaneous fibroma levels similar to historical controls	Yasui *et al* (1997)
Female F344 rats	60 Hz, 2, 20, 200 μT or 2 mT for 2 years	No effect on tumour incidence	Site-specific tumour incidence close to historical controls	Mandeville *et al* (1997)
Male and female F344 rats	60 Hz, 2, 200 μT or 1 mT continuous or 1 mT intermittent for 2 years	No effect on incidence of most tumours; no overall effect	–	Boorman *et al* (1999a), NTP (1999a)

which were not sham-exposed, experienced stray fields of up to 50 μT. The authors reported that the three first-generation exposed animals had, on sacrifice, generalised lymphoid hyperplasia, whereas no abnormal pathology was found in the three control animals. In the second generation, six (about 14%) of the female animals in the exposed group had developed premalignant changes or lymphoma; again no abnormal pathology was found in the control group. No statistical analysis was presented for these results. In the third generation, 16 (about 17%) of the male and female animals in the exposed group had developed premalignant changes and 37 (about 40%) were diagnosed as having lymphoma, whereas in the control group two mice (about 5%) developed early lymphoma which the authors considered to be close to the expected background. Statistical analysis of the data for the difference in the prevalence of lymphoma between the exposed and control groups in the third generation showed highly significant differences for the male groups, female groups and all animals combined.

10 However, there are some problems with the interpretation of this study. The exposed animals may well have been stressed due to possible noise and vibration from the coils and nearby cooling fans; the latter keeping coil temperatures below 45 °C. In addition, there were too few animals in the first generation to draw any sensible conclusion. In the second generation, the control animals were killed at different times to the exposed animals to the extent that the four exposed animals that developed lymphoma were about four times the age of the oldest control animal (418 versus 103 days, respectively). Thus, spontaneous lymphomas may have contributed to or even account for this excess. A highly significant excess of lymphomas was reported in the third-generation exposed group compared to the controls; in this case, age at sacrifice was similar in both groups (between 133 and 408 days in the exposed group and between 141 and 455 days for the control group). However, the pathology figures presented in the paper were, according to some reviewers, more indicative of age-related lymphocytic infiltrates (McCann *et al.* 2000) or hyperplasia (Boorman *et al.* 2000a) than neoplasia.

11 More recently, a large-scale study by Harris *et al* (1998) was carried out using transgenic (Eμ-*pim-1*) mice which are predisposed to spontaneously develop thymic lymphoblastic (T-cell) lymphoma when young, and non-lymphoblastic (B-cell) lymphoma in older mice. Steps were taken to reduce noise, vibration and heating during exposure; 'double-blind' procedures were used and major components of the study, such as histopathology and statistical analysis, were carried out independently at different institutions. The authors reported a lack of effect of prolonged exposure to continuous or intermittent power frequency magnetic fields on the incidence of either lymphoma.

12 McCormick *et al* (1998) carried out a study of the effects of exposure to power frequency magnetic fields for a short time (23 weeks) on the incidence of lymphoma using two transgenic model systems with different incidences and kinetics of lymphoma induction: a 'high incidence' lymphoma model (chemically induced tumours in Eμ-*pim-1* mice, see paragraph 31) and a 'low incidence' lymphoma model (spontaneous tumours in heterozygous TSG-*Trp53* knockout mice). For the low incidence spontaneous lymphoma model, groups of 30 male or female heterozygous TSG-*Trp53* knockout mice (which lack one copy of the *Trp53* tumour suppressor gene) were exposed or sham-exposed to 60 Hz continuous magnetic fields. The incidence of malignant lymphoma in all experimental groups of mice at the end of the exposure was low, 7% or less (ie only two per group or less). There was no statistically significant difference between the exposed and sham-exposed groups.

Mammary tumours

13 For mammary tumours, Beniashvili *et al* (1991) reported an increased incidence of mammary tumours in rats chronically exposed to power frequency magnetic fields compared to a zero incidence reported in untreated controls. This formed a part of a larger study (paragraph 36) of the effect of electromagnetic field exposure on the development of mammary tumours in rats following injection with the carcinogen nitrosomethyl urea (NMU). A difficulty with the interpretation of these data is whether the incidence seen in the control group really reflects the background level of mammary tumour development generally seen in stock animals of the strain (unspecified) of rat used.

Brain tumours

14 There are no natural animal models of spontaneous brain tumours. Several large-scale studies have reported a lack of effect of exposure to electromagnetic fields on brain tumour incidence (paragraphs 15–18), but, generally, the number of tumours reported has been too low to allow a meaningful conclusion to be drawn. However, a recently developed model of spontaneous medulloblastoma in *Ptch*-knockout mice (Hahn *et al*, 1999), and more particularly, a hemizygous (*Nf1;Trp53*) knockout mouse model of astrocytomas (Reilly *et al*, 2000), a leading cause of brain cancer in humans, may prove useful in the further investigation of these effects.

All tumour types

15 Four large-scale studies of the effects of magnetic field exposure for two years (most of their lives) on the background tumour incidence in rats and mice have been recently completed; the effects on tumour incidence are described in detail in an appendix (Tables A1–A6). Yasui *et al* (1997) reported that exposure to power frequency magnetic fields for two years did not affect the tumour incidence in Fischer (F344) rats (Table A1). With regard to specific tumours, the incidence of tumours of the haemopoietic system, particularly the large granulocytic (mononuclear cell) leukaemias to which this strain is prone, was unaffected. In addition, there was no excess incidence of mammary tumours in the exposed animals and the incidence of skin tumours was low in all groups. A total of five brain tumours, evenly distributed throughout the different groups, was identified in the 288 animals used in the study. Similar results were reported in a larger and more detailed investigation by Mandeville *et al* (1997) of the effects of chronic exposure to power frequency magnetic fields on the spontaneous tumour incidence in female rats of the same strain (Table A2). In this study, care was taken to minimise the effects of potentially confounding variables such as vibration. The histopathology was examined in a 'blinded manner and was checked by independent quality assurance procedures'. The overall proportion of malignant cancers tended to be evenly distributed between exposed and control animals, and there was no evidence of a significant trend in dose-response relationship for either benign or malignant neoplasms. Only one brain tumour was found in the 300 animals used in this study.

16 More recently, the results of a study of the effects of exposure to power frequency magnetic fields for about two years on the background tumour incidence in a total of 1000 male and female rats of the same strain used in the studies described above and in a total of 1000 male and female mice have been described (Boorman *et al*, 1999a; McCormick *et al*, 1999; NTP, 1999a). A complete pathological examination was carried out of both neoplastic and non-neoplastic lesions in all animals in the study which was subject to quality assurance procedures. There were no significant differences in the survival of exposed and sham-exposed animals except that the survival of intermittently exposed male mice was significantly reduced.

17 Overall, the histopathological evaluation of tissues from rats exposed to magnetic fields revealed few statistically significant effects (Tables A3 and A4). Benign and malignant lesions in all groups in the study were generally similar to historical background values. With regard to leukaemia, brain cancer and mammary cancer, there was no evidence of increased risk. The incidence of mononuclear cell leukaemia was not increased by exposure to magnetic fields – exposure to an intermittent field of 1 mT significantly decreased the risk in male rats; this effect was not seen in females. The incidence of brain (glial) tumours in the study was very small (four cases); there was no evidence of an effect of magnetic field exposure. With regard to mammary tumours, magnetic field exposure did not significantly affect the incidence of malignant or benign tumours in female or in male rats; the incidence in the latter was quite small. The study did find that thyroid C-cell adenomas and carcinomas were significantly elevated in two groups of male rats. However, this may have been a chance event since the effect was not related to field intensity, there was no comparable increase in the levels of C-cell hyperplasia in these groups, and the effect was not seen in male F344 rats in other studies (Mandeville *et al*, 1997; Yasui *et al*, 1997). The few other significant effects noted on individual tumour incidence may also have been a chance observations, given the large number of significance tests carried out based on pairwise comparisons.

18 In mice, exposure resulted in a slight but significant reduction in tumour incidence in some groups (Tables A5 and A6). The overall incidence of malignant tumours was significantly reduced in two groups of female mice and the incidence of benign and malignant tumours significantly decreased in a third group. With regard to individual tumour types, malignant lymphoma was significantly reduced in one group of female mice and the incidence of lung adenoma significantly reduced in two groups of male mice and one group of females. However, the biological significance of these findings is not clear; these may also have been chance observations resulting from the large number of significance tests based on pairwise comparisons. The incidence of benign and malignant mammary tumours in female mice was very low and was not significantly increased by magnetic field exposure. There were no diagnoses of mammary tumours in male mice and no primary glial tumours were identified in either male or female mice.

Tumour promotion and co-promotion

19 A number of studies have examined the possible promotional or co-promotional effects of magnetic fields on the induction by chemicals or ionising radiation of pre-neoplastic lesions in the liver, on skin tumours, on leukaemia/lymphoma, on mammary tumours and brain tumours. The recent evidence is summarised in Table 4.2.

TABLE 4.2 Animal cancer studies – tumour (co-)promotion

Animal model	Exposure	Response	Comment	Authors
Pre-neoplastic lesions				
Partial hepatectomy plus DENA initiated liver lesions in Sprague-Dawley rats	50 Hz, 0.5–500 μT for about 20 h per week for 12 weeks	No effect	Increase in positive control group	Rannug *et al* (1993a)
Partial hepatectomy plus DENA and phenobarbital induced liver lesions in Sprague-Dawley rats	50 Hz, 0.5 or 500 μT for about 20 h per week for 12 weeks	Slight inhibitory effect	–	Rannug *et al* (1993b)
Skin tumours				
Sub-carcinogenic DMBA initiated or DMBA and sub-optimal (1 μg) TPA induced skin tumours in SENCAR mice	60 Hz, 2 mT for 6 h per day, 5 days per week for 21 weeks	No tumours in DMBA treated mice; for DMBA plus TPA, test insensitive due to 90% incidence in controls	–	McLean *et al* (1991), Stuchly *et al* (1991)
DMBA and sub-optimal (0.3 μg) TPA induced skin tumours in SENCAR mice	60 Hz, 2 mT for 6 h per day, 5 days per week from week 2 to week 23 of age	No consistent effect in replicate studies	3 replicate studies; some heterogeneity in results	Stuchly *et al* (1992) McLean *et al* (1997)
DMBA and sub-optimal (0.3 μg) TPA induced skin tumours in SENCAR mice	60 Hz, 2 mT for 6 h per day, 5 days per week from week 24 to week 52 of age	Increase in malignant conversion of papillomas to carcinomas	Continuation of study by Stuchly *et al* (1992)	McLean *et al* (1995)
DMBA and sub-optimal (0.85–3.4 nmol) TPA induced skin tumours in SENCAR mice	60 Hz, 2 mT for 6 h per day, 5 days per week for 23 weeks	No effect	Extension of study by Stuchly *et al* (1992)	Sasser *et al* (1998)
Early markers of skin tumourigenesis in DMBA and sub-optional TPA-treated SENCAR mice	60 Hz, 2 mT for 6 h per day 5 days per week for 1, 2 and 5 weeks of promotion	No consistent effect	Extension of study by Sasser *et al* (1998)	DiGiovanni *et al* (1999)
DMBA-induced skin tumours in NMRI mice	50 Hz, 50 or 500 μT for about 20 h per day for 2 years	No effect on skin tumour incidence	Increase in positive control group	Rannug *et al* (1993c)
DMBA-induced skin tumours in SENCAR mice	50 Hz continuous or intermittent, 50 or 500 μT, for about 20 h per day for 2 years	No effect of continuous or intermittent exposure compared to control groups	Increase in positive control group	Rannug *et al* (1994)
UVR induced skin tumours in transgenic (K2) and non-transgenic mice	50 Hz continuous at 100 μT or variable 1.3–130 μT for 10.5 months	No effect on final tumour incidence but earlier appearance in exposed transgenic mice	Small numbers of mice	Kumlin *et al* (1998)
Lymphoma/leukaemia				
Possible lymphoma or leukaemia in SENCAR mice painted with DMBA and TPA	60 Hz, 2 mT for 6 h per day, 5 days per week for 21 weeks	Larger spleens and increased mononuclear cells in spleen	Leukaemia/ lymphoma insufficiently identified	McLean *et al* (1991)
X-ray induced lymphoma in CBA/S mice	20 kHz, sawtooth field of 15 μT peak–peak until death	No effect of exposure	Experiment unable to detect increase	Svendenstål and Holmberg (1993)
DMBA-induced thymic lymphoma in Swiss mice	50 Hz, 1 mT 3 h per day, 6 days per week for 16 weeks	No effect on tumour incidence	Inconsistent effect on metatstatic infiltration	Shen *et al* (1997)

Animal model	Exposure	Response	Comment	Authors
ENU-induced lymphoblastic lymphoma in *pim-1* transgenic mice	60 Hz, 2, 200 μT or 1 mT continuous or 1 mT intermittent (1 h on/off) 18.5 h per day for 23 weeks	No effect except decreased incidence in 1 mT continuous group	Small numbers of mice	McCormick *et al* (1998)
Gamma-radiation-induced lymphomas in C57BL/6 female mice	60 Hz, circularly polarised 1.42 mT for 18 h per day for up to 29 months	No effect on incidence of haemopoietic neoplasms including lymphoma	Large-scale study (2660 mice) rigorously monitored	Babbitt *et al* (2000)
Mammary tumours				
NMU-induced mammary tumours in female rats (unidentified strain)	50 Hz, 20 μT 0.5 or 3 h per day for 2 years	Increased incidence in 3 h per day group, plus increased malignancy	Experimental procedures not adequately described	Beniashvili *et al* (1991)
DMBA-induced mammary tumours in female Sprague-Dawley rats	50 Hz, 0.3–1.0 μT for 13 weeks	No effect on visible or histologically identified tumour incidence	Well-designed, fully described experiment	Mevissen *et al* (1993a;b), Löscher *et al* (1994)
DMBA-induced visible mammary tumours in Sprague-Dawley female rats	50 Hz, 10 μT for 13 weeks	No effect on incidence of visible tumours at autopsy	Well-designed, fully described experiment	Mevissen *et al* (1996a)
DMBA-induced mammary tumours in female Sprague-Dawley rats	50 Hz, 50 μT for 13 weeks	Increased incidence of visible tumours at autopsy	Well-designed, fully described experiment	Mevissen *et al* (1996b)
DMBA-induced mammary tumours in female Sprague-Dawley rats	50 Hz, 100 μT for 13 weeks	Increased incidence of visible tumours, no effect on histologically identified incidence, increased malignancy	Low incidence of visible tumours in the sham-exposed group	Löscher *et al* (1993), Baum *et al* (1995)
DMBA-induced mammary tumours in female Sprague-Dawley rats	50 Hz, 100 μT for 13 weeks	Increased incidence of visible tumours at autopsy	Replicate of above experiment	Mevissen *et al* (1998a)
DMBA-induced mammary tumours in female Sprague-Dawley rats	50 Hz, 100 μT for 27 weeks	Increased mammary tumour incidence in exposed group	Well-designed, fully described experiment	Thun-Battersby *et al* (1999)
DMBA-induced visible mammary tumours in female Sprague-Dawley rats	50 Hz, 30 mT for 13 weeks	Opposite results in replicate studies but no overall effect	Well-designed, fully described experiment	Mevissen *et al* (1993a)
DMBA-induced mammary tumours in female Sprague-Dawley rats	50/60 Hz, 100 or 500 μT for 13 or 26 weeks	No effect. Sham tumour incidence very high in 2 of 3 experiments	Repeat and extension of study by Löscher *et al* (1993)	Anderson *et al* (1999), Boorman *et al* (1999b), NTP (1999b)
DMBA-induced mammary tumours in female Sprague-Dawley rats	50 Hz intermittent fields of 250 or 500 μT for 21 weeks	No effect	Somewhat brief description of experimental protocol, analysis and results	Ekström *et al* (1998)
Brain tumours				
ENU-induced tumours of the nervous system of female F344 rats	60 Hz magnetic fields of 2, 20, 200 or 2000 μT for 20 h per day for 65 weeks	No effect of magnetic field exposure	Exposure to ENU and magnetic fields begun *in utero*	Mandeville *et al* (2000)

high blood mononuclear cell counts. Natural killer cell activity was lower in the spleen and blood of the exposed group, but not significantly so. The authors tentatively suggested that the changes indicated the possible development of leukaemia, perhaps due to a field-induced suppression of the immune system. However, the effect on the immune system was not statistically significant and, in most cases, the evidence of leukaemia was weak.

29 Svedenstål and Holmberg (1993) found no effect of almost a lifetime exposure to pulsed 20 kHz magnetic fields on the incidence of lymphomas in x-irradiated mice; the experiment was well described but unexpectedly high levels of x-ray-induced thymic lymphomas in the control animals (around 66%) rendered the study insensitive, according to the authors, to any promotional effect.

30 Shen *et al* (1997) found no effect of exposure to power frequency magnetic fields on the incidence of DMBA-induced thymic lymphoma in mice. The authors also reported that significantly more animals with advanced lymphoma in the exposed group had dense metastatic infiltration of the liver compared to the sham-exposed group (16/36 in the exposed group versus 6/37 in the sham-exposed group). However, these values were similar for both groups if the numbers of animals with moderate and dense infiltration were combined (22/36 versus 19/37, respectively). In addition, metastatic infiltration of the spleen was similar in both exposed and sham-exposed groups, suggesting that the observation of greater metastatic invasion in the liver in the exposed group was spurious.

31 McCormick *et al* (1998) carried out a study of the effects of exposure to power frequency magnetic fields for 23 weeks on the incidence of lymphoma using two transgenic model systems with different incidences and kinetics of lymphoma induction: a 'low incidence' lymphoma model (spontaneous tumours in heterozygous TSG-*Trp53* knockout mice, see paragraph 12) and a 'high incidence' lymphoma model (chemically induced tumours in *pim-1* mice). For the 'high incidence' model, groups of 30 male or female *pim-1* transgenic mice (which carry the *pim-1* oncogene) were injected with N-ethyl-N-Nitrosourea (ENU) in order to induce lymphoblastic lymphoma and then exposed or sham-exposed to power frequency magnetic fields. Similar patterns of tumour-related mortality were seen in all groups of *pim-1* animals in the study; clinical observations were generally associated with the development of malignant lymphoma. At the end of exposure, there were no significant differences in survival nor in the mortality-adjusted incidence of malignant lymphoma, except in the group of males continuously exposed at 1 mT in which survival was significantly increased compared to animals sham-exposed and lymphoma incidence significantly decreased.

32 Babbitt *et al* (2000) conducted a large-scale study of the effects of a lifetime exposure to circularly polarised power frequency magnetic fields on the incidence of gamma radiation induced lymphoma and other haemopoietic neoplasias in a total of 2660 mice. Sections from ten lymphoid tissues were evaluated histopathologically for haemopoietic neoplasia; diagnoses were subject to independent internal and external peer review. Test of significance included pairwise comparisons of the lifetime incidence of lymphoma, adjusted for survival, between exposed and sham-exposed groups. The authors reported that the study had a statistical power of greater than 80%

to detect odds ratios above 1.5 for an effect of chronic magnetic field exposure on the incidence of radiation-induced lymphoma.

33 Analysis of the data (Table A7) revealed a convincing lack of effect of magnetic field exposure on mortality and on the incidence of radiation-induced haemopoietic neoplasia, especially lymphomas and histiocytic sarcoma. The relative frequencies and general occurrence of haemopoietic neoplasia were similar for both exposed and sham-exposed mice that had received the same ionising radiation treatment. Chronic exposure to the magnetic field did not change the relative incidence of neoplasia in mice, with the exception of a marginally reduced relative risk ($p = 0.05$) for lymphoblastic lymphoma in mice exposed to the magnetic field and treated with 5.1 Gy. A non-significant reduction in the incidence of lymphoblastic lymphoma in one group and a non-significant earlier appearance (by 50 days) of lymphomas and histiocytic sarcomas in mice exposed only to magnetic fields suggested a possible promoting effect and the authors thought that further investigation was warranted. However, these observations may have been due to chance since, as the authors noted, formal allowance for multiple comparisons was not made.

34 The same group (Kharazi *et al*, 1999) examined brain tissue from mice used in the above study in order to determine any possible effect of electromagnetic field exposure on radiation-induced brain tumour incidence. The authors found that exposure to ionising radiation slightly increased the incidence of primary brain tumours in mice but there was no detectable effect of exposure to power frequency magnetic fields. However, the low incidence of spontaneous and radiation-induced brain tumours prevented any firm conclusion being drawn.

Mammary tumours

35 The induction of mammary tumours in female rats has been used as a standard assay in the investigation of potential carcinogenesis, often using a carcinogen such as DMBA as an initiator in the two-stage initiator–promoter model of carcinogenesis. Four groups of workers have investigated the possible effects of magnetic field exposure on chemically induced mammary tumour incidence.

36 Beniashvili *et al* (1991) found that chronic exposure to power frequency magnetic fields for 3 h per day, but not 0.5 h per day, significantly increased the incidence of NMU-induced mammary tumours (43/46 in the exposed group compared to 27/46 in the control group) and decreased the latency (46 versus 74 days, respectively). The exposed rats also had a higher total number of large malignant mammary tumours (adenocarcinomas) than the control group (57/75 malignant tumours in the exposed group compared to 16/31 in the control group). The experimental details were, however, rather briefly summarised. In particular, no detailed description of the exposure system was given, the strain and background mammary tumour incidence were not given, and the method of counting tumour incidence and assessing tumour latency were not clearly described.

37 A series of medium-term studies of magnetic field effects on mammary tumour incidence was carried out by Löscher and colleagues (Löscher *et al*, 1993, 1994, 1997; Baum *et al*, 1995; Löscher and Mevissen, 1995; Mevissen *et al*, 1993a,b, 1996a,b, 1998). The evidence from these studies relating to the incidence of macroscopically visible tumours in rats exposed or sham-exposed to 50 Hz magnetic fields is summarised in

Figure 4.1 and Table 4.3. The authors attempted to control a number of potentially confounding factors, such as the noise, heat and vibration from the electromagnets, and to remove sources of subjective bias by conducting the assessments (tumour palpation etc) 'blind', ie without knowledge of the exposure conditions. The evidence from a full histopathological analysis of mammary tissue showed that, under two different exposure conditions (0.3–1.0 μT, Löscher *et al*, 1994, and 100 μT, Baum *et al*, 1995), there was no statistically significant effect on tumour incidence.

38 In contrast, the incidence of palpable tumours (detected during exposure) and, more particularly, macroscopically visible tumours (detected during post-mortem examination) was significantly increased following exposure to 50 μT (Mevissen *et al*, 1996b) and to 100 μT (Löscher *et al*, 1993). Indeed, the percentage increase in the incidence of macroscopically visible tumours compared to their concurrent sham-exposed control showed a highly linear dose–response relationship over the flux density range 0.3–1.0 μT up to 100 μT (Löscher and Mevissen, 1995) but not up to 30 mT (Mevissen *et al*, 1993a). Thus, Löscher and Mevissen (1995) argued that magnetic field exposure did not alter the incidence of (neoplastic) mammary lesions but accelerated tumour growth, so that a higher number of tumours was macroscopically visible when the rats were sacrificed. In addition, Baum *et al* (1995) reported that there was a statistically significant increase in the number of rats exposed to 100 μT with mammary gland adenocarcinomas, a malignant tumour type, compared to sham-exposed animals (63% incidence in the exposed group compared to 49% in the sham-exposed group). However, the total number of malignant tumours in the exposed group was not statistically significantly increased (R G E Haylock, NRPB, personal communication).

39 A difficulty with the interpretation of these studies is that there is considerable variation from experiment to experiment in tumour incidence in the sham-exposed groups (Figure 4.1 and Table 4.3). In particular, in the first 100 μT experiment (Löscher *et al*, 1993; Baum *et al*, 1995) there was an unusually low incidence (34%) of macroscopically visible tumours in the sham-exposed group compared to the overall mean sham incidence of 51% in the four studies from which the linear dose–response was derived (Löscher and Mevissen, 1995). In addition, opposite results were seen in replicate studies carried out at 30 mT. These observations suggest the possibility that the authors lacked control over a factor or factors which influenced the outcome of their experiments. In an analysis of these data, Löscher *et al* (1997) noted the possibility of seasonal influences on mammary tumour incidence. In particular, the low sham incidence of 34% coincided with exposure during autumn and early winter, in contrast to the other experiments. A replicate 100 μT study (Mevissen *et al*, 1998a) carried out at a different time of year to the original reported that the incidence of macroscopically visible tumours in the sham-exposed group was 62%, almost double the incidence in the earlier study. In addition, significantly more (83%) of the exposed animals had developed macroscopically visible tumours. A re-analysis of all these data still revealed a statistically significant linear correlation between increase in tumour incidence and flux density (Mevissen *et al*, 1998a). However, this analysis did not account for the variability seen in the sham-exposed data. More recently, these authors (Thun-Battersby *et al*, 1999) reported a significantly increased incidence of mammary tumours following 10 μT exposure for 27 weeks following initiation by only 10 mg DMBA.

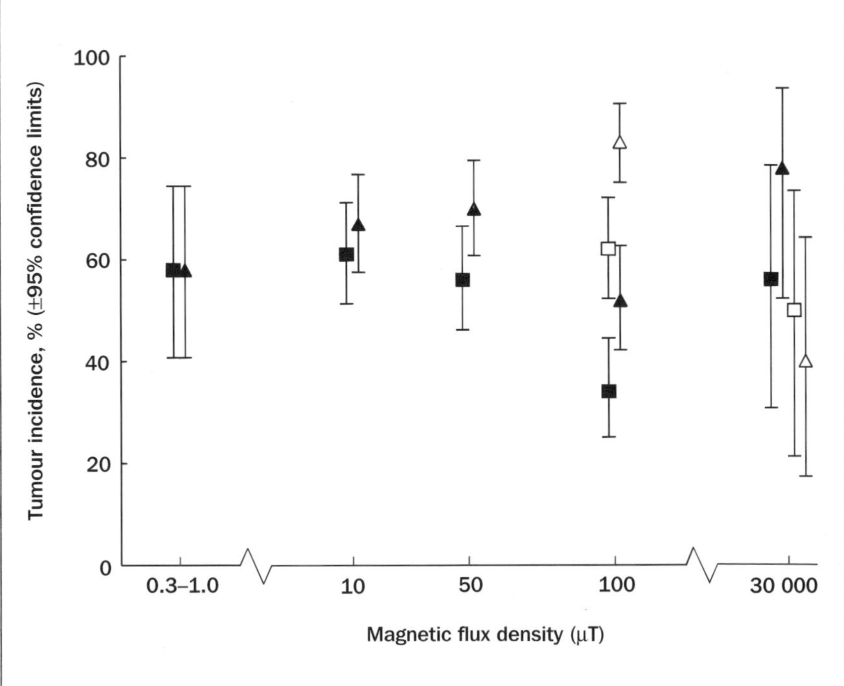

Square = sham-exposed; triangle = exposed; solid squares/triangle = first experiment; open squares/triangles = second experiment)

FIGURE 4.1 Studies by Löscher and colleagues of 50 Hz magnetic field exposure for 13 weeks on DMBA-induced macroscopically visible mammary tumours in female rats

TABLE 4.3 Studies by Löscher and colleagues of 50 Hz magnetic field exposure for 13 weeks on DMBA-induced macroscopically visible mammary tumours in female rats

Field (μT)	Replicate experiments	Number of animals per group	Sham tumour incidence (%)	Exposed tumour incidence (%)	Authors
0.3–1.0	-	36	58	58	Mevissen *et al* (1993a)
10	-	99	61	67	Mevissen *et al* (1996a)
50	-	99	56	70*	Mevissen *et al* (1996b)
100	R1 + R2	198	48	67*	
100	*R1*	*99*	*34*	*52**	*Löscher et al (1993)*
100	*R2*	*99*	*62*	*83**	*Mevissen et al (1998a)*
30 000	R1 + R2	33–36	53	61	Mevissen *et al* (1993a)
30 000	*R1*	*18*	*56*	*78*	*Mevissen et al (1993a)*
30 000	*R2*	*15–18*	*50*	*40*	*Mevissen et al (1993a)*

*$p < 0.05$.

Replicate studies italicised (R1, R2) and summed (R1 + R2).

40 It is clearly important for other research groups to attempt to replicate the positive findings reported by Löscher and colleagues. An attempted repeat and extension of the study by Löscher *et al* (1993) using the same outbred Sprague-Dawley strain of rat has been reported by one laboratory (Anderson *et al*, 1999; Boorman *et al*, 1999b; NTP, 1999b). These authors found no evidence that magnetic field exposure was associated with an earlier onset or an increased multiplicity of mammary tumours, nor was the mammary tumour incidence significantly increased in the one experiment (of three) in which an increased incidence could have been detected (Table A8). There were, however, clear differences in the responsiveness of the rats used in the NTP study to DMBA compared to those used by Löscher and colleagues and other differences in experimental protocol (Anderson *et al*, 2000); use of 20 mg DMBA in the first 13 week NTP study (Anderson *et al*, 1999) or 10 mg in the 26 week study (Boorman *et al*, 1999b) resulted in a high incidence of mammary tumours (more than 90%, Table A8) in the sham-exposed groups, diminishing the sensitivity of these experiments. However, the second 13 week study, using only 8 mg DMBA, resulted in an incidence of around 40%–50% in the sham-exposed group (Anderson *et al*, 1999). Ekström *et al* (1998) found no effect on DMBA-induced mammary tumour incidence in the same rat strain following prolonged exposure to intermittent power frequency magnetic fields. There were no statistically significant differences in the number of tumour-bearing animals and no differences in the total number of tumours between the different groups. In addition, the rate of tumour appearance was the same in all groups. However, the description of the experimental protocol, statistical analysis and results was somewhat brief.

Brain tumours

41 Mandeville *et al* (2000) studied the potential of 60 Hz magnetic fields to act as promoters of neurogenic tumours initiated transplacentally by N-ethyl-N-nitrosourea (ENU), a potent carcinogen primarily affecting the nervous system. Although ENU does not induce glioblastomas, the most frequent human malignant glioma, according to the authors ENU-induced rat neurogenic tumours are considered as a representative model for human nervous system tumours.

42 The experimental data are summarised in Table A9. Body weight, mortality, and clinical observations were evaluated in all groups. Necropsy was performed on all exposed and control animals that died, were found moribund or sacrificed at termination of the study. Histopathology was carried out on brains, spinal cord, cranial nerves and major organs. All observations were made under 'blinded' conditions. The study was periodically audited by independent quality assessment procedures. Tumour incidence was analysed by pairwise comparison using logistic regression. The authors reported that the study had a 90% power to detect a change in tumour incidence as small as 30%.

43 Survival varied between 48% and 62% per group and did not differ significantly between the exposed and sham-exposed groups. All groups of rats treated with ENU developed tumours of the central and peripheral nervous system. The total number of animals bearing neurogenic tumours varied from 38% to 60%; the incidence in the exposed groups was lower than that seen in the sham-exposed group. Glial tumours were the most common lesions, varying in number between 15 and 23 per group and were not found to be associated with any level of magnetic field exposure. Schwannomas were found in the peripheral nervous system and the incidence was also unaffected by exposure. Thus, overall, magnetic field exposure had no statistically significant effect on the survival of female F344 rats or on the number of animals bearing neurogenic tumours. Slight increases and decreases in tumour incidence were seen in the exposed groups which were of borderline significance ($0.1 > p > 0.05$) but these might have reflected chance observations from multiple comparisons. The results support the view that power frequency magnetic fields do not have a promoting effect on neurogenic tumours in female rats exposed transplacentally to ENU.

Tumour progression

44 Few studies have investigated the effect of power frequency electromagnetic fields on the growth of transplanted tumours. The recent evidence is summarised in Table 4.4. Possible electromagnetic field effects on specific factors such as circulating levels of the hormone melatonin and immune responsiveness which may affect tumour growth are considered in later sections.

45 In its earlier report on electromagnetic fields and the risk of cancer (NRPB, 1992), the Advisory Group noted a report by Thomson *et al* (1988) of a lack of effect on the progression of leukaemia in mice implanted with mouse leukaemia cells and exposed until death. More recently, Sasser *et al* (1996) reported a lack of effect of exposure on the progression of large granular lymphocytic (LGL) leukaemia in rats following the injection of LGL cells derived from older rats of the same strain. In general, it was noted that there were no significant or consistent differences between the exposed or sham-exposed groups; in contrast, enlarged spleens appeared earlier and survival was significantly depressed in a positive control group exposed to 5 Gy gamma radiation prior to leukaemia cell injection. Similar results were reported by Morris *et al* (1999) in an extension of the study by Sasser *et al* (1996).

TABLE 4.4 Animal cancer studies – tumour transplantation

Animal model	Exposure	Response	Comment	Authors
Leukaemia/lymphoma				
P388 mouse leukaemia cells into DBNA female mice	60 Hz, 1.4, 200 or 500 μT for 6 h per day, 5 days per week until death	No effect	Some heterogeneity in control values	Thomson *et al* (1988)
LGL leukaemia cells into male Fischer rats	60 Hz, 1 mT for 20 h per day until death	No effect	Increase in positive control group	Sasser *et al* (1996)
LGL leukaemia cells into male Fischer rats	60 Hz linearly polarised fields of 1 mT for 20 h per day for up to 11 weeks	No effect	Extension of the study by Sasser *et al* (1996); questionable comparison with ambient control values	Morris *et al* (1999)
Acute myeloid leukaemia cells into Brown Norway rats	50 Hz magnetic fields of 100 μT for 18 h per day until death	No effect on leukaemic progression	Transitory differences in haemoglobin levels	Devary *et al* (2000)

46 Devary *et al* (2000) examined the effect of chronic exposure to 50 Hz magnetic fields on the progression of acute myeloid leukaemia (AML) in rats, the most frequent type of leukaemia reported in occupational studies (see Chapter 6). The authors reported that this model of AML exhibited characteristics closely related to human acute myeloid leukaemia, including infiltration of bone marrow and spleen, prolonged transit time of leukaemic cells in the blood and suppression of normal haemopoiesis. A total of 340 rats were used in four independent, replicate, experiments. No significant differences were seen in survival between exposed and unexposed leukaemic groups, average survival was 26 days for both groups. Similarly, in the terminal stage of leukaemia when the rats were sacrificed, there were no differences in white blood cell count, or differential white blood cell count, or the degree of bone marrow infiltration or bone marrow differential cell count at sacrifice. Thus, exposure had no significant effect on the parameters involved in leukaemic progression.

Summary

47 Many studies investigating the possible effects of exposure to mostly power frequency electromagnetic fields on spontaneous and chemically induced tumour incidence, and on the growth of transplanted tumour cells, that have been carried out since publication of the earlier Advisory Group report (NRPB, 1992) are summarised where possible according to tumour type. Generally, the more recent large-scale studies of animal carcinogenesis, including those using transgenic animals, which find no evidence of carcinogenicity have been more carefully conducted than some of the earlier studies reporting either negative or positive effects. These later studies have often used independent quality assurance procedures.

48 The results of four large-scale studies of the effects of lifetime exposure on spontaneous tumour incidence in rats and mice were mostly negative.

49 With regard to the studies of chemically induced pre-neoplastic liver lesions and skin tumours, the evidence is almost uniformly negative. No effect of exposure to power frequency electromagnetic fields has been seen on the induction of chemically induced pre-neoplastic lesions in the rat liver; such lesions are generally taken as additional evidence of carcinogenicity. Three different research groups found a lack of consistent effects of exposure to power frequency magnetic fields on chemically induced skin tumours. A fourth group reported that exposure to continuous or intermittently variable power frequency magnetic fields had no effect on the overall incidence of UVR-induced skin tumours in normal and transgenic mice, although the tumours appeared earlier in the transgenic animals exposed to magnetic fields.

50 The evidence that exposure to power frequency electromagnetic fields can affect the incidence of leukaemia/lymphoma is not compelling. The most marked effect was seen in a study of lymphoid hyperplasia and lymphoma in mice exposed over three generations to an intense power frequency 'travelling wave' magnetic field compared to controls exposed to stray magnetic fields; however, there were a number of deficiencies in the study making it difficult to place a high degree of confidence on the experimental outcome. Otherwise, no effect was seen on the spontaneous incidence of thymic and non-lymphoblastic lymphoma in a large-scale transgenic mouse study, nor on the spontaneous incidence of leukaemia or lymphoma in four large-scale studies of rats and mice exposed to electromagnetic fields for most of their lives. In addition, no effect was seen on the incidence of radiation-induced lymphoma and leukaemia in a large-scale mouse study, nor on chemically induced thymic lymphoma in mice, nor on the incidence of spontaneous or chemically induced lymphoma in a smaller scale transgenic mouse study. The transgenic mouse model used in two of the studies mentioned above develops a disease with some similarities to childhood acute lymphoblastic leukaemia. Further studies found no effect on the progression of transplanted leukaemia cells.

51 The evidence concerning electromagnetic field effects on chemically induced mammary tumours is equivocal. Two laboratories have reported an increased incidence, possibly due to increased growth rates, of chemically induced mammary tumours in female rats exposed to power frequency magnetic fields. However, the work of one laboratory was inadequately described, making it difficult to judge how well the study had been carried out. A series of well-planned experiments from the other laboratory suffered from inter-experimental variability, suggesting some sort of experimental confounding. In contrast to these positive observations, two different laboratories have reported a lack of effect of power frequency magnetic field exposure on chemically induced mammary tumours in the same strain of female rats used in the series of experiments outlined above. One laboratory found no effects following an attempt to repeat and extend some of the positive effects reported; however, there were clear differences in the responsiveness to the carcinogen of the rats in this study compared to those in the original studies, leading to a reduced sensitivity of some of the experiments. The study from the other laboratory, albeit somewhat briefly described, found no effect on chemically induced mammary tumour incidence following exposure to intermittent power frequency magnetic fields.

52 A large-scale study which examined the potential of power frequency magnetic fields to act as promoters of chemically induced nervous system tumours in female rats reported that, overall, magnetic field exposure had no statistically significant effect on survival nor on the number of animals bearing nervous system tumours.

53 No significant effect on spontaneous mammary tumour incidence was seen in three large lifetime studies using rats of a different strain. A low incidence of brain tumours (generally one or less per experimental group) was found in these studies. In one study, thyroid C-cell tumours were significantly elevated in two groups of exposed male rats; this effect was not seen in female rats nor in male rats of the same strain in the other studies and is thought to be a chance result.

54 There is no convincing evidence of increased malignant conversion after electromagnetic field exposure. Although two studies reported an increased incidence of malignant mammary tumours following the exposure of female rats treated with a chemical carcinogen, there are difficulties in the interpretation of both: in one study, the methodology was described somewhat briefly and it is difficult to judge how well the study was carried out; in the other study there was an unusually low number of visible tumours in the sham-exposed group and this may have affected the outcome. A third study reported an increase in the malignant conversion of chemically induced benign skin tumours to malignant squamous cell carcinomas. However, no difference was seen in squamous cell carcinoma incidence in a study of power frequency magnetic field effects on UVR-induced skin tumours in normal and transgenic mice. In two large-scale studies of electromagnetic field effects on spontaneous tumour incidence in rats, the overall proportion of malignant tumours tended to be evenly distributed between exposed and control animals, and there was no evidence of a significant trend in dose-response relationship. In a large-scale mouse study, there was evidence of a decrease in the incidence of malignant tumours in exposed females.

MELATONIN, CANCER AND ELECTROMAGNETIC FIELDS

55 Stevens (1987) first suggested that chronic exposure to electric fields may reduce melatonin secretion by the pineal gland and increase the risk of breast cancer. This followed reports, particularly by Wilson *et al* (1981), of a significant overall reduction in pineal melatonin in rats chronically exposed to power frequency electric fields and by Tamarkin *et al* (1981) and Shah *et al* (1984) of increased DMBA-induced mammary carcinogenesis in rats with reduced melatonin levels following removal of the pineal gland or exposure to constant light. The possibility has aroused wide interest and attention and has stimulated considerable experimental and epidemiological research.

56 Melatonin is a hormone produced by the pineal gland in a distinct daily or circadian rhythm which is governed by day length; serum melatonin levels are very low during the day and are elevated at night in nocturnal animals and in diurnal animals including humans (Hastings, 1991). The primitive role of melatonin in lower vertebrates is to regulate pigment dispersion in melanophores controlling skin colour. In mammals, melatonin is implicated in the control of daily activities such as the sleep/wake cycle and, more convincingly, in seasonal rhythms such as those of reproduction (Hastings, 1991). In particular, the changes at dawn and dusk in the activity of the rate-limiting enzyme for melatonin production in the pineal gland (N-acetyl transferase or NAT) are very abrupt; determinations of pineal and serum melatonin concentrations reveal that the melatonin signal varies in direct proportion to the length of the night (Hastings, 1991) and this photoperiodic cue is used to trigger neuroendocrine responses that co-ordinate the various physical and physiological changes that occur, for example, in seasonal breeders. These animals, mostly from temperate or polar regions, show annual cycles of fertility and infertility, along with corresponding changes in the gonads and secondary sexual characteristics. There are, however, many species differences. For example, seasonal breeders with a short gestational period, such as Djungarian hamsters, become reproductively depressed in the late summer and autumn as night length increases, leading to the view that melatonin has an 'antigonadotrophic' function (Reiter, 1980); however, those with a long gestational period, such as sheep, tend to become reproductively active during this period (Tamarkin *et al*, 1985). Both strategies ensure that offspring are not produced during winter when food is scarce.

57 In humans, the relevance of altered day length and serum melatonin levels to reproductive activity are not well established. Arendt (1995) noted some evidence for seasonal influences on human reproduction but acknowledged that these were overlaid with social, behavioural and cultural factors. Reiter (1997) reported that it was generally believed that melatonin had a negative impact on human reproductive physiology but that any changes were slight compared to those seen in experimental animals. Thus, the view that reduced night-time melatonin levels may increase the risk of breast cancer in humans via induced changes in circulating levels of sex hormones is less compelling than that for laboratory animals.

58 The hypothesis that reduced pineal function may promote the development of breast cancer in humans had been previously suggested by Cohen *et al* (1978). Several mechanisms whereby changes in pineal or serum melatonin levels may affect the risk of breast cancer have been proposed. These include the observation, at least in some animal species, that decreased melatonin levels cause elevations in circulating levels of oestrogen and progesterone which increase cell proliferation in the stem cell population of the breast and so increase the risk of cancer in these cells (Cohen *et al*, 1978). Other suggestions are that melatonin may directly suppress the growth of mammary tumour cells (Blask and Hill, 1986) and other cancer cells, particularly melanoma, prostate cancer, ovarian cancer, bladder cancer and leukaemia (Stevens, 1994) and that melatonin may act as a scavenger of free radicals, preventing oxidative damage to DNA (Reiter *et al*, 1995), at least at pharmacological levels (Cridland *et al*, 1996). It has also been suggested that melatonin may modulate immune responsiveness (Maestroni *et al*, 1986).

Electromagnetic field effects on melatonin levels

59 Studies of the effects of electromagnetic fields on melatonin levels have mostly been carried out using laboratory rats; other animals investigated have included mice, Djungarian hamsters, sheep and primates, particularly humans. Djungarian hamsters and sheep are both seasonal breeders, the former becoming reproductively inactive and the latter reproductively active as day length shortens; tests in these species were carried out of electromagnetic field effects on serum melatonin and reproductive status.

Laboratory rodents

60 With regard to studies on common laboratory animals such as the rat and the mouse, the results are equivocal. Few studies have been carried out using mice; one large-scale study (McCormick *et al*, 1995) has briefly reported that exposure to continuous or intermittent power frequency magnetic fields had no effect on serum or pineal melatonin. In contrast, a later study (Picazo *et al*, 1998) described a significant reduction in the night-time serum melatonin levels of mice exposed up to sexual maturity for four generations. However, as a part of a tumour promotion study, Heikkinen *et al* (1999) found no effect of chronic exposure to power frequency magnetic fields of varying intensity on the night-time excretion of a urinary metabolite of melatonin in mice exposed to ionising radiation (4 Gy). A great many more studies have been carried out using rats. The effects of electric fields were investigated before interest turned predominantly to magnetic fields.

Electric fields

61 Several studies by one group of authors (Wilson *et al*, 1981, 1983, 1986; Reiter *et al*, 1988), mentioned in the earlier Advisory Group publication (NRPB, 1992), reported that the exposure to electric fields significantly suppressed pineal melatonin and the activity in the pineal gland of an enzyme (NAT) important in the synthesis of melatonin, and that this effect was transient, appearing within three weeks of exposure but recovering within three days following the cessation of exposure. A similar suppression of pineal melatonin was reported by these authors following the prenatal and neonatal exposure of rats to power frequency electric fields; no simple dose–response relationship was apparent. More recently, however, workers from the same laboratory (Sasser *et al*, 1991) briefly reported that they were unable to reproduce the reduction in pineal

65 Four further groups which have investigated magnetic field effects on serum and pineal melatonin levels in rats came to inconsistent but mostly negative conclusions. One group of authors (Selmaoui and Touitou, 1995) reported that the acute exposure of rats to horizontally polarised power frequency magnetic fields significantly depressed night-time serum melatonin levels and NAT activity in the pineal gland; chronic exposure had a similar effect. In contrast, Bakos *et al* (1995, 1997, 1999) reported that exposure to a vertical or horizontal power frequency magnetic field had no effect on the circadian excretion of the major urinary metabolite of melatonin. As part of a larger study of electromagnetic field effects on DMBA-induced mammary tumours and pineal function, Mevissen *et al* (1996a) found no effect of magnetic field exposure on pineal melatonin levels in rats not treated with DMBA. In addition, Löscher *et al* (1998) were unable to identify any consistent effects of power frequency magnetic field exposure for up to 13 weeks in night-time serum melatonin levels. Further, John *et al* (1998) reported that the exposure of rats for up to six weeks to power frequency magnetic fields under a variety of conditions intended to maximise magnetic field sensitivity had no effect on the circadian excretion of the major urinary metabolite of melatonin.

Seasonal breeders

66 Four different laboratories have investigated the effects of electromagnetic field exposure on pineal activity, serum melatonin levels and reproductive development in animals which breed seasonally (Table 4.6). Three laboratories examined these effects in Djungarian hamsters in which the duration of melatonin secretion during the shortening days of autumn and winter inhibit reproductive activity. In an early study, Wilson *et al* (1993) briefly confirmed work fully published later by Yellon (1994) that acute exposure to a power frequency magnetic field before the onset of darkness reduced and delayed the night-time rise in serum melatonin.

67 The most complete data come from a series of studies by Yellon and colleagues. In the first study, Yellon (1994) found that acute exposure to a power frequency magnetic field two hours before the onset of darkness reduced and delayed the night-time rise in serum and pineal melatonin, but that this effect was diminished in a subsequent replicate study and absent in the third replicate study. Similarly, variable results on pineal and serum melatonin were reported by Yellon (1996) and Truong *et al* (1996). In addition, both studies found that magnetic field exposure had no effect on reproductive development, even in reproductively repressed hamsters on 'short day' (winter) schedules which might be thought to be sensitive to reduced and delayed night-time melatonin elevation. A fourth study (Truong and Yellon, 1997) found no effect on the night-time melatonin levels of different magnetic field exposure parameters to those used in the previous experiments. Finally, Yellon and Truong (1998) reported that a brief exposure to power frequency magnetic fields prior to the night-time rise in pineal and serum melatonin levels had no effect even in complete darkness, ie in the absence of a strong photoperiodic cue.

68 In contrast to the work of Yellon and his colleagues, Niehaus *et al* (1997) reported that the chronic exposure of Djungarian hamsters on 'long day' (summer) schedules to 'rectangular' power frequency magnetic fields resulted in increased testis cell numbers and night-time levels of serum melatonin, whereas exposure to sinusoidal power frequency magnetic fields had little effect. The authors concluded that the *in vivo* effects

TABLE 4.6 Melatonin levels: seasonal breeders

Assay	Exposure	Response	Comment	Authors
Djungarian hamsters				
Night-time pineal melatonin levels	60 Hz, 100 μT for 15 min, 2 h before dark period	Suppression of night-time peak	Meeting abstract	Wilson *et al* (1993)
Night-time pineal and serum melatonin levels	60 Hz, 100 μT for 15 min, 2 h before dark period	Reduced and delayed night-time peak; this effect diminished and absent in 2nd and 3rd replicate study	Considerable variability between replicate studies	Yellon (1994)
Night-time pineal and serum melatonin levels	60 Hz, 100 μT for 15 min, 2 h before dark period	Reduced and delayed night-time peak; this effect diminished in 2nd replicate study	Considerable variability between replicate studies	Yellon (1996)
Night-time pineal and serum melatonin levels; adult male reproductive status	60 Hz, 100 μT for 15 min, 2 h before dark period for 3 weeks	No effect on pineal and serum melatonin; no effect on melatonin-induced sexual atrophy	Second part of above paper	Yellon (1996)
Night-time pineal and serum melatonin levels; male puberty, assessed by testes weight	60 Hz, 100 μT for 15 min, 2 h before dark period from 16–25 days of age	Reduced and delayed night-time peak; this effect absent in 2nd replicate study. No effect on development of male puberty	Considerable variability of melatonin levels between replicate studies	Truong *et al* (1996)
Night-time pineal and serum melatonin levels	60 Hz, 10 or 100 μT before or after dark onset or intermittent 100 μT; 15 or 60 min	No effect	-	Truong and Yellon (1997)
Night-time rise in pineal and serum melatonin levels; testicular weight	60 Hz, 100 μT in complete darkness; 15 min per day for up to 21 days	No effect, even in absence of photoperiodic cue	-	Yellon and Truong (1998)
Night-time pineal and serum melatonin levels; testis cell numbers	50 Hz, 450 μT (peak) sinusoidal or 360 μT (peak) rectangular fields, 56 days	Increased cell number and night-time serum melatonin after rectangular field exposure	Animals on long day schedules; difficult interpretation	Niehaus *et al* (1997)
Night-time pineal melatonin levels, serum prolactin levels and testis and seminal vesicle weights in short day (regressed) animals	60 Hz,100 or 500 μT; CW and/or intermittent, starting 30 min or 2 h before onset of darkness; for up to 3 h for up to 42 days	Reduced pineal melatonin after acute (15 min) exposure; reduced gonad weight but not melatonin after 42 day exposure	Authors suggest a stress-like effect	Wilson *et al* (1999)
Suffolk sheep				
Night-time serum melatonin levels and female puberty, detected by rise in serum progesterone	60 Hz, 6 kV m^{-1} and 4 μT fields generated by overhead power lines; 10 months	No effect of EMFs; strong seasonal effects	Two replicate studies; open air conditions	Lee *et al* (1993, 1995)

of magnetic fields may have been dependent on their waveform, and that the rapidly changing waveform of the rectangular fields was a more effective biological stimulus. However, the results are not easy to interpret; increased melatonin levels in the Djungarian hamster are usually accompanied by decreased testicular activity.

69 More recently, in an extension of earlier work, Wilson *et al* (1999) investigated the effect of exposure to power frequency magnetic fields on pineal melatonin levels, serum prolactin levels and testicular and seminal vesicle weights in Djungarian hamsters moved to a 'short day' light regime in order to induce sexual regression. Night-time pineal melatonin levels were reduced following acute exposure but this effect diminished with prolonged exposure. In contrast, induced sexual regression, as indicated by the testicular and seminal vesicle weights, seemed to be enhanced rather than diminished by prolonged magnetic field exposure, suggesting a possible stress response.

70 The fourth set of studies of electromagnetic field effects on seasonal breeders concerned Suffolk sheep; these have a long gestational period and become reproductively active in the autumn, as day length shortens. In two replicate studies (Lee *et al*, 1993, 1995), Suffolk lambs were exposed outdoors to the magnetic fields generated by overhead transmission lines for about ten months. The authors reported no effect of exposure on serum melatonin levels or on the onset of puberty.

Non-human primate and volunteer studies

71 Non-human primates are close, in evolutionary terms, to humans and share many similar characteristics; the results of studies of both human and non-human primates are summarised in Table 4.7.

72 Using male baboons, Rogers *et al* (1995a) reported that chronic exposure to power frequency electric and magnetic fields had no effect on night-time serum melatonin levels. However, a preliminary study from the same authors (Rogers *et al*, 1995b), based on data from only two baboons, reported that a three week exposure to an irregular, intermittent sequence of combined electric and magnetic fields in which switching transients were generated resulted in a marked suppression of the night-time rise in melatonin.

73 Volunteer studies of the effects of power frequency electromagnetic fields on the night-time elevation in serum melatonin clearly give information of direct relevance to exposed humans. Wilson *et al* (1990) examined the possible effects of chronic exposure to low frequency electromagnetic fields. In this study, exposure was to the pulsed electromagnetic fields generated by mains or DC powered electric blankets over a 6–10 week period. Overall, no effect of exposure was seen on the urinary excretion of the major urinary metabolite of melatonin; however, transient increases in night-time excretion were seen in the periods following the onset of use of an electric blanket and following cessation of its use in 7 of 28 users of one type of electric blanket. This observation may, however, be rather weak given the apparent lack of control over life-style factors such as sleeping habits (the exposures took place at home) which may have influenced night-time melatonin levels, the lack of correspondence of the effect with field condition and the fact that responsiveness was only identified following the analysis of the excretion data from each of 42 volunteers, of which some analyses may have turned out positive by chance.

TABLE 4.7 Melatonin levels: non-human primates and volunteers

Assay	Exposure	Response	Comment	Authors
Non-human primates				
Night-time serum melatonin levels in baboons	60 Hz, 6 kV m^{-1} and 50 μT (6 weeks); 30 kV m^{-1} and 100 μT (3 weeks)	No effect	–	Rogers *et al* (1995a)
Night-time serum melatonin levels in baboons	60 Hz; irregular and intermittent sequence of 6 kV m^{-1} and 50 μT or 30 kV m^{-1} and 100 μT for 3 weeks	Reduced serum melatonin levels	Preliminary study on two baboons	Rogers *et al* (1995b)
Human studies				
Early morning excretion of urinary metabolite of melatonin	60 Hz EMFs generated by pulsed AC or DC current supply to electric blankets at night for 7–10 weeks	No overall effect; transient increases in 7/28 users of one type of blanket	Realistic, but concomitant lack of control over lifestyle etc	Wilson *et al* (1990)
Night-time serum melatonin levels	60 Hz, intermittent fields of 1 or 20 μT for 8 h at night	No effect; possible effect on low melatonin subjects not replicated in larger study	–	Graham *et al* (1996)
Night-time serum melatonin levels	60 Hz, continuous fields of 20 μT for 8 h at night	No effect	–	Graham *et al* (1997)
Night-time serum melatonin levels and excretion of its major urinary metabolite	50 Hz, continuous or intermittent fields of 10 μT for 9 h at night	No effect	–	Selmaoui *et al* (1996)
Night-time serum melatonin levels	50 Hz intermittent sinusoidal or square wave fields of 20 μT for 1.5–4 h at night	Possible delay and reduction of night-time melatonin levels in subgroup	Inconsistent, variable data; incomplete volunteer participation	Wood *et al* (1998)
Early morning excretion of urinary melatonin and its metabolite	60 Hz circularly polarised magnetic field of 28.3 μT overnight for 4 consecutive nights	No effect on night-time levels	Exposed subjects showed less intra-individual consistency on night 4	Graham *et al* (2000)

74 Three acute studies (Graham *et al,* 1996, 1997; Selmaoui *et al,* 1996) have been carried out in which volunteers, screened for various factors which might have influenced melatonin levels, were exposed or sham-exposed overnight to circularly or horizontally polarised intermittent or continuous power frequency magnetic fields. No significant effects of exposure on night-time serum melatonin levels were found in the studies, nor, in one study (Selmaoui *et al,* 1996), of any effect on the excretion of the major urinary metabolite of melatonin. An initial report (Graham *et al,* 1996) of a magnetic field induced reduction of night-time serum melatonin levels in volunteers with normally low basal melatonin levels was not confirmed using a larger number of volunteers.

75 More recently, Wood *et al* (1998) exposed or sham-exposed male subjects to an intermittent, circularly polarised, power frequency magnetic field at various times during the dusk or night and measured the effect on night-time serum melatonin levels. The study was conducted 'blind' and was carried out over a two-year period between the months of February and September. The results indicated that exposure prior to the night-time rise in serum melatonin may have delayed the onset of the rise by about half an hour and may have reduced peak levels, possibly in a sensitive subgroup of the study population. However, these effects were not consistent and it is difficult to regard them as conclusive. In particular, the high variation in melatonin rhythmicity may have confounded attempts to distinguish the effects of several different experimental variables using, in these circumstances, a comparatively small number (30) of subjects. Exposure categorisation (into groups whose exposure began before, during or after the onset of the night-time rise in serum melatonin) was made after, rather than before, exposure. Other acknowledged difficulties included the apparent failure of some volunteers to attend all their scheduled sessions whilst others contributed several data points to one experiment, leading to an underestimation of variability within treatment groups and thus an overestimation of the significance of differences between groups (R G E Haylock, NRPB, personal communication). In addition, the exposure periods were not clearly defined. Further study would be required to corroborate these preliminary findings.

76 The effect of exposure to power frequency magnetic fields over four consecutive nights has been investigated by Graham *et al* (2000). Thirty men aged between 18 and 35 years were used in a randomised, double-blind trial. Each man slept in the Midwest Research Institute facility from Monday through Thursday over the spring and summer. Half of the men selected were exposed every night to a circularly polarised 60 Hz magnetic field of 20 μT along each axis (giving a resultant field of 28.3 μT). Urine samples were collected each morning in order to determine the overnight levels of excretion of melatonin or its major metabolite 6-OHMS.

77 Analysis failed to reveal any statistical differences in mean concentrations of melatonin or 6-OHMS in morning urine as a function of four consecutive nights of magnetic field exposure. However, whereas individual urinary measures collected across the four test nights in the sham control conditions were highly ($p < 0.01$) correlated with one another, those collected in the magnetic field exposure condition showed a similar high degree of consistency only across the first three nights. The measures collected after exposure on night 4 were substantially different from those obtained after the previous nights, and two of the correlation comparisons (2–4 and 3–4) were significantly different ($p < 0.01$). So whilst the results indicated that there was no overall effect of magnetic fields on night-time circulating levels of melatonin, there was some suggestion of a cumulative effect of magnetic field exposure on the stability of melatonin measurement, indicating a need for further investigation.

Magnetic field effects on melatonin levels and tumour growth

78 Several studies by Löscher, Mevissen and their colleagues attempted to correlate magnetic field induced changes in the incidence and growth of DMBA-induced mammary tumours in rats with changes in the nocturnal levels of serum melatonin (Table 4.8). In two experiments (Löscher *et al*, 1994; Mevissen *et al*, 1996a), the authors reported that exposure for three months to a power frequency magnetic field which had no significant effect on the incidence of DMBA-induced mammary tumours in female rats was associated with significantly decreased nocturnal melatonin levels. In two other experiments, the authors (Mevissen *et al*, 1996b, 1998a) reported a significantly increased incidence of DMBA-induced mammary tumours in female rats; however, nocturnal melatonin levels were not significantly affected. Thus, in these experiments, magnetic field induced changes in DMBA-induced mammary tumour incidence were not correlated with changes in nocturnal melatonin levels.

TABLE 4.8 Melatonin levels and tumour incidence

Assay	Exposure	Response	Comment	Authors
Mammary tumour incidence and night-time serum melatonin levels in DMBA-treated Sprague-Dawley rats	50 Hz, 0.3–1.0 μT for 13 weeks	No significant increase in tumour incidence; significant reduction of serum melatonin after 8–9 weeks exposure	A small part of a larger mammary tumour study	Löscher *et al* (1994)
Mammary tumour incidence and night-time pineal and serum melatonin levels in DMBA-treated Sprague-Dawley rats	50 Hz, 10 μT for 13 weeks	No significant increase in visible tumour incidence; serum, but not pineal melatonin reduced after 13 weeks exposure	As above	Mevissen *et al* (1996a)
Mammary tumour incidence and night-time serum melatonin levels in DMBA-treated Sprague-Dawley rats	50 Hz, 50 μT for 13 weeks	Significant increase in visible tumour incidence; no effect on night-time serum melatonin after 9 or 12 weeks exposure	As above	Mevissen *et al* (1996b)
Mammary tumour incidence and night-time serum melatonin levels in DMBA-treated female Sprague-Dawley rats	50 Hz, 100 μT for 13 weeks	Significant increase in visible tumour incidence; no effect on night-time serum melatonin after 12 weeks exposure	As above	Mevissen *et al* (1998a)

Summary

79 Some, but not all, studies of power frequency electromagnetic field effects on rat pineal and serum melatonin levels reported that exposure to power frequency electric or magnetic fields resulted in suppression. The results of the early studies of electric field effects could not be replicated and may have suffered from technical difficulties. The evidence from a series of more recent studies by another group reporting

that circularly polarised magnetic fields suppressed night-time melatonin levels was sometimes weakened by inappropriate comparisons between exposed animals and historical controls. The data from other experiments were equivocal but mostly negative. Studies by one group found no correlation between electromagnetic field effects on melatonin suppression and mammary tumour incidence in female rats treated with a chemical carcinogen.

80 The evidence for an effect of exposure to power frequency electromagnetic fields on melatonin levels and melatonin-dependent reproductive status in seasonally breeding animals, Djungarian hamsters and Suffolk sheep, is mostly negative. A series of studies by one group reported reduced and delayed night-time peaks in pineal and serum melatonin in Djungarian hamsters that could not be successfully replicated; no effects were seen on changes in reproductive status. Another study reported that 'rectangular' power frequency magnetic fields increased night-time serum melatonin levels and testis cell number; contrary to the expected inhibitory effect of melatonin in this species. A third group reported that sexual regression in male hamsters, induced by a short day length, was enhanced rather than inhibited by magnetic field exposure. Finally, two replicate studies by another group found no effect on serum melatonin and the onset of puberty in sheep.

81 No convincing effect on melatonin levels has been seen in non-human primates chronically exposed to power frequency electromagnetic fields, although a preliminary study reported melatonin suppression in response to an irregular and intermittent exposure. Similarly, most evidence indicates that human melatonin rhythms are not delayed or suppressed by acute exposure to continuous or intermittent power frequency magnetic fields, although one recent study provided preliminary evidence suggesting that exposure prior to the night-time rise in serum melatonin may have had this effect, possibly in a sensitive subgroup of the study population. In addition, night-time melatonin levels were not suppressed by chronic exposure to the weak, pulsed electromagnetic fields generated by electric blankets.

IMMUNE SYSTEM RESPONSES RELEVANT TO CANCER

82 In principle, ELF electromagnetic fields might affect tumour growth via induced changes in immune system responses involved in tumour eradication. The extent, however, to which the immune system is involved in tumour eradication is not fully clear. There is good evidence (summarised, for example, by IARC, 1992) from people whose immune system has been compromised, such as transplant recipients treated with immunosuppressive drugs and patients with AIDs (acquired immunodeficiency syndrome), that cancers of a definite or possible viral origin such as non-Hodgkin's lymphoma and Kaposi's sarcoma are increased in incidence by severe immune impairment. The slightly increased risk in this group of patients for other cancers in which viruses are not known to play a role suggests that surveillance against these other tumours is generally less effective (Abbas *et al*, 1994; Roitt *et al*, 1996).

Electromagnetic field effects on immune response

83 Electromagnetic field studies have been carried out on a variety of immunological and haematological parameters. However, the effector cells and molecules that are considered, at least experimentally, to be most relevant to tumour suppression (reviewed, for example, by Abbas *et al*, 1994; Roitt *et al*, 1996) are the cytotoxic T-lymphocytes, natural killer cells, macrophages and, possibly less importantly, antibodies secreted by B-lymphocytes.

84 Most studies have carried out a rather heterogeneous mix of tests, they have been subdivided here for clarity into functional aspects and are summarised in Table 4.9. Whilst *in vivo* studies examine the responsiveness of the complex and highly regulated action of the immune system, standard tests of discrete immunological functions have been carried out *in vitro* on cells taken from the peripheral blood and spleen of exposed animals.

Lymphocyte proliferation

85 In general, lymphocytes respond to specific, 'foreign' antigens such as proteins by proliferation and functional activation. Studies of the ability of T- and B-lymphocytes to proliferate *in vitro* in response to chemical (mitogenic) signals have produced varied results. Mevissen *et al* (1996b) reported a depression of spleen T-lymphocyte proliferation in rats chronically exposed to power frequency magnetic fields. In a follow-up study, these authors (Mevissen *et al*, 1998b) found that spleen T-lymphocyte proliferation was initially increased (2 weeks) and then decreased (13 weeks) compared to sham-exposed animals following similar exposure. In addition, a pilot experiment by Murthy *et al* (1995) reported a significant decrease in a predominantly B-lymphocyte mitogenic response and a non-significant decrease in the T-lymphocyte response in baboons following exposure to power frequency electric and magnetic fields. However, effects on mitogen-induced B- or T-lymphocyte proliferation attributable to exposure were not seen following a larger investigation of the effects of exposure to more intense power frequency electric and magnetic fields. In humans, Fotopoulos *et al* (1987) found no effect of an acute exposure to power frequency electromagnetic fields on the proliferation of peripheral blood T- or B-lymphocytes.

T-lymphocyte function *in vivo*

86 Activated cytotoxic T-lymphocytes specifically recognise and kill cells expressing foreign (such as viral or mutant) molecules on their surface and are strongly implicated in anti-tumour responses. Two tests have been carried out of T-lymphocyte mediated responses *in vivo* in mice (House *et al*, 1996). A delayed-type hypersensitivity test measured the T-cell mediated inflammatory response following the application of a 'foreign' agent (oxazolone) to which the animal has been previously sensitised. The susceptibility of mice to infection by the intracellular bacteria *Listeria moncytogenes* was also used to test T-cell mediated immune responsiveness. In both sets of experiments, no effects of prolonged exposure to power frequency magnetic fields were found.

Natural killer cell activity

87 Natural killer cells are less specific than cytotoxic T-lymphocytes but also kill target cells and are strongly implicated in anti-tumour responses. A number of tests of natural killer cell function following *in vivo* electromagnetic field exposure have been carried out. McLean *et al* (1991) reported that natural killer cell activity was lower, but not significantly so, in mice treated with DMBA and weekly, sub-optimal doses of the tumour promoter TPA and exposed to power frequency magnetic fields. House *et al*

TABLE 4.9 Immune system responses relevant to cancer

Assay	Exposure	Response	Comment	Authors
Lymphocyte proliferation				
Sprague-Dawley rats: spleen lymphocyte proliferation	50 Hz, 50 μT for 13 weeks	Depressed T-cell proliferation	-	Mevissen *et al* (1996b)
Sprague-Dawley rats: spleen lymphocyte proliferation	50 Hz, 100 μT for 2, 4, 8, or 13 weeks	Increased then decreased T-cell proliferation	-	Mevissen *et al* (1998b)
Baboons: peripheral blood lymphocyte proliferation	60 Hz, 9 kV m^{-1} and 20 μT, 5 weeks (pilot study); 60 Hz, 30 kV m^{-1} and 50 μT, 5 weeks (main study)	No effect in main study; reduced B-lymphocyte response in pilot study	Considerable heterogeneity in sham-exposed results	Murthy *et al* (1995)
Humans: peripheral blood lymphocyte proliferation	60 Hz, 9 kV m^{-1} and 20 μT for 6 h	No effect	-	Fotopoulos *et al* (1987)
T-lymphocyte function				
B6C3F1 mice: delayed-type hypersensitivity to oxazolone	60 Hz, 2, 200, 1000 μT continuous or 1000 μT intermittent for 4 or 13 weeks	No effect	-	House *et al* (1996)
Mice (BALB/C?) resistance to *Listeria monocytogenes* infection	60 Hz, 2, 200, 1000 μT continuous or 1000 μT intermittent for 4 or 13 weeks	No effect	Experimental and control data not shown	House *et al* (1996)
NK cell activity				
Spleen and blood NK cells from SENCAR mice painted with DMBA and TPA	60 Hz, 2 mT for 21 weeks	No significant effect	-	McLean *et al* (1991)
Spleen natural killer cells from B6C3F1 male and female mice	60 Hz, 2, 200, 1000 μT continuous or 1000 μT intermittent for 4, 6 or 13 weeks	Consistently reduced NK activity in female but not male mice	Replicate experiments	House *et al* (1996)
Spleen natural killer cells from mature B6C3F1 female mice	60 Hz, 2, 200, 1000 μT continuous or 1000 μT intermittent for 13 weeks	Reduced NK activity in female mice exposed to 1 mT continously	Repeat of above experiment using mature mice	House and McCormick (2000)
Spleen natural killer cells from F344 rats	60 Hz, 2, 200, 1000 μT continuous or 1000 μT intermittent for 6 or 13 weeks	No consistent effect in males or females	Replicate experiments	House *et al* (1996)
Spleen natural killer cells from F344 rats	60 Hz, 2, 20, 200 μT or 2 mT; 20 h per day for 6 weeks	Trend for enhanced activity with exposure	Significant effects with control group rather than sham-exposed comparison	Tremblay *et al* (1996)
Macrophage activity				
Peritoneal macrophages from F344 rats	60 Hz, 2, 20, 200 μT or 2 mT; 20 h per day for 6 weeks	Trend for enhanced hydrogen peroxide release with exposure	Significant effects with control group rather than sham-exposed comparison	Tremblay *et al* (1996)
Antibody (B-cell) activity				
Plaque-forming spleen cells in immunised BALB/C mice	60 Hz, 500 μT for 5 h on 3 alternate days	No effect	-	Putinas and Michaelson (1990)
Plaque-forming spleen cells in immunised B6C3F1 mice	60 Hz, 2, 200, 1000 μT continuous or 1000 μT intermittent for 3 or 13 weeks	No effect	Positive controls	House *et al* (1996)

(1996) reported that the natural killer cell activity of female mice was reduced by exposure to continuous or intermittent power frequency magnetic fields but this did not occur with any degree of consistency in male mice, nor in male or female rats. However, a repeat of this experiment (House and McCormick, 2000) using older female mice resulted in a similar depression in natural killer cell activity. In contrast, Tremblay *et al* (1996) reported that spleen natural killer cell activity was enhanced in the same strain of rats used by House *et al* (1996) exposed to power frequency magnetic fields, reflecting a statistically significant trend with 'dose' over the range. However, the significance of this increase disappeared when comparison was made with the sham-exposed group rather than the cage control group.

Macrophage activity

88 Macrophages are also are less specific than cytotoxic T-lymphocytes but are nevertheless implicated in anti-tumour responses; however, few studies have examined electromagnetic field effects on their activity. Tremblay *et al* (1996) reported that a subgroup of peritoneal macrophages exposed to power frequency magnetic fields showed a dose-dependent increase in hydrogen peroxide release, a measure of macrophage activity, when compared with cage control animals; comparison with sham-exposed animals revealed a significant increase only at higher levels of exposure. In contrast, there were no effects of exposure on two other measures of activity, the production of nitric oxide and tumour necrosis factor.

Antibody (B-lymphocyte) activity

89 Both natural killer cells and macrophages express IgG antibody receptors and can, at least *in vitro*, be targeted to tumour cells coated with this antibody. Two studies on mice (Putinas and Michaelson, 1990; House *et al*, 1996) found no effect of exposure to power frequency or pulsed magnetic fields on antibody cell function assessed using the plaque-cell forming assay which is based on the number of clear areas (plaques) formed when spleen cells are mixed with cells (sheep red blood cells) to which the mice had been sensitised.

Electromagnetic field effects on immune response and tumour growth

90 Whilst possible effects of electromagnetic field exposure on tumour progression might be inferred, but not demonstrated, by these experiments of the effects of power frequency electromagnetic field exposure on the function of immune cells, only two experiments have attempted to correlate electromagnetic field induced changes in immune function directly with tumour growth (Table 4.10). In addition, separate studies of electromagnetic field induced changes in immune function and tumour incidence in the same mouse strain are compared.

91 In a co-promotion study of power frequency magnetic field effects on DMBA- and TPA-induced skin tumours in SENCAR mice (McLean *et al*, 1991), the authors found increased numbers of exposed mice with enlarged spleens and extremely high blood mononuclear cell counts. In addition, natural killer cell activity was lower in the exposed groups, but not significantly so. The authors speculated that the changes indicated the possible development of leukaemia (or lymphoma), possibly due to a field-induced suppression of the immune system, but acknowledged that the evidence of immune

system neoplasia was weak. In a study of magnetic field effects on the growth of DMBA-induced mammary tumours in rats, Mevissen *et al* (1996b) reported that the exposure of DMBA-treated rats significantly increased the number of mammary tumours and reduced the proliferative responsiveness of T-lymphocytes. However, this latter effect was not significant and the suggestion that the effect on the immune system contributed to the increased tumour growth was therefore rather speculative. Finally, whilst House *et al* (1996) and House and McCormick (2000) reported reduced natural killer cell activity in female mice exposed to electromagnetic fields for up to 13 weeks, McCormick *et al* (1999) found no overall effect of similar levels of exposure for two years on the spontaneous tumour incidence in the same mouse strain. If anything, the tumour incidence in female mice was slightly reduced.

TABLE 4.10
Immune response and tumour growth

Assay	Exposure	Response	Comment	Authors
SENCAR mice painted with DMBA and TPA	60 Hz, 2 mT for 6 h per day, 5 days per week for 21 weeks	More mice with enlarged spleens and high mononuclear cell count; insignificant drop in NK activity	No correlation; leukaemia/ lymphoma insufficiently identified	McLean *et al* (1991)
DMBA-induced mammary tumours in female Sprague-Dawley rats	50 Hz, 50 μT for 13 weeks	Increased incidence of visible tumours at autopsy; no significant change in T-cell mitogen response (in DMBA-treated rats)	No correlation	Mevissen *et al* (1996b)
Spontaneous tumours in B6C3F1 male and female mice	60 Hz, 2, 200, 1000 μT continuous or 1000 μT intermittent for up to 13 weeks or 2 years	Reduced NK activity in female but not male mice; no overall effect on spontaneous tumour incidence	No correlation; exposure durations different	House *et al* (1996), McCormick *et al* (1999), NTP (1999a), House and McCormick (2000)

Summary

92 There is little consistent evidence of any inhibitory effect of power frequency electromagnetic field exposure on the various aspects of immune system function relevant to tumour suppression that have been examined; these included *in vivo* assays of T-lymphocyte mediated immune responsiveness to infection and antigen stimulation and, following *in vivo* exposure, *in vitro* assays of lymphocyte proliferation, of natural killer cell activity, macrophage activity and B-lymphocyte (antibody) cell activity. Consistently reduced natural killer cell activity was seen in female mice exposed to magnetic fields but this was not seen in exposed male mice nor in male or female rats. This could not be correlated with any change in spontaneous tumour incidence seen in a separate study. In addition, two other studies were unable to correlate possible electromagnetic field induced changes in tumour incidence with significant changes in immune function.

CONCLUSIONS

93 Overall, no convincing evidence has been found from experimental studies supporting the hypothesis that exposure to power frequency electromagnetic fields increases the risk of cancer. This conclusion is well supported by the results of a number of recent large-scale studies of animal carcinogenesis including those using transgenic animals, which have generally been more carefully conducted, often using independent quality assurance procedures, than some of the earlier studies reporting either positive or negative effects.

Animal tumour studies

Leukaemia/lymphoma, mammary tumours and brain tumours

94 Rodents, particularly mice, have been used extensively in studies of adult leukaemogenesis; there is, however, currently no natural animal model of the most common form of childhood leukaemia, acute lymphoblastic leukaemia. Most studies reported a lack of effect of power frequency magnetic fields on leukaemia or lymphoma in rodents, mostly mice. These included several recent large-scale studies of spontaneous tumour incidence in normal and transgenic mice, and of radiation-induced lymphoma and leukaemia in mice. The transgenic mouse model used in two of the studies mentioned above develops a disease with some similarities to childhood acute lymphoblastic leukaemia. Further studies found no effect on the progression of transplanted leukaemia cells in mice or rats. The most marked effect reported in one study was an increase in lymphoid hyperplasia and lymphoma in mice exposed over three generations; however, there were a number of deficiencies making it difficult to place a high degree of confidence in the experimental outcome.

95 Rat mammary carcinomas represent a standard laboratory animal model in the study of human breast cancer. Three recent large-scale studies of rats found that lifetime magnetic field exposure had no effect on the incidence of spontaneous mammary tumours. The evidence concerning electromagnetic field effects on chemically induced mammary tumours is more equivocal. Two studies suggested that exposure to power frequency electromagnetic fields increased the incidence or growth of chemically induced mammary tumours in female rats. However, the work of one laboratory was inadequately described and there was considerable inter-experimental variability in the results from the other laboratory. Two more recent studies have not been able to corroborate these findings; there were, however, clear differences in experimental protocol between these studies and the earlier studies reporting positive effects. Further experimental investigation may be warranted to resolve this uncertainty.

96 Whilst there is no natural animal model of spontaneous brain tumour, a recent large-scale study reported a lack of effect of exposure to power frequency magnetic fields on chemically induced nervous system tumours in female rats. In addition, the low incidence of brain cancers in three recent large-scale rat studies was not elevated by magnetic field exposure.

Other tumours

97 With regard to the studies of pre-neoplastic liver lesions and chemically induced skin tumours, the evidence is almost uniformly negative. In addition, there is no convincing evidence of increased malignant conversion. In particular, in three recent

large-scale studies of electromagnetic field effects on spontaneous tumour incidence in rodents, the overall proportion of malignant tumours tended to be evenly distributed between exposed and control animals and there was no evidence of a significant trend in dose–response relationship.

Electromagnetic field effects on serum melatonin

98 Melatonin is involved in the control of reproductive activity in seasonally breeding animals via inhibitory effects on circulating levels of sex hormones; any role in human reproduction is less clear.

Humans and non-human primates

99 Most evidence suggests that human melatonin rhythms are not delayed or suppressed by chronic exposure to the weak, pulsed electromagnetic fields generated by electric blankets nor by acute exposure to continuous or intermittent power frequency magnetic fields, although one recent study provided preliminary data indicating that exposure prior to the night-time rise in serum melatonin may have had this effect in a sensitive subgroup of the study population. No convincing effect on melatonin levels has been seen in non-human primates chronically exposed to power frequency electromagnetic fields.

Seasonally breeding animals and laboratory rodents

100 The evidence for an effect of exposure to power frequency electromagnetic fields on melatonin levels and melatonin-dependent reproductive status in seasonally breeding animals is mostly negative. There were no effects on Suffolk sheep. Initial reports of reduced and delayed night-time peaks in pineal and serum melatonin in Djungarian hamsters could not be successfully replicated; no effects were seen on changes in reproductive status.

101 In contrast, a number of studies reported that exposure to power frequency electric or magnetic fields resulted in suppression of rat pineal and serum melatonin levels. Many other studies found no effect. Several suffered from technical difficulties or poor experimental design. Overall, the evidence is inconsistent, no clear effect emerges. In addition, studies by one group were unable to correlate possible electromagnetic field induced changes in tumour incidence with melatonin suppression.

Electromagnetic field effects on immune response

102 In principal, electromagnetic field exposure might affect tumour growth via induced changes in immune system responses involved in tumour eradication. There is, however, little consistent evidence of any inhibitory effect of power frequency electromagnetic field exposure on the various aspects of immune system function relevant to tumour suppression that have been examined. These have included *in vivo* assays of T-lymphocyte mediated immune responsiveness to infection and antigen stimulation and, following *in vivo* exposure, *in vitro* assays of lymphocyte proliferation, of natural killer cell activity, macrophage activity and B-lymphocyte (antibody) cell activity. Consistently reduced natural killer cell activity was seen in female mice exposed to magnetic fields but this could not be correlated with any change in spontaneous tumour incidence seen in a separate study. In addition, two other studies were unable to correlate possible electromagnetic field induced changes in tumour incidence with significant changes in immune function.

ACKNOWLEDGEMENTS

103 The comments and suggestions of Dr R Cox, NRPB, are gratefully acknowledged.

REFERENCES

Abbas A A, Lichtman A H and Pober J S (1994). *Cellular and Molecular Immunology*. Philadelphia, W B Saunders.

Anderson L E, Boorman G A, Morris J E, *et al* (1999). Effect of 13 week magnetic field exposures on DMBA-initiated mammary gland carcinomas in female Sprague-Dawley rats. *Carcinogenesis*, **20**(8), 1615–20.

Anderson L E, Morris J E, Sasser L B, *et al* (2000). Effects of 50- or 60-hertz, 100 mT magnetic field exposure in the DMBA mammary cancer model in Sprague-Dawley rats: possible explanations for different results from two laboratories. *Environ Health Perspect*, **108**, 797–802.

Arendt J (1995). *Melatonin and the Mammalian Pineal Gland*. London, Chapman and Hall.

Babbitt J T, Kharazi A I, Taylor J M G, *et al* (2000). Hematopoietic neoplasia in C57BL/6 mice exposed to split-dose ionizing radiation and circularly polarised 60 Hz magnetic fields. *Carcinogenesis*, **21**(7), 101–11.

Bakos J, Nagy N, Thuróczy G, *et al* (1995). Sinusoidal 50 Hz, 500 μT magnetic field has no acute effect on urinary 6-sulphatoxymelatonin in Wistar rats. *Bioelectromagnetics*, **16**, 377–80.

Bakos J, Nagy N, Thuróczy G, *et al* (1997). Urinary 6-sulphatoxymelatonin excretion is increased in rats after 24 hours of exposure to vertical 50 Hz, 100 μT magnetic field. *Bioelectromagnetics*, **18**, 190–92.

Bakos J, Nagy N, Thuróczy G, *et al* (1999). Urinary 6-sulphatoxymelatonin excretion of rats is not changed by 24 hours of exposure to a horizontal 50-Hz, 100-μT magnetic field. *Electro- Magnetobiol*, **18**(1), 23–31.

Balmain A and Harris C C (2000). Carcinogenesis in mouse and human cells: parallels and paradoxes. *Carcinogenesis*, **21**, 371–7.

Baum A, Mevissen M, Kamino K, *et al* (1995). A histopathalogical study on alterations in DMBA-induced mammary carcinogenesis in rats with 50 Hz, 100 μT magnetic field exposure. *Carcinogenesis*, **16**, 119–25.

Bellossi A (1991). Effect of pulsed magnetic fields on leukemia-prone AKR mice. No-effect on mortality through five generations. *Leukemia Res*, **15**, 899–902.

Beniashvili D Sh, Bilanishvili V G and Menabde M Z (1991). Low-frequency electromagnetic radiation enhances the induction of rat mammary tumours by nitrosomethyl urea. *Cancer Lett*, **61**, 75–9.

Blask D E and Hill S M (1986). Effects of melatonin on cancer: studies on MCF-7 human breast cancer cells in culture. *J Neural Transm*, **21** (Suppl), 433–49.

Boorman G A, McCormick D L, Findlay J C, *et al* (1999a). Chronic toxicity/oncogenicity evaluation of 60 Hz (power frequency) magnetic fields in F344/N rats. *Toxicol Pathol*, **27**(3), 267–78.

Boorman G A, Anderson L E, Morris J E, *et al* (1999b). Effect of 26 week magnetic field exposures in a DMBA initiation-promotion mammary gland model in Sprague-Dawley rats. *Carcinogenesis*, **20**(5), 899–904.

Boorman G A, Rafferty C N, Ward J M, *et al* (2000a). Leukaemia and lymphoma incidence in rodents exposed to low-frequency magnetic fields. *Radiat Res*, **153**, 627–36.

Boorman G A, McCormick D L, Ward J M, *et al* (2000b). Magnetic fields and mammary cancer in rodents: a critical review and evaluation of published literature. *Radiat Res*, **153**, 617–26.

Brady J V and Reiter R J (1992). Neurobehavioural effects. IN *Health Effects of Low-frequency Electric and Magnetic Fields*. Prepared by an Oak Ridge Associated Universities Panel for the Committee on Interagency Radiation Research and Policy Coordination. Oak Ridge Associated Unversities, ORAU 92/F8, Chapter 7, pp vii-1–vii-56.

Carron C, Cormier F, Janin A, *et al* (2000). TEL-JAK2 transgenic mice develop T-cell leukaemia. *Blood*, **95**(12), 3891–9.

Cohen M, Lippman M and Chabner B (1978). Role of pineal gland in aetiology and treatment of breast cancer. *Lancet*, **2**, 814–16.

Cridland N A, Sienkiewicz Z J, Kowalczuk C I, *et al* (1996). Recent biological studies relevant to carcinogenesis. IN *Biological Effects of Magnetic and Electromagnetic Fields* (S Ueno, Ed). New York, Plenum Press, pp 221–38.

Devary L, Patinot C, Debray M, *et al* (2000). Absence of the effects of 50 Hz magnetic fields on the progression of acute myeloid leukaemia in rats. *Int J Radiat Biol*, **76**, 853–62.

DiGiovanni J, Johnston D A, Rupp T, *et al* (1999). Lack of effect of a 60 Hz magnetic field on biomarkers of tumour promotion in the skin of SENCAR mice. *Carcinogenesis*, **20**(4), 685–9.

Ekström T, Mild K H and Holmberg B (1998). Mammary tumours in Sprague-Dawley rats after initiation with DMBA followed by exposure to 50 Hz electromagnetic fields in a promotional scheme. *Cancer Lett*, **123**, 107–11.

Fam W Z and Mikhail E L (1993). A system for the exposure of small laboratory animals to a 25-mT 60 Hz alternating or travelling magnetic field. *IEEE Trans Biomed Eng*, **40**, 708–11.

Fam W Z and Mikhail E L (1996). Lymphoma induced in mice chronically exposed to very strong low-frequency electromagnetic field. *Cancer Lett*, **105**, 257–69.

Fotopoulos S S, Cook M R, Gerkovich M M, *et al* (1987). 60-Hz field effects on human neuroregulatory, immunologic, haematologic and target organ activity. IN *Interactions of Biological Systems with Static and ELF Electric and Magnetic Fields*. Proceedings 23rd Hanford Life Sciences Symposium (L E Anderson, B J Kelman and R J Weigel, Eds). CONF-841041, pp 455–70.

Fry R J M and Carnes B A (1989). Age, sex and other factors in radiation carcinogenesis. IN *Low Dose Radiation: Biological Basis of Risk Assessment* (K F Baverstock and J W Stather, Eds). London, Taylor and Francis, pp 196–206.

Gibbons D L, MacDonald D, McCarthy K P, *et al* (1999). An Eμ-BCL-2 transgene facilitates leukaemogenesis by ionising radiation. *Oncogene*, **18**, 3870–77.

Griffiths S D, Healy L E, Ford A M, *et al* (1992). Clonal characteristics of acute lymphoblastic cells derived from BCR/ABL p190 transgenic mice. *Oncogene*, **7**, 1391–9.

Graham C, Cook M R, Riffle D W, *et al* (1996). Nocturnal melatonin levels in human volunteers exposed to intermittent 60 Hz magnetic fields. *Bioelectromagnetics*, **17**, 263–73.

Graham C, Cook M R and Riffle D W (1997). Human melatonin during continuous magnetic field exposure. *Bioelectromagnetics*, **18**, 166–71.

Graham C, Cook M R, Sastre A, *et al* (2000). Multinight exposure to 60 Hz magnetic fields: effects on melatonin and its enzymatic metabolite. *J Pineal Res*, **28**, 1–8.

Grota L J, Lu S-T, Reiter R, *et al* (1991). Melatonin secretion by rats exposed to electric fields. IN Abstracts, 13th Annual Meeting of the Bioelectromagnetics Society, Salt Lake City, Utah, June 1991, p 106.

Grota L J, Reiter R J, Keng P, *et al* (1994). Electric field alters serum melatonin but not pineal melatonin synthesis in male rats. *Bioelectromagnetics*, **15**, 427–37.

Hahn H, Wojnowski L and Miller G (1999). The patched signalling pathway in tumourigenesis and development: lessons from animal models. *J Mol Med*, **77**, 459–68.

Hastings M H (1991). Neuroendocrine rhythms. *Pharmac Ther*, **50**, 35–71.

Harris A W, Basten A, Gebski V, *et al* (1998). A test of lymphoma induction by long-term exposure of E-*PIM1* transgenic mice to 50 Hz magnetic fields. *Radiat Res*, **149**, 300–307.

Heikkinen P, Kumlin T, Laitinen J T, *et al* (1999). Chronic exposure to 50-Hz magnetic fields or 900-MHz electromagnetic fields does not alter nocturnal 6-hydroxymelatonin sulphate secretion in CBA/S mice. *Electro- Magnetobiol*, **18**(1), 33–42.

House R V and McCormick D L (2000). Modulation of natural killer cell function after exposure to 60 Hz magnetic fields: confirmation of the effect in mature B6C3F1 mice. *Radiat Res*, **153**, 722–4.

House R V, Ratajczak H V, Gauger J R, *et al* (1996). Immune function and host defence in rodents exposed to 60-Hz magnetic fields. *Fundam Appl Toxicol*, **34**, 228–39.

Hoyes K P, Hendry J H and Lord B I (2000). Modifications of murine adult haemopoiesis and response to methyl nitrosourea following exposure to radiation at different developmental ages. *Int J Radiat Biol*, **76**, 77–85.

IARC (1980). Long-term and short term screening assays for carcinogens: a critical appraisal. IN IARC Monographs on the Evaluation of the Carcinogenic Risk of Chemicals to Humans, Supplement 2. Lyon, International Agency for Research on Cancer.

IARC (1992). Mechanisms of Carcinogenesis in Risk Identification (H Vaino, P N Magee, D B McGregor and A J McMichael, Eds). IARC Scientific Publications No. 116. Lyon, International Agency for Research on Cancer.

John T M, Liu G-Y and Brown G M (1998). 60 Hz magnetic field exposure and urinary 6-sulphatoxymelatonin levels in the rat. *Bioelectromagnetics*, **19**, 172–80.

Kato M and Shigemitsu T (1997). Effects of 50 Hz magnetic fields on pineal function in the rat. IN *The Melatonin Hypothesis, Breast Cancer and Use of Electric Power* (R G Stevens, B W Wilson and L E Anderson, Eds). Richland, Battelle Press, pp 337–76.

Kato M, Honma K, Shigemitsu T, *et al* (1993). Effects of exposure to a circularly polarised 50-Hz magnetic field on plasma melatonin levels in rats. *Bioelectromagnetics*, **14**, 97–106.

Kato M, Honma K, Shigemitsu T, *et al* (1994a). Recovery of nocturnal melatonin concentration takes place within one week following cessation of 50 Hz circularly polarised magnetic field exposure for six weeks. *Bioelectromagnetics*, **15**, 489–92.

Kato M, Honma K, Shigemitsu T, *et al* (1994b). Circularly polarised 50-Hz magnetic field exposure reduces pineal gland and blood melatonin concentrations of Long-Evans rats. *Neurosci Lett*, **166**, 59–62.

Kato M, Honma K, Shigemitsu T, *et al* (1994c). Horizontal or vertical 50-Hz, 1-μT magnetic fields have no effect on pineal gland or plasma melatonin concentrations of albino rats. *Neurosci Lett*, **168**, 205–8.

Kato M, Honma K, Shigemitsu T, *et al* (1994d). Circularly polarised, sinusoidal, 50 Hz magnetic field does not influence plasma testosterone levels of rats. *Bioelectromagnetics*, **15**, 513–18.

Kharazi A I, Babbitt J T and Hahn T (1999). Primary brain tumour incidence in mice exposed to split-dose ionizing radiation and circularly polarised 60 Hz magnetic fields. *Cancer Lett*, **147**, 149–56.

Kowalczuk C I and Saunders R D (1990). Dominant lethal studies in male mice after exposure to a 50-Hz electric field. *Bioelectromagnetics*, **11**, 129–37.

Kowalczuk C I, Robbins L, Thomas J M, *et al* (1995). Dominant lethal studies in male mice after exposure to a 50 Hz magnetic field. *Mutat Res*, **328**, 229–37.

Kroese E D, Dortant P M, van Steeg H, *et al* (1997). Use of Eμ-*PIM-1* transgenic mice for short-term *in vivo* carcinogenicity testing: lymphoma induction by benzo[α]pyrene, but not by TPA. *Carcinogenesis*, **18**, 975–80.

Kumlin T, Kosma V-M, Alhonen L, *et al* (1998). Effects of 50 Hz magnetic fields on UV-induced tumorigenesis in ODC-transgenic and non-transgenic mice. *Int J Radiat Biol*, **73**, 113–21.

Lee J M, Stormshak F, Thompson J M, *et al* (1993). Melatonin secretion and puberty in female lambs exposed to environmental electric and magnetic fields. *Biol Reproduct*, **49**, 857–64.

Lee J M, Stormshak F, Thompson J M, *et al* (1995). Melatonin and puberty in female lambs exposed to EMF: a replicate study. *Bioelectromagnetics*, **16**, 119–23.

Löscher W and Mevissen M (1995). Linear relationship between flux density and tumour copromoting effect of magnetic field exposure in a rat breast cancer model. *Cancer Lett*, **96**, 175–89.

Löscher W, Mevissen M, Lehmacher W, *et al* (1993). Tumour promotion in a breast cancer model by exposure to a weak alternating magnetic field. *Cancer Lett*, **71**, 75–81.

Löscher W, Wahnschaffe U, Mevissen M, *et al* (1994). Effects of weak alternating magnetic fields on nocturnal melatonin production and mammary carcinogenesis in rats. *Oncology*, **51**, 288–95.

Löscher W, Mevissen M and Häußler M (1997). Seasonal influence on 7,12-dimethylbenz[α]anthracene-induced mammary carcinogenesis in Sprague-Dawley rats under controlled laboratory conditions. *Pharmacol Toxicol*, **81**, 265–70.

Löscher W, Mevissen M and Lerchl A (1998). Exposure of female rats to a 100-μT 50 Hz magnetic field does not induce consistent changes in nocturnal levels of melatonin. *Radiat Res*, **150**, 557–67.

McCann J, Dietrich F, Rafferty C, *et al* (1993). A critical review of the genotoxic potential of electric and magnetic fields. *Mutat Res*, **297**, 61–95.

McCann J, Kavet R and Rafferty C N (2000). Assessing the potential carcinogenic activity of magnetic fields using animal models. *Environ Health Perspect*, **108**, 79–100.

McCormick D L, Cahill M A, Ryan B M, *et al* (1995). Pineal function in B6C3F1 mice exposed to 60 Hz magnetic fields: time course studies. IN Abstracts, 17th Annual Meeting of the Bioelectromagnetics Society, June 1995, Boston, Massachusetts, p 81.

McCormick D L, Ryan B M, Findlay J C, *et al* (1998). Exposure to 60 Hz magnetic fields and risk of lymphoma in PIM transgenic and TSG-*p53* (*p53* knockout) mice. *Carcinogenesis*, **19**, 1649–53.

McCormick D L, Boorman G A, Findlay J C, *et al* (1999). Chronic toxicity/oncogenicity evaluation of 60 Hz (power frequency) magnetic fields in B6C3F1 mice. *Toxicol Pathol*, **27**(3), 279–85.

McLean J R N, Stuchly M A, Mitchel R E J, *et al* (1991). Cancer promotion in a mouse-skin model by a 60-Hz magnetic field: II. Tumour development and immune response. *Bioelectromagnetics*, **12**, 273–87.

McLean J, Thansandote A, Lecuyer D, *et al* (1995). A 60-Hz magnetic field increases the incidence of squamous cell carcinomas in mice previously exposed to chemical carcinogens. *Cancer Lett*, **92**, 121–5.

McLean J R N, Thansandote A, Lecuyer D, *et al* (1997). The effect of 60-Hz magnetic fields on co-promotion of chemically induced skin tumours on SENCAR mice: a discussion of three studies. *Environ Health Perspect*, **105**, 94–6.

Maestroni G J M, Conti A and Pierpaoli W (1986). Role of pineal gland in immunity: circadian synthesis and release of melatonin modulates the antibody response and antagonizes immunosuppressive effect of corticosterone. *J Neuroimmunol*, **13**, 19–30.

Mandeville R, Franco E, Sidrac-Ghali S, *et al* (1997). Evaluation of the potential carcinogenicity of 60 Hz linear sinusoidal continuous-wave magnetic fields in Fischer F344 rats. *FASEB J*, **11**, 1127–36.

Mandeville R, Franco E, Sidrac-Ghali S, *et al* (2000). Evaluation of the potential promoting effect of 60 Hz magnetic fields on N-ethyl-N-nitrosourea induced neurogenic tumours in female F344 rats. *Bioelectromagnetics*, **21**, 84–93.

Martínez Soriano F, Giménez González F, Armañazas E, *et al* (1992). Pineal 'synaptic ribbons' and serum melatonin following the pulse cation of 52-Gs (50-Hz) magnetic fields: an evolutive analysis over 21 days. *Acta Anat*, **143**, 289–93.

Mevissen M, Stamm A, Buntenkötter S, *et al* (1993a). Effects of magnetic fields on mammary tumour development induced by 7,12-dimethylbenz(a)anthracene in rats. *Bioelectromagnetics*, **14**, 131–43.

Mevissen M, Wahnschaffe U, Löscher W, *et al* (1993b). Effects of AC magnetic field on DMBA-induced mammary carcinogenesis in Sprague-Dawley rats. IN *Electricity and Magnetism in Biology and Medicine* (M Blank, Ed). San Francisco, San Francisco Press, pp 413–15.

Mevissen M, Lerchl A and Löscher W (1996a). Study on pineal function and DMBA-induced breast cancer formation in rats during exposure to a 100 mG, 50-Hz magnetic field. *J Toxicol Environ Health*, **48**, 169–85.

Mevissen M, Lerchl A, Szamel M, *et al* (1996b). Exposure of DMBA-treated female rats in a 50-Hz, 50 μtesla magnetic field: effects on mammary tumour growth, melatonin levels and T lymphocyte activation. *Carcinogenesis*, **17**, 903–10.

Mevissen M, Häußler M, Lerchl A, *et al* (1998a). Acceleration of mammary tumourigenesis by exposure of 7,12-dimethylbenz[α]anthracene-treated female rats in a 50-Hz 100-μT magnetic field: replication study. *J Toxicol Environ Health*, **53**, 401–18.

Mevissen M, Häussler M, Szamel M, *et al* (1998b). Complex effects of long-term 50 Hz magnetic field exposure *in vivo* on immune functions in female Sprague-Dawley rats depend on duration of exposure. *Bioelectromagnetics*, **19**, 259–70.

Morris J E, Sasser L B, Miller D L, *et al* (1999). Clinical progression of transplanted large granular lymphocytic leukaemia in Fischer 344 rats exposed to 60 Hz magnetic fields. *Bioelectromagnetics*, **20**, 48–56.

Murphy J C, Kadan D A, Warren J and Sivak A (1993). Power frequency electric and magnetic fields: a review of genetic toxicology. *Mutat Res*, **296**, 221–40.

Murthy K K, Rogers W R and Smith H D (1995). Initial studies on the effects of combined 60 Hz electric and magnetic field exposure on the immune system of non-human primates. *Bioelectromagnetics*, Supplement, **3**, 93–102.

NRPB (1992). Electromagnetic fields and the risk of cancer. Report of an Advisory Group on Non-ionising Radiation. *Doc NRPB*, **3**(1), 1–138.

NTP (1999a). NTP technical report on the toxicology and carcinogenesis studies of 60-Hz magnetic fields in F344/N rats and B6C3F1 mice. Washington DC, National Toxicology Program, NTP TR 488, NIH Publication No. 99-3978.

NTP (1999b). NTP technical report on studies of magnetic field promotion (DMBA initiation) in Sprague-Dawley rats (gavage/whole-body exposure studies). Washington DC, National Toxicology Program, NTP TR 489, NIH Publication No. 99-3979.

Niehaus M, Brüggemeyer H, Behre H M, *et al* (1997). Growth retardation, testicular stimulation and increased melatonin synthesis by weak magnetic fields (50 Hz) in Djungarian hamsters *Phodoporus sungorus*. *Biochem Biophys Res Comm*, **237**, 707–11.

Pattengale P K (1990). Classification of mouse lymphoid cell neoplasms. IN *Hemopoietic System* (T C Jones, J M Ward, U Mohr and R D Hunt, Eds). Berlin, Springer-Verlag, pp 137–43.

Pattengale P K (1994). Tumours of the lymphohaematopoietic system. IN Pathology of Tumours in Laboratory Animals. Volume II: Tumours of the Mouse. IARC Scientific Publications No. 111, Volume 2 (V S Turosov and U Mohr, Eds). Lyon, International Agency for Research on Cancer, pp 651–70.

Pattengale P K and Taylor C R (1983). Experimental models of lymphoproliferative disease: the mouse as a model for human Non-Hodgkin's lymphomas and related leukaemias. *Am J Pathol*, **113**, 237–65.

Picazo M L, Catalá M D, Romo M A, *et al* (1998). Inhibition of melatonin in the plasma of third-generation male mice under the action of ELF magnetic fields. *Electro- Magnetobiol*, **17**, 75–85.

Putinas J and Michaelson S M (1990). Humoral responsiveness of mice exposed to a 500 μT 60 Hz magnetic field. *Biochem Bioenerg*, **24**, 371–4.

Rannug A, Holmberg B and Mild K H (1993a). A rat liver foci promotion study with 50 Hz magnetic fields. *Environ Res*, **62**, 223–9.

Rannug A, Holmberg B, Ekström T, *et al* (1993b). Rat liver foci study on coexposure with 50 Hz magnetic fields and known carcinogens. *Bioelectromagnetics*, **14**, 17–27.

Rannug A, Ekström T, Hansson Mild K, *et al* (1993c). A study on skin tumour formation in mice with 50 Hz magnetic field exposure. *Carcinogenesis*, **14**, 573–8.

Rannug A, Holmberg B, Ekström T, *et al* (1994). Intermittent 50 Hz magnetic field and skin tumour promotion in SENCAR mice. *Carcinogenesis*, **15**, 153–7.

Reilly K M, Loisel D A, Bronson R T, *et al* (2000). Nf1;Trp53 mutant mice develop glioblastoma with evidence of strain-specific effects. *Nature Genet*, **26**, 109–13.

Reiter R J (1980). The pineal and its hormones in the control of reproduction in mammals. *Endocrine Rev*, **1**, 109–31.

Reiter R J (1993). Static and extremely low frequency electromagnetic field exposure: reported effects on the circadian production of melatonin. *J Cell Biochem*, **51**, 394–403.

Reiter R J (1997). Melatonin biosynthesis, regulation and effects. IN *The Melatonin Hypothesis, Breast Cancer and Use of Electric Power* (R G Stevens, B W Wilson and L E Anderson, Eds). Richland, Battelle Press, pp 25–48.

Reiter R J, Anderson L E, Buschbom R L, *et al* (1988). Reduction in the nocturnal rise in melatonin levels in rats exposed to 60-Hz electric fields *in utero* and for 23 days after birth. *Life Sci*, **42**, 2203.

Reiter R J, Melchiorri D, Sewerynek E, *et al* (1995). A review of the evidence supporting melatonin's role as an antioxidant. *J Pineal Res*, **18**, 1–11.

Rogers W R, Reiter R J, Barlow-Walden L, *et al* (1995a). Regularly scheduled, day-time, slow-onset 60 Hz electric and magnetic field exposure does not depress serum melatonin concentration in nonhuman primates. *Bioelectromagnetics*, Supplement, **3**, 111–18.

Rogers W R, Reiter R J, Smith H D, *et al* (1995b). Rapid-onset/offset, variably scheduled 60 Hz electric and magnetic field exposure reduces nocturnal serum melatonin concentration in non-human primates. *Bioelectromagnetics*, Supplement, **3**, 119–22.

Roitt I, Brostoff J and Male D (1996). *Immunology* (4th Ed). London, Mosby.

Russo I H and Russo J (1996). Mammary gland neoplasia in long-term rodent studies. *Environ Health Perspect*, **104**, 938–67.

Sasser L B, Morris J E, Buschbom R L, *et al* (1991). Effect of 60 Hz electric fields on pineal melatonin during various times of the dark period. IN Project Resumes, DOE Annual Review of Research on Biological Effects of 50 and 60 Hz Electric and Magnetic Fields, November 1991, Milwaukee, Wisconsin, p A-24.

Sasser L B, Morris J E, Miller D L, *et al* (1996). Exposure to 60 Hz magnetic fields does not alter clinical progression of LGL leukemia in Fischer rats. *Carcinogenesis*, **17**, 2681–7.

Sasser L B, Anderson L E, Morris J E, *et al* (1998). Lack of a co-promoting effect of a 60 Hz magnetic field on skin tumourigenesis in Sencar mice. *Carcinogenesis*, **19**, 1617–21.

Selmaoui B and Touitou Y (1995). Sinusoidal 50-Hz magnetic fields depress rat pineal NAT activity and serum melatonin. Role of duration and intensity of exposure. *Life Sci*, **57**, 1351–8.

Selmaoui B, Lambrozo J and Touitou Y (1996). Magnetic fields and pineal function in humans: evaluation of nocturnal acute exposure to extremely low frequency magnetic fields on serum melatonin and urinary 6-sulfatoxymelatonin circadian rhythms. *Life Sci*, **58**, 1539–49.

Shah P N, Mhatre M C and Kothari L S (1984). Effect of melatonin on mammary carcinogenesis in intact and pinealectomized rats in varying photoperiods. *Cancer Res*, **44**, 3403.

Shen Y H, Shao B J, Chiang H, *et al* (1997). The effects of 50 Hz magnetic field exposure on dimethylbenz(α)anthracene induced thymic lymphoma/leukaemia in mice. *Bioelectromagnetics*, **18**, 360–64.

Stevens R G (1987). Electric power use and breast cancer: a hypothesis. *Am J Epidemiol*, **125**, 556–61.

Stevens R G (1994). Electric power and the risk of hormone-related cancers. IN *Biological Effects of Electric and Magnetic Fields*, Volume 2 (D O Carpenter and S Ayrapetyan, Eds). San Diego, Academic Press, pp 263–78.

Stuchly M A, Lecuyer D W and McLean J (1991). Cancer promotion in a mouse-skin model by a 60-Hz magnetic field: I. Experimental design and exposure system. *Bioelectromagnetics*, **12**, 261–71.

Stuchly M A, McLean J R N, Burnett R, *et al* (1992). Modification of tumour promotion in the mouse skin by exposure to an alternating magnetic field. *Cancer Lett*, **65**, 1–7.

Svedenstål B-M and Holmberg B (1993). Lymphoma development among mice exposed to X-rays and pulsed magnetic fields. *Int J Radiat Biol*, **64**, 119–25.

Tamarkin L, Cohen M, Roselle D, *et al* (1981). Melatonin inhibition and pinealectomy enhancement of 7,12-dimethylbenz(a)anthracene-induced mammary tumours in the rat. *Cancer Res*, **41**, 4432–6.

Tamarkin L, Baird C J and Almeida O F X (1985). Melatonin: a coordinating signal for mammalian reproduction? *Science*, **227**, 714–20.

Thomson R A E, Michaelson S M and Nguyen Q A (1988). Influence of 60-hertz magnetic fields on leukaemia. *Bioelectromagnetics*, **9**, 149–58.

Thun-Battersby S, Mevissen M and Löscher W (1999). Exposure of Sprague-Dawley rats to a 50-hertz, 100-μtesla magnetic field for 27 weeks facilitates mammary tumourigenesis in the 7,12-dimethylbenz[α]anthracene model of breast cancer. *Cancer Res*, **59**, 3627–33.

Tremblay L, Houde M, Mercier G, *et al* (1996). Differential modulation of natural and adaptive immunity in Fischer rats exposed for 6 weeks to 60 Hz linear sinusoidal continuous-wave magnetic fields. *Bioelectromagnetics*, **17**, 373–83.

Truong H and Yellon S M (1997). Effect of various acute 60 Hz magnetic field exposures on the nocturnal melatonin rise in the adult Djungarian hamster. *J Pineal Res*, **22**, 177–83.

Truong H, Smith J C and Yellon S M (1996). Photoperiod control of the melatonin rhythm and reproductive maturation in the juvenile Djungarian mamster. *Biol Reproduct*, **55**, 455–60.

UNSCEAR (1993). Sources and Effects of Ionizing Radiation. Report to the General Assembly with Scientific Annexes. New York, United Nations.

Verbeel S, van Lohuizen M, van der Valk M, *et al* (1991). Mice bearing the Eμ-myc and Eμ-pim-1 transgenes develop pre-B-cell leukaemia prenatally. *Mol Cell Biol*, **11**, 1176–9.

Wilbourn J, Haroun L, Heseltine E, *et al* (1986). Response of experimental animals to human carcinogens: an analysis based upon the IARC Monographs programme. *Carcinogenesis*, **7**, 1853–63.

Wilson B W, Anderson L E, Hilton D I, *et al* (1981). Chronic exposure to 60-Hz electric fields: effects on pineal function in the rat. *Bioelectromagnetics*, **2**, 371.

Wilson B W, Anderson L E, Hilton D I, *et al* (1983). Chronic exposure to 60-Hz electric fields: effects on pineal function in the rat. *Bioelectromagnetics*, **4**, 293.

Wilson B W, Chess E K and Anderson L E (1986). 60-Hz electric-field effects on pineal melatonin rhythms: time course for onset and recovery. *Bioelectromagnetics*, **7**, 239.

Wilson B W, Wright C W, Morris J E, *et al* (1990). Evidence for an effect of ELF electromagnetic fields on human pineal gland function. *J Pineal Res*, **9**, 259–69.

Wilson B W, Morris J E, Sasser L B, *et al* (1993). Changes in the hypothalamus and pineal gland of Djungarian hamsters from short-term exposure to 60-Hz magnetic fields. IN Abstracts, DOE Annual Review of Research on Biological Effects of Electric and Magnetic fields from the Generation, Delivery and Use of Electricity, October/November 1993, Savannah, Georgia, pp 97–8.

Wilson B W, Matt K S, Morris J E, *et al* (1999). Effects of 60 Hz magnetic field exposure on the pineal and hypothalamic-pituitary-gonadal axis in the Siberian hamster (*Phodopus sungorus*). *Bioelectromagnetics*, **20**, 224–32.

Wood A W, Armstrong S M, Sait M L, *et al* (1998). Changes in human plasma melatonin profiles in response to 50 Hz magnetic field exposure. *J Pineal Res*, **25**, 116–27.

Yasui M, Kikuchi T, Ogawa M, *et al* (1997). Carcinogenicity test of 50 Hz magnetic fields in rats. *Bioelectromagnetics*, **18**, 531–40.

Yellon S M (1994). Acute 60 Hz magnetic field exposure effects on the melatonin rhythm in the pineal gland and circulation of the adult Djungarian hamster. *J Pineal Res*, **16**, 136–44.

Yellon S M (1996). 60 Hz magnetic field exposure effects on the melatonin rhythm and photoperiod control of reproduction. *Am J Physiol*, **270**, E816–21.

Yellon S M and Truong H N (1998). Melatonin rhythm onset in the adult Siberian hamster: influence of photoperiod but not 60-Hz magnetic field exposure on melatonin content in the pineal gland and in circulation. *J Biol Rhythms*, **13**, 52–9.

5 Recent Epidemiological Studies on Residential Electric and Magnetic Fields and Cancer

INTRODUCTION

1 The 1992 Advisory Group report on electromagnetic fields and the risk of cancer (NRPB, 1992) gave detailed consideration to the early studies on residential exposure and cancer, with particular emphasis on findings in children. The report concluded that while there was suggestive evidence of an association in children, methodological shortcomings were such that the evidence did not allow conclusions to be drawn. For example, the controls were not always comparable with the cases and the tendency for wire configuration to show stronger relationships with childhood cancer than other measures of extremely low frequency (ELF) electromagnetic field (EMF) exposure may have been due to an association of wire codes with other characteristics besides electromagnetic field exposure, ie confounding. This possibility was supported by the observation that studies contributing most weight to the significant results selected controls by methods which may have been biased with respect to socioeconomic status and stability of residence. In addition, the proportion of houses for which direct measurements of exposure were possible was low. Pooled results showing an association between measured electromagnetic fields and all childhood cancers combined were heavily weighted by a large excess of cancers other than leukaemia and brain tumours from a single study. Thus, the studies considered had sufficient methodological problems to indicate 'extreme caution' in the interpretation of their findings. In the case of adults, data on exposure were sparse and the available evidence did not suggest that this was a risk factor.

2 Since the 1992 report, four studies from the Nordic region on a range of cancers in children based on similar methods of ascertainment of cases and selection of controls have been published. In addition, the results of several studies, including those from the UK, USA and Canada, in which detailed measurements have been made using direct in-residence estimates of electromagnetic field exposure, have become available. These and the Nordic studies have generally been of considerably higher quality than those considered previously. Selection biases and confounding are less likely explanations for their findings than in the earlier studies. Several other studies in adults as well as children have been published, some of these too including more direct measures of exposure than previously. This chapter reviews these new studies, starting with a summary of each and then considering them collectively with some of the earlier studies according to methods used and reliability. Recent residential studies are summarised in Table 5.1.

Text continues on page 109

TABLE 5.1
Summary of main features of recent residential studies
A: Childhood studies

Study	**Feychting and Ahlbom (1993)**			
Country	Sweden			
Type	Case-control, ages 0–16 years			
Exposure Main method(s)	Residence within 300 m of lines. Spot measurements in central room with and without appliances running (62% of homes) Calculated fields closest to diagnosis			
Cases	142 from National Board of Health and Welfare Registry			
Controls	558, ie four for each case			
Allowance for confounding	Extensive			
Main results		*Relative risks (RR)*		
		All cancer	*Leukaemia*	*CNS* tumours*
	≤0.09 μT	1.0	1.0	1.0
	0.1–0.19 μT	1.5	2.1	1.0
	≥0.2 μT	1.1	2.7	0.7
Comments	Contemporary and historical fields compared and validated against measured fields. Relation with leukaemia only in one-family homes			

Study	**Olsen *et al* (1993)**				
Country	Denmark				
Type	Case-control, ages 0–15 years				
Exposure Main method(s)	Dwellings with exposure ≥0.1μT Historical fields using magnetic field programme				
Cases	1707 from Danish cancer registry				
Controls	Two to five, total 4788, from central population register				
Allowance for confounding	Partial				
Main results		*Odds ratios (OR)*			
		All cancer	*Leukaemia*	*CNS tumours*	*Lymphoma*
	Not exposed	1.0	1.0	1.0	1.0
	Exposed (≥0.10 μT)	1.4	1.0	1.0	5.0
Comments	Lymphoma result based on 3 cases and 3 controls				

Study	**Verkasalo *et al* (1993)**			
Country	Finland			
Type	Cohort, ages 0–19 years. Observed/expected comparison			
Exposure Main method(s)	Buildings within 500 m of lines Calculated historical fields and cumulative exposure			
Cases	140 (145 expected) from cancer registry			
Controls	From remainder of 68 300 boys and 66 500 girls			
Allowance for confounding	Not described			
Main results		*Incidence ratios*		
		All cancer	*Leukaemia*	*CNS tumours*
	0.01–0.19 μT	0.94	0.89	0.85
	≥0.20 μT	1.5	1.6	2.3
Comments	CNS result based on 3 tumours (out of 7) in one boy with neurofibromatosis. Cumulative exposure in μT years gives similar results. Only 1 lymphoma case			

* CNS = central nervous system.

TABLE 5.1

A: Childhood studies (continued)

Study	**Tynes and Haldorsen (1997)**
Country	Norway
Type	Nested case–control, ages 0–14 years
Exposure Main method(s)	Calculated historical fields
Cases	532 from Norwegian Cancer Registry
Controls	2112, ie up to five for each case from same cohort
Allowance for confounding	Partial
Main results	*Odds ratios*

	All cancer	*Leukaemia*	*CNS tumours*	*Lymphoma*
≤0.05 µT	1.0	1.0	1.0	1.0
0.05–0.14 µT	1.9	1.8	1.9	1.0
≥0.14 µT	0.9	0.3	0.7	2.5

Comments	Liittle support for association between exposure and leukaemia

Study	**UK Childhood Cancer Study (1999)**
Country	UK
Type	Case–control, ages 0–14 years
Exposure Main method(s)	(a) Phase 1 - 90-minute family room measurement and bedroom spot measurements, and school measurements (b) Phase 2 - 48-hour residential assessment on top 10% of Phase 1 residential exposures (0.1 µT and above) (c) Allowance for specified appliance, electricity supply and historical load situations
Cases	2226 (acute lymphoblastic leukaemia, ALL, in 84% of leukaemia cases) registered with health authorities having magnetic field measurements (3838 in main study)
Controls	2226 randomly selected from same health authorities as cases (7629 in main study)
Allowance for confounding	Extensive
Main results	*OR < 0.2 µT compared with > 0.1 µT*

ALL	*All leukaemia*	*CNS tumours*	*All malignancies*
0.92	0.90	0.46	0.87

Comments	No evidence of association of exposure with leukaemia, CNS tumours or other cancers. Magnetic field measurements in 50% eligible cases and 40% controls

Study	**Linet *et al* (1997)**
Country	USA
Type	Case–control, under 15 years
Exposure Main method(s)	24-hour measurements in bedroom and 30-second measurements in other rooms and outside front door. Also wire-code catergories
Cases	638 with ALL registered with Children's Cancer Group
Controls	620 selected by random digit dialling
Allowance for confounding	Extensive
Main results	OR for ALL 1.24 (not significant) at exposures of ≥ 0.200 µT compared with <0.065 µT, 1.53 (not significant) in matched analysis. See text on home and leisure appliances
Comments	No conclusive evidence of risk due to magnetic field exposure. 63% participation by controls

TABLE 5.1
A: Childhood studies (continued)

Study	**McBride *et al* (1999)**
Country	Canada
Type	Case–control, ages 0–14 years
Exposure Main method(s)	Included 48-hour personal measurements. Also residential fields and wire coding
Cases	399 (88% ALL) within 100 km of principal cities of 5 provinces
Controls	399 at random from health insurance records
Allowance for confounding	Extensive
Main results	ORs 0.95 and 0.93 for all leukaemia and ALL, respectively, using personal measurements
Comments	No evidence of risk. 76% of eligible controls participated. Personal measurements available for 75% cases and 86% controls
Study	**Dockerty *et al* (1998, 1999a,b)**
Country	New Zealand
Type	Case–control, ages 0–14 years
Exposure Main method(s)	24-hour measurements in child's main day room and in bedroom
Cases	303 from New Zealand cancer registry, 121 with leukaemia, 58 CNS tumours, 124 other solid tumours
Controls	303 from birth records, electoral rolls and telephone books
Allowance for confounding	Partial
Main results	OR $\geq 0.2\ \mu T$ compared with $< 0.1\ \mu T$ 1.4 (not significant) for leukaemia
Comments	Few children in highest exposure categories. Consult original papers for re-analysis and erratum. No evidence for association of EMF exposure with leukaemia or other cancers
Study	**Michaelis *et al* (1997)**
Country	Germany
Type	Population-based case–control, ages 0–14 years
Exposure Main method(s)	Magnetic field over 24 hours
Cases	129 leukaemia cases from German Childhood Cancer Registry
Controls	238 from local government records
Allowance for confounding	Partial
Main results	OR 3.2 (not significant) for median of 24-hour measurement in bedroom using cutoff point of $0.2\ \mu T$
Comments	Possible selection bias (low response rate). Results might indicate 8 cases of leukaemia per annum in 13 million children. Further results in Michaelis *et al* (1998)

TABLE 5.1

A: Childhood studies (continued)

Study	**Petridou *et al* (1997)**
Country	Greece
Type	Case–control, ages 0–14 years
Exposure Main method(s)	Distance from centre of residence to two nearest transmission/ distribution lines. Voltage/distance and square and cube of distance (ie three measures). Modified Wertheimer-Leeper code
Cases	117 cases through nationwide group of paediatric oncologists
Controls	202 patients in hospital for other conditions
Allowance for confounding	Partial
Main results	No significant trends for association of any measure with leukaemia, but ORs highest (1.50, 1.65, 1.71 – none significant) for top compared with lowest quintiles of each of three distance measures
Comments	No direct measurements. Probable selection bias in controls, especially. No support for a causal link
Study	**Preston-Martin *et al* (1996a)**
Country	USA, Los Angeles
Type	Case–control, ages 0–19 years
Exposure Main method(s)	24-hour residential field monitors, wire codes
Cases	298 brain tumours in residents of Los Angeles County
Controls	298 by random digit dialling
Allowance for confounding	Extensive
Main results	No significant trends
Comments	Apparent increase in risk with underground wiring probably an artefact
Study	**Gurney *et al* (1996)**
Country	USA, Seattle
Type	Case–control, ages 0–19 years
Exposure Main method(s)	Wire codes
Cases	133 brain tumours in Cancer Surveillance System
Controls	270 by random digit dialling
Allowance for confounding	Extensive
Main results	No significant trends
Comments	Incomplete information on exposure

TABLE 5.1
B: Adult studies

Study	**Feychting and Ahlbom (1994)**
Country	Sweden
Type	Case-control, age 16 years or more
Exposure Main method(s)	Residence within 300 m of lines. Calculated and cumulative historical fields. Spot measurements. *See childhood section under same authors*
Cases	Swedish Cancer Registry: 325 leukaemia, 233 CNS tumours
Controls	1091 from study base
Allowance for confounding	Extensive
Main results	

	Relative risks	
	Leukaemia	*CNS tumours*
≤1.0 μT years	1.0	1.0
1.0–1.9 μT years	1.0 (AML* 1.5)	1.1
≥0.2 μT years	1.5 (AML 2.3)	0.7

Comments	Selection bias unlikely, high proportion exposed ('corridor' method). Contrast between possible effect on myeloblastic leukaemia in residential studies compared with lymphoblastic in occupational studies

Study	**Verkasalo *et al* (1996)**
Country	Finland
Type	Nationwide cohort, age 20 years or more
Exposure Main method(s)	Buildings within 500 m of lines. Cumulative exposure. *See childhood section under same authors*
Cases	8415 (all sites) from Finnish Cancer Registry
Controls	From remainder of 383 700 subjects
Allowance for confounding	Partial
Main results	No consistent associations for any site
Comments	Criticised for not analysing by higher exposure among those in ≥ 2.00 μT years category

Study	**Li *et al* (1997)**
Country	Taiwan
Type	Case-control, age 15 years or more
Exposure Main method(s)	Distance from lines. Calculated fields in year of diagnosis
Cases	National Cancer Registry: 870 leukaemia, 577 CNS tumours, 1980 breast cancer
Controls	National Cancer Registry: 3321 other cancers
Allowance for confounding	Indirect
Main results	

	Relative risks		
	Leukaemia	*CNS tumours*	*Breast cancer*
< 0.10 μT	1.0	1.0	1.0
0.1–0.2 μT	1.3	0.9	1.1
≥0.2 μT	1.4	1.1	1.1

Comments	Leukaemia results clearer using distance from lines. Selection bias possible. Only contemporary residential exposure available

* AML = acute myeloblastic leukaemia.

TABLE 5.1
B: Adult studies (continued)

Study	**Wrensch *et al* (1999)**
Country	USA
Type	Case-control
Exposure Main method(s)	(a) wire codes for residences over previous 7 years (b) EMDEX spot measurements
Cases	492 adult glioma via Northern California Cancer Center ascertainment program 1991–94
Controls	462 by random-digit dialling. Matching for age, gender and ethnicity
Allowance for confounding	Partial
Main results	Odds ratio 0.9 for longest residence comparing high vs low wire code groups. No significant trend with front door spot measurements
Comments	Potential exposure misclassification. 63% participation by controls. No support for or against association

STUDIES OF LEUKAEMIA AND OTHER MALIGNANCIES IN CHILDREN

Nordic region

Swedish study

3 Feychting and Ahlbom (1993) identified and listed all properties from the Central Board for Real Estate Data located totally or partially within a corridor of 325 m on either side of power lines. The population registry was used to identify individuals who had lived on the listed properties. Individuals were followed up from 1960 or from birth or movement on to a corridor property till 1985, whether or not they were still living within the corridor. Magnetic field exposure was assessed first by spot measurements. These were performed in homes where the cases and controls lived at the time of diagnosis of the case. A three-dimensional magnetic density flux meter able to detect flux densities of 50–60 Hz was designed specifically for the study. High power measurements were made in the most central room, with all appliances running when the investigators entered the house left on. Then the main current was turned off and low power measurements taken in three rooms located perpendicularly to the line. These measurements were almost certainly less accurate for those living in apartments than in houses. Measurements were performed in 62% of the homes. Each home was characterised by the mean value of the low power measurements across all rooms. Secondly, calculated fields were established using a computer program that calculated the maximum value of the magnetic field. The method took account of other nearby lines but not buried cables. The station responsible for the operation of the line provided the full details needed. To allow for the possibility that the load on the line was not the same at the time the station gave its information as at the 'aetiologically relevant period', the annual average of the load on each line was obtained for every year during 1958–85 (and some even earlier information for cases and controls where it was deemed necessary), giving historical fields. Contemporary fields were also derived. In defining exposure, most emphasis was placed on the calculated historical fields. The cutoff points

used were 0.10, 0.20 and 0.30 μT, although it is not clear whether these were predetermined or decided upon after inspection of the data. Higher cutoffs were not considered useful because of the small numbers in such categories. Most emphasis was placed on the three-level scale ≤0.09, 0.10–0.19 and ≥0.20 μT. Cutoffs for the spot measurements were the same as for the calculated fields. Cutoffs for distances were <50, 51–100 and ≥101 m.

4 Cancer cases were identified through record linkage to the files of the registry operated by the National Board of Health and Welfare. Four controls were selected at random for each case from those included in the study population during the year of diagnosis of the case, of the same gender, born in the same year and living near the same power line in the same parish during the year of diagnosis. The data were stratified according to age, gender, year of diagnosis, residence in the county of Stockholm or not and single-family house or apartment. Matching to several censuses enabled a socioeconomic index to be included in the analyses and air pollution from traffic was also estimated.

5 In all, 127 282 children were included in the study. A total of 142 cancers were identified, compared with 138 expected. The relative risk for leukaemia increased with exposure, being estimated at 2.7 (95% CI 1.0, 6.3) for 0.2 μT or more using calculated fields closest to diagnosis. The test for trend was $p = 0.02$ or 0.005 if the cutoff point of 0.30 μT or more was used. There was no relation of exposure with all cancers combined or for central nervous system tumours or lymphoma. The results were similar for boys and girls, in different age groups, for residence or not in Stockholm county and whether living in the corridor at diagnosis or having lived in it for at least half the lifetime. However, the relation of exposure with leukaemia was confined to one-family homes. Analysis by proximity to power line gives a relative risk of 2.9 for those living within 50 m compared to those living more than 100 m away. Using spot measurements, there was no excess risk for total cancer or leukaemia but for tumours of the central nervous system (CNS) there was a relative risk of 2.5 for intermediate exposure and 1.5 for high exposure (neither statistically significant). There was no relation between exposure and brain tumours. The main results are shown in Table 5.2 (and are given in further detail in Tables 5.5 and 5.6, along with the results of other studies that have made direct or calculated field measurements of exposure).

TABLE 5.2 Results of the Nordic studies

Country	Number of cases/ controls	High exposure, definition (μT)	Relative risk * (95% CI)		
			Leukaemia	CNS tumours	Lymphoma
Sweden	38/554	≥0.20	2.7 (1.0, 6.3)	0.7 (0.1, 2.7)	1.3 (0.2, 5.1)
Denmark	833/1666	≥0.25	1.5 (0.3, 6.7)	1.0 (0.2, 5.0)	5.0 (0.3, 82.0)
Finland	-	≥0.20	1.6 (0.3, 4.5)	1.4 (0.3, 0.41)	0.0 (0.0, 4.2)
Norway	148/529	≥0.14	0.3 (0.0, 2.1)	0.7 (0.2, 2.1)	2.5 (0.4, 15.5)

* High exposure compared to 'unexposed', ie Sweden <0.1 μT; Denmark outside area or <0.1 μT; Finland incidence in whole country; Norway <0.05 μT.

Danish study

6 Olsen *et al* (1993) studied 1707 children under 15 years newly diagnosed as having leukaemia, a central nervous system tumour or malignant lymphoma between 1968 and 1986.

7 Trained local representatives of the electrical utilities checked addresses against maps of existing or former 50–400 kV connections (overhead or underground). The criteria used to define the area of potential exposure ensured that all dwellings with an exposure to fields of at least 0.1 µT would be included, amounting to 57 dwellings occupied by 55 children. The areas classified as 'view distant' covered vicinities close to overhead lines but not exposed to any measurable extent, amounting to 66 dwellings occupied by 65 children. For dwellings within the potential exposure area, historical magnetic field strengths were determined using a magnetic field programme based on the distance between dwelling and installation, category of line, type of pylon, ordering of phases, current flow and date of construction. Children were considered exposed to the average magnetic field strength calculated at the dwelling for as long as the family was there. The lower cutoff point of the average magnetic field exposure was set at 0.1 µT since lower values did not clearly outweigh the combined exposures to 50 Hz fields from other sources. An intermediate cutoff point was 0.25 µT. The cumulative dose of magnetic fields ever received by a child was the product of the number of months exposed and the average field at the residence (µT months).

8 Cases were identified from the Danish cancer registry. The three tumours (leukaemia, central nervous system (CNS) tumours and malignant lymphoma) make up 65% of childhood neoplasms in Denmark. Controls were drawn from the central population register.

9 Using the 0.1 µT cutoff to categorise children as ever or never exposed, there were no significant associations for leukaemia or CNS tumours but an increased risk, ie an odds ratio of 5.0 for malignant lymphomas which was, however, barely significant and based on only 3 cases and 3 controls. Using the cutoff of 0.25 µT, the odds ratio for leukaemia was 1.5 (95% CI 0.3, 6.7) and the risks for CNS tumours and lymphoma were unaltered. Children under one year at the onset of exposure to 0.25 µT or more had an odds ratio of cancer of 3.4 (95% CI 0.9, 13) compared with those first exposed at a later age for whom the odds ratio was 0.4 (95% CI 0.0, 3.0). Higher cumulative doses were 'generally' found among cases than among controls. The dose category above 9.7 µT months (median exposure) was associated with an increased but not statistically significant risk, the odds ratio being 1.8 (95% CI 0.6, 4.5). There was no association between the distance of residence and cancer risk. Adjustment for population density, socioeconomic class and family mobility did not change any results. The main results are shown in Table 5.2.

10 The paper also shows a 30-fold increase in electricity consumption since 1945, contrasting with a much smaller increase in all childhood cancers and no consistent increase in childhood leukaemia.

Finnish study

11 Verkasalo *et al* (1993) identified children aged between 0 and 19 years living at any time in 1979–89 within 500 m of overhead lines and followed for their cancer incidence in a cohort rather than case–control study. Data for about 90% of the total length of

power lines in Finland were available and were linked to the register of buildings of the central population register. Buildings within 500 m of power lines were identified. Magnetic fields at the central point of these buildings were calculated separately for each of the years 1970–89, taking account of current locations of phase conductors in power lines and the shortest distance to the centre of the building. Further data collection was restricted to buildings with annual magnetic fields of 0.01 μT or more for one or more years between 1970 and 1989, this low limit being likely to include most buildings in Finland with increased magnetic fields from power lines. Study subjects were classified into categories according to

(a) magnetic field in microtesla,
(b) cumulative exposure in microtesla years.

The cutoff points used were selected *a priori* on the basis of the distribution of the number of exposed children.

12 Children in the relevant buildings were identified from the personal data file of the central population register. Cases of cancer in the cohort so defined were identified from the Finnish cancer registry. Calculation of person years began at the start of 1974 or on the day when the child first met the exposure criteria. Observed numbers of cancers and years at risk were categorised by age, gender, calendar period and exposure category. Expected numbers of cases were calculated in five year age groups by multiplying the stratum-specific number of person years by the corresponding cancer incidence in Finland. There were 68 300 boys and 66 500 girls in the cohort, contributing nearly one-million person years. Only 5.4% of the children had been exposed to fields of 0.20 μT or more. The mean length of follow up was 7.3 years. A total of 140 cases of cancer were observed, compared with 145 expected. There were no significantly increased risks for leukaemia, lymphomas or other cancers in any magnetic field or cumulative exposure categories, the standardised incidence ratio for leukaemia being 1.6 (95% CI 0.3, 4.5) for exposure at 0.20 μT or more. The standardised incidence ratio for CNS tumours for those exposed to 0.20 μT or more was 2.3 (95% CI 0.8, 5.4) and was also 2.3 for those with a cumulative exposure of 0.40 μT years or more (95% CI 0.94, 4.8). All the CNS tumours occurred in boys. One of the four boys who developed a CNS tumour had neurofibromatosis type 2 and had three CNS tumours. In this analysis, he has been treated as one case, the resulting incidence ratio being 1.4 (95% CI 0.3, 4.1). No CNS tumours were found in girls in the same exposure categories. The main results are shown in Table 5.2.

Norwegian study

13 Tynes and Haldorsen (1997) studied 532 cancer cases and 2112 controls in Norwegian children aged up to 14 years. Calculated magnetic fields were the main basis for classifying exposure, the historical load being estimated as the yearly average. All high voltage power lines carrying 11 kV or more were considered in calculating exposure, which also took account of the height of towers, distance between phases and ordering of phases. Underground cables were not considered. The distance of addresses from power lines were recorded from maps. Analyses were also based on calculated fields closest in time to diagnosis and during the first year of life. To validate estimates of exposure, a special study was undertaken of 65 school children living close to a 300 kV power line in which 24 hour measurements were obtained with a personal dosemeter. The line owner supplied information on current load for the period during which the dosemeter was used. A questionnaire provided information on where the child had spent the 24 hours. Children living closer than 50 m to the line were exposed to between 0.4 and 1.6 μT for 75% of the day, while those living more than 150 m away from the line were exposed to less than 0.1 μT for 83% of the time. Using average background exposure levels in a typical Norwegian home, background exposure was considered as less than 0.05 μT. Those exposed above this level were divided into two groups by use of the median value for the controls, ie 0.14 μT. Exposure to electric fields was also assessed. (No association of electric fields with cancers was found, although this result may have been 'unreliable' because of shielding from these fields.)

14 The study population was children aged up to 14 years who had lived in a census ward crossed by a high voltage power line during at least one of years 1960, 1970, 1980, 1985, 1987 or 1989. Wards were selected by comparing maps of high voltage power lines and maps of census wards. The cohort was linked to notifications in the Cancer Registry of Norway by each individual's unique 11 digit identification number. All cases of cancer among children aged up to 14 years diagnosed from 1965 to 1969 were identified (new cases of cancer in Norway having been recorded by the Registry since 1953). Five controls were selected at random from the cohort to be alive at the time of diagnosis of the cases and matched for gender, year of birth and municipality. A residential history based on detailed addresses was collected for cases and controls from local population registries as far back as 1952.

15 For leukaemia, the odds ratio for those exposed to 0.14 μT or more was 0.3 (95% CI 0.0, 2.1). Only ten cases (four brain tumours, two lymphomas, two osteosarcomas, one Wilm's tumour and one testicular tumour) were exposed to levels above 0.2 μT. There was a technically significant excess risk for cancers at all sites for the intermediate exposure category, ie 0.05–0.14 μT. There were increased odds ratios in the two highest exposure categories for cancers at 'other' sites. There were no significant associations of exposure with brain tumours or lymphoma. Using distance from power lines, the odds ratios for 'other' sites and for lymphoma were 2.8 (95% CI 1.5, 5.0) and 1.9 (95% CI 0.6, 6.4), respectively. According to magnetic field closest in time to diagnosis, the odds ratio for 'other' sites was 2.9 (95% CI 1.1, 5.9) in those exposed to more than 0.14 μT. There was no excess of leukaemia at exposure of 0.2 μT or more and, for comparison with the Swedish study, no excess of leukaemia in one-family houses. Based on calculated fields during first year of life, odds ratios for cancer at all sites and at 'other' sites were increased, although not significantly. Several other subgroup analyses were carried out, from which a possible relation between magnetic field closest in time to diagnosis and osteosarcoma emerged, the odds ratio being 10.9 (95% CI 1.1, 107.8) and based on three cases in the higher exposure category. Adjustment for socioeconomic status and number of residences did not affect the results. The main results are shown in Table 5.2.

UK studies

United Kingdom Childhood Cancer Study

16 The main hypothesis of the electromagnetic field component of the UK Childhood Cancer Study (UKCCS, 1999) was that a mean exposure of 0.2 μT or above in the year prior to diagnosis would increase the risk of childhood leukaemia, specifically acute lymphoblastic leukaemia (ALL), and cancers of the central nervous system, compared with a mean exposure of less than 0.1 µT in the year preceding diagnosis. A further hypothesis was that the risk of the same diagnoses would increase smoothly with increasing mean exposure in the year preceding diagnosis.

17 From 1991 in Scotland and 1992 in England and Wales, all children aged 0–14 years with a pathologically confirmed diagnosis of one of the index conditions were considered eligible for the full study. Accrual of the 3838 cases mainly ended in December 1994 but continued until the end of 1996 for leukaemia. Of those with leukaemia, 84% had ALL. For each case, two controls (a total of 7629 controls) matched for gender and date of birth were selected from lists of the same health authorities. All controls were assigned a 'pseudo-diagnosis' date on which they were the same age as the corresponding case at diagnosis. The study included personal interviews with the parents of cases and controls covering full residential and occupational histories, parental health, social habits and family illnesses and, from mothers, sections on the pregnancy and the index child's health, schooling and social history.

18 For the electromagnetic field component of the study one control was matched with each case. Eligibility for the electromagnetic field component stipulated residency for each member of the case–control pair in the same home throughout the year prior to diagnosis or pseudo-diagnosis and continuing through the period of electromagnetic field measurements. A total of 2283 case–controls pairs participated in a study using a two-phase electromagnetic field measurement protocol. The protocol was designed specifically to estimate the average electromagnetic field exposure in the year before diagnosis or pseudo-diagnosis.

19 In the first phase a residential exposure assessment was conducted for all participants. The assessment consisted of a 90 minute family room measurement separating two sets of bedroom spot measurements. Magnetic flux density, over the broadband frequency range of 40–800 Hz, was recorded using an EMDEX II magnetic field meter and readings were not displayed to technicians. A school exposure assessment was also carried out where relevant. In the second phase, a further residential assessment was made for those children (and matching case or control) indicated during phase 1 to be in the top 10% of residential exposures, taken as those at 0.1 µT or above. The phase 2 assessment included a 48 hour measurement at the child's bedside. Children identified in phase 1 to have exposure from night storage heaters or underfloor heating were also selected for phase 2 (and matching case or control). In addition, children were included who lived within certain threshold distances of high voltage overhead power lines or underground cables, or where local distribution circuits were reported not to be operating typically during phase 1. Altogether, about 20% of case–control pairs had phase 2 measurements.

20 Measurements were residence- rather than individual-based, and were made after the period of interest. However, analysis of repeat measurements, and a separate validation study based on personal exposure monitoring of healthy children, suggested that the UKCCS measurement protocol provided adequate surrogate data for exposure during the year of interest. In addition, historical exposure for the year of interest was reconstructed, where high voltage electricity distribution and transmission circuits had the potential to influence exposure classification, and where operational details were available.

21 Statistical analysis was based on four exposure categories, < 0.1, 0.1–< 0.2, 0.2–< 0.4 and ≥0.4 µT, based on previously reported categories, the primary analysis combining the top two categories. Analysis preserved case and control matching through the use of conditional logistic regression. Findings were adjusted for any differences between cases and controls, particularly deprivation index (derived from unemployment, overcrowding and car ownership data for census enumeration districts).

22 Of all eligible cases, 87% were included with at least one of the parents interviewed, the corresponding figure among controls being 64% with evidence in the controls of under-representation of those living in the most deprived census areas. Exposure could not be measured for all the interviewed cases and controls but measurements were obtained for 2226 eligible case–control pairs (58% of all interviewed case–control sets and 50% of all eligible cases). From census-based small-area deprivation indices, the most deprived category was strikingly under-represented compared with the full set of the first-choice controls. However, the distribution of deprivation indices differed little between the cases and controls with electromagnetic field measurements. The main results are shown in Table 5.3. Adjustment for deprivation had only a small effect on odds ratios. Risk did not differ by age. Tests for trend of odds ratios were performed for each diagnostic category, p values ranging from 0.33 to 0.80. For magnetic fields, there was no evidence supporting either of the hypotheses of the electromagnetic field study for any category of malignant disease. Compared with those who had exposures of less than 0.1 µT, there was no excess among children with exposures of more than 0.2 µT nor was there any evidence of increasing risk with increasing exposure. Possible effects of refusal bias were investigated by issuing questionnaires to a random sample of 1000 of the 1582 first-choice controls who had refused to take part in the full study. It is unlikely that participation bias not taken account of by deprivation index might have concealed any substantial positive association.

23 The study also examined distance to power lines, 11 to 400 kV, and electricity sub-stations. Distances were obtained from the maps available from electricity companies and the grid references of the relevant residences of cases and controls. These addresses were available for nearly 90% of eligible cases and first-choice controls, irrespective of whether the parents were interviewed. No association was seen between distance to a power line, of any voltage, and risk for any of the diagnostic categories shown in Table 5.3. The magnetic fields associated with power lines were also calculated for all relevant residences on the basis of line load data for the period of interest. Using the same exposure categories as for measured exposure, no excess risk was seen with increasing exposure and tests for trend were not significant (UKCCS, 2000).

Coghill study

24 Coghill *et al* (1996) reported a small case–control study on ALL, assessing low frequency (50 Hz) electric as well as magnetic field exposure. The 56 cases were obtained by media advertising, personal introduction and through the Wessex Health Authority. Parents for the cases were asked to identify a control child of the same sex and age living nearby. There were no differences between cases and controls using magnetic field measure-ments. Electric field readings (V m^{-1}) were significantly higher in cases than in controls. However, the authors themselves recognise 'a number of poor design elements' as well as other reasons, including the possibility of instrumental inaccuracy, for questioning whether the results indicate an association and the study is not summarised in Table 5.1.

TABLE 5.3 Odds ratios and ratios adjusted for deprivation index for acute lymphoblastic leukaemia, all leukaemias, cancers of the central nervous system, and other malignant disease by exposure in the UKCCS (1999)

	Exposure range (μT)				
	< 0.1	0.1– < 0.2	≥0.2	0.2– < 0.4	≥0.4
Acute lymphoblastic leukaemia					
Cases	845	44	17	14	3
Controls	825	63	18	16	2
Odds ratio (95% CI)	1.00	0.69 (0.46, 1.02)	0.90 (0.47, 1.76)	0.84 (0.41, 1.73)	1.40 (0.23, 8.40)
Adjusted odds ratio (95% CI)	1.00	0.69 (0.47, 1.03)	0.92 (0.47, 1.79)	0.84 (0.41, 1.74)	1.51 (0.25, 9.18)
Total leukaemia					
Cases	995	57	21	16	5
Controls	977	73	23	20	3
Odds ratio (95% CI)	1.00	0.77 (0.54, 1.10)	0.89 (0.49, 1.61)	0.78 (0.41, 1.51)	1.62 (0.39, 6.77)
Adjusted odds ratio (95% CI)	1.00	0.78 (0.55, 1.12)	0.90 (0.49, 1.63)	0.78 (0.40, 1.52)	1.68 (0.40, 7.10)
Cancers of central nervous system					
Cases	359	25	3	3	0
Controls	371	10	6	4	2
Odds ratio (95% CI)	1.00	2.50 (1.20, 5.21)*	0.50 (0.13, 2.00)	0.75 (0.17, 3.35)	-
Adjusted odds ratio (95% CI)	1.00	2.44 (1.17, 5.11)	0.46 (0.11, 1.86)	0.70 (0.16, 3.17)	-
Other malignant disease					
Cases	713	38	15	12	3
Controls	706	45	15	11	4
Odds ratio (95% CI)	1.00	0.84 (0.53, 1.31)	0.98 (0.47, 2.06)	1.07 (0.45, 2.53)	0.75 (0.17, 3.35)
Adjusted odds ratio (95% CI)	1.00	0.81 (0.52, 1.28)	0.97 (0.46, 2.05)	1.08 (0.45, 2.56)	0.71 (0.16, 3.19)
Total malignant disease					
Cases	2067	120	39	31	8
Controls	2054	128	44	35	9
Odds ratio (95% CI)	1.00	0.93 (0.72, 1.20)	0.88 (0.57, 1.36)	0.88 (0.54, 1.43)	0.89 (0.34, 2.29)
Adjusted odds ratio (95% CI)	1.00	0.93 (0.72, 1.19)	0.87 (0.56, 1.35)	0.87 (0.53, 1.42)	0.89 (0.34, 2.32)

* The 95% confidence interval (of 1.20, 2.00) in the UKCCS publication (1999) is incorrect.

American study

25 Linet *et al* (1997) recruited participants from a group of 1914 children with ALL under 15 years of age and from 1987 controls taking part in a nationwide telephone-interview study conducted by the Children's Cancer Group and, like UKCCS, studying several possible causes of cancer in children. Cases were diagnosed between 1989 and 1994. Eligible controls were selected by random-digit telephone dialling and were matched to cases according to the initial digits of the telephone number, age and ethnic group. Eligibility for the assessment of magnetic field exposure was restricted to those living in one of nine states on the reference date defined as the date of diagnosis of ALL for each patient. Overall, 78% of eligible patients participated compared with 63% of the controls, resulting in final numbers of 638 and 620, respectively. Exposure was assessed, first, by magnetic field measurements. Technicians, unaware of whether the child was a case or a control, used an EMDEX-C meter measuring electromagnetic fields in the range 40 to 300 Hz. The standardised procedure included a 24 hour measurement in the child's bedroom, 30 second measurements in the centre of the child's bedroom, the family room, the kitchen and the room in which the mother slept during the index pregnancy, and a 30 second outdoor measurement made within 0.9 m of the front door. The study included a high proportion exposed to 0.4 μT or more by comparison with others. Secondly, technicians (also unaware of whether the child was a case or a control) drew diagrams and recorded the distance from home of any overhead power lines within 46 m of the residence including transmission lines and subsidiary lines. A computer algorithm assigned a wire code to each residence according to the five-category Wertheimer-Leeper classification. Measured field levels rose with increasing wire-code category. Further information about measurements of exposure is given in the section on Overviews (see paragraph 66).

26 The primary measure of exposure for each child was an average of the summary level for all the eligible measured homes weighted according to duration of residence, categorised according to *a priori* criteria. The risk of childhood ALL was not linked with this measure. In an unmatched analysis, the odds ratio for ALL was 1.24 (95% CI 0.86, 1.79) at exposures of 0.200 μT or greater as compared with less than 0.065 μT, although it was 1.53 (95% CI 0.91, 2.56) but still not significantly raised in a matched analysis. There was a tendency for risk to be higher at exposures of 0.300 μT or more but numbers of children with these levels were small and tests for trend with level of exposure were not significant. The risk of ALL was not increased among children whose main residences were in the highest wire-code category (odds ratio as compared with the lowest category 0.88; 95% CI 0.48, 1.63). The risk was not significantly associated with either residential magnetic field levels or the wire codes of the homes in which the mothers lived when pregnant with the subjects. Findings on electrical appliances are described later (Hatch *et al*, 1998).

27 More recently, the American group has analysed different components of wire coding (Kleinerman *et al*, 2000), creating an exposure index of distance of homes within 40 m of transmission and three-phase primary distribution lines and strength of multiple power lines. Neither distance nor exposure index was related to the risk of ALL.

Canadian studies

Trans-Canadian study

28 McBride *et al* (1999) recruited children aged 0–14 years with leukaemia between 1990 and 1994 resident in census tracts within 100 km of the principal cities of a number of Canadian provinces. Ascertainment of cases during the first year was retrospective but subsequently cases were approached as they were diagnosed. Most cases had ALL (88%), the remainder having acute myeloblastic leukaemia (10%) or other subtypes (2%). For each case with agreement to participate, a control child matched for age, area and gender was selected at random from provincially based government health insurance rolls. Initial contact for controls was by letter with telephone follow-up. After five unsuccessful attempts, another potential control was selected. The diagnosis date of the case was taken as the reference date of the matched control for the electromagnetic field exposure assessment and interview. Of the 675 potential controls identified, 149 could not be contacted leaving 526 for participation in the study.

29 Electromagnetic field exposure assessment consisted of a personal 48 hour magnetic and electric field exposure measurement using a Positron electromagnetic field meter worn in a small backpack and a 24 hour electromagnetic field measurement of the child's bedroom. In addition, local power line characteristics were recorded and magnetic field measurements of the residence perimeter and front door were recorded for residence of the mother from one year before the birth of the child until birth and for residences of the child from birth to the diagnosis or reference date. Of the 445 eligible cases, 399 (90%) took part along with 399 controls (76% of the 526 eligible controls contacted). Interviews were completed for all participants. Bedroom measurements were available for 75% of the cases and 86% of the controls. Valid personal electromagnetic field measurements were obtained for 73% of the cases and 85% of the controls. Among participants with personal measurements, about three-quarters were at least 75% complete and half were at least 90% complete. For contemporaneous measures, risks as odds ratios according to percentile were not significantly elevated – for example, 1.05 (95% CI 0.61, 1.80) and 0.68 (95% CI 0.37, 1.25) for the 75th–90th percentile and more than the 90th percentile, respectively. Using the cutoff point of $\geq$0.2 µT, the adjusted odds ratio was 1.12 (95% CI 0.69, 1.80). Predicted exposure two years before the diagnosis or reference date also showed no significantly increased odds ratios nor did predicted lifetime exposure. No tests for trend were significant. Similarly, there were no significant associations of contemporaneous or previous wire configuration codes with risk.

Ontario study

30 Green *et al* (1999a,b) carried out a case–control study based on 201 cases of childhood leukaemia aged 0 to 14 years from an oncology registry and 406 controls contacted by telephone. Residential point-in-time measurements of magnetic fields were made 'where possible'. Personal monitoring was carried out in 88 cases and 133 controls. The analyses are based on many fewer cases and controls than initially identified and most exposure categories used were well within what would generally be considered as background levels. The authors concluded that there was no support for an association between leukaemia and proximity to power lines with high current configurations. The results using personal monitoring were considered to support an

association but because of the further selection that evidently occurred in obtaining the data on personal monitoring, the validity of this conclusion is open to serious doubt. For a variety of reasons, these studies are largely if not completely uninterpretable and are not summarised in Table 5.1.

Other countries

New Zealand study

31 Dockerty *et al* (1998) carried out a case-control study in New Zealand. Children who developed cancer aged from 0 to 14 years were ascertained between 1990 and 1993 from national databases including the New Zealand Cancer Registry. A total of 303 took part (participation 88%). The 303 age- and gender-matched controls were selected randomly from birth records (participation 69%). Mothers were interviewed about appliance exposures (all cases and controls), and 24 hour residential measurements of electromagnetic fields were made. For the various appliance exposures, there were some odds ratios above 1.0 and others below 1.0. Leukaemia risk was increased for the highest category of the mean measured bedroom magnetic field (≥0.2 μT *cf* < 0.1 μT), with an adjusted odds ratio of 15.5 (95% CI 1.1, 224). A gradient in odds ratio with exposure was not shown, and there was no association with exposure categorised into thirds based on the exposure of controls. The adjusted odds ratio for leukaemia in relation to the measured daytime room magnetic field level (≥0.2 μT *cf* < 0.1 μT) was 5.2 (95% CI 0.9, 30.8). However, a subsequent correction necessitated by one child with leukaemia initially classified into the ≥0.2 μT exposure group (instead of 0.1–< 0.2 μT) has been published (Dockerty *et al.* 1999a) so that 'leukaemia risk was non-significantly increased for the highest category of the mean measured bedroom magnetic field ... with an adjusted relative risk of 8.8' should be substituted in the abstract and corresponding text of Dockerty *et al* (1998). A further re-analysis to facilitate comparison with other studies (Dockerty *et al.* 1999b) showed no association with leukaemia of time-weighted average exposure in the bedroom and living room combined.

German study

32 Michaelis *et al* (1997) carried out a case–control study of electromagnetic fields and childhood leukaemia during 1992–95 based on 129 and 328 controls.

33 For each child, exposure to magnetic fields was measured over a period of 24 hours using the EMDEX II field meter and by indoor spot measurements. The 24 hour measurements were carried out in the child's bedroom and in the room where the child had been longest before diagnosis. Measurements were made in more than one house if the child's family had moved during the relevant period. A predetermined cutoff point of 0.2 μT was used, based on previous analyses from other studies suggesting increased risk above this level. All newly diagnosed cases of leukaemia occurring from July 1988 to June 1993 in children aged less than 15 years at diagnosis were ascertained from the German Childhood Cancer Registry. Ascertainment through the Registry was considered to be 95% complete and 219 cases were identified. Controls were drawn from local government office files. For each case, one control was selected from the same registration office and a second from a registration office chosen at random in Lower Saxony. Questionnaires were mailed to cases and controls requesting information on residential history. The response to requests for 24 hour magnetic field measurements was 59% for the cases and 54% for the controls so that, with some other reasons for

exclusion, full data were available for only 129 cases and 328 controls. Adjustments were made for age, gender, socioeconomic status and degree of urbanisation.

34 According to the cutoff point of 0.2 μT, the odds ratio for the main exposure measure, ie over 24 hours in the child's bedroom, was 3.2 but not statistically significant (95% CI 0.7, 14.9) and the data for this assessment are, of course, not independent of the other analyses based on 24 hour measurements. Further analyses based on five exposure categories suggested no trend between exposure and risk. Analyses using spot measurements suggested no risk.

35 Michaelis *et al* (1998) later expanded their study to include electromagnetic field measurements in Berlin, applying the same methods of exposure assessment and pooling the data of the two studies. There were 24 hour measurements for a total of 176 cases and 414 controls. Comparing those exposed to median 24 hour measurements of 0.2 μT or more with those exposed to lower levels, regression analyses gave an odds ratio of 2.3 (95% CI 0.8, 6.7).

Greek study

36 Petridou *et al* (1997) recruited 117 incident cases of leukaemia between 1993 and 1994 in children aged up to 14 years through a nationwide network of paediatric oncologists and compared them with 202 controls matched for age, gender and place of residence. The Public Power Corporation of Greece provided information on exposure based on distance from the centre of each residence of the two closest transmission or distribution lines. The voltage of each of these was divided by the distance, the square and the cube of the distance, giving V m^{-1}, V m^{-2}, V m^{-3}, and a modified Wertheimer-Leeper wire code was also used. In multiple regression analyses, there were no significant trends by quintile of exposure with risk for any of the four measures.

Italian study

37 Bianchi *et al* (2000) identified 101 cases of leukaemia in children aged between 0 and 14 years, diagnosed between 1976 and 1992 in the Province of Varese, Lombardy, Italy. For each case, four controls, 410 in total allowing for exclusion of a few cases, were 'selected randomly' in 1996 from Italian Health Service Archives and matched for gender, date of birth (within five days) and residence in the study area. Data on exposure were provided by the Italian National Electricity Board through information on the distribution of high-voltage power lines. Children living within 150 m of a power line were defined as exposed and the average magnetic field strengths in microtesla in the homes of each of the 20 exposed subjects were calculated. The relative risk of leukaemia in those exposed to between 0.001 and 0.1 μT was 3.2 (95% CI 1.11, 9.73) (six cases, eight controls) and 4.51 (95% CI 0.88, 23.17) for those exposed to more than 0.1 μT (three cases, three controls). The authors consider that possible biases arising from the different recruitment periods did not 'seem to have influenced the risk estimates'. However, the small numbers of cases exposed (nine) should be noted and the levels of exposure of all but perhaps three of the twenty exposed subjects were noticeably lower than the levels considered to be of possible significance in most other studies. The study is not included in Table 5.1 because of uncertainty about the results arising from the long interval between recruitment of the cases and controls and from the small numbers and the definitions of those exposed.

OTHER STUDIES OF CHILDREN SPECIFICALLY LIMITED TO CNS TUMOURS

Los Angeles study

38 Preston-Martin *et al* (1996a) reported a case–control study on 298 subjects under the age of 20 years with a primary brain tumour diagnosed between 1984 and 1991 and 298 controls identified by random digit dialling. Magnetic field exposure was assessed, first, by Wertheimer-Leeper codes. Addresses of cases and controls were sent to the relevant utilities (before approaches for interviews had been made, so that data on those refusing or unavailable for interview were also available) and these utilities provided circuit maps. Computer map files and data on wiring features were used to assign Wertheimer-Leeper codes. Secondly, exterior measurements included fields over the water meter and water pipes, static magnetic field, front door fields and STAR magnetic field profiles. Thirdly, for interior measurements, EMDEX meters were initially left in 163 homes for 24 hours. Then 48 further homes were included to ensure adequate representation across several strata (eg case or control, wire code) for all 211 homes. EMDEX measurements were taken every 10 seconds in the child's bedroom and in a second room, where the child spent most time. A tripod-mounted magnetometer in the child's bedroom was also used.

39 Patients were residents of Los Angeles County with benign or malignant primary brain tumours of any type diagnosed during the 7.5 year period between 1984 and 1991. Controls were selected from a 'pool of potential random digit dial controls' to be of the same sex and aged within a year of the corresponding case. However, interviewing of cases and controls did not take place concurrently in the earlier stages of the study, some cases being seen some time before their controls. Response rates were 70% of those eligible for both cases and controls. Besides gender and age at diagnosis (or reference), details on ethnicity and socioeconomic status were obtained.

40 For the mean, median and 90th percentiles, odds ratios tended to be raised among children in homes at or above the 90th percentile for each 'metric'. There was a corresponding tendency for higher odds ratios in those for whom mean fields were more than 0.3 μT. None of the trends was significant. There appeared to be an increase in risk associated with underground wiring but this was attributed to an artefact in the selection of controls, who (see above) were not recruited concurrently with the cases during the earlier stages of the study.

Seattle study

41 Gurney *et al* (1996) assessed the relation between exposure to residential magnetic fields and childhood brain tumours in a population-based case–control study of 133 subjects younger than 20 years of age when diagnosed between 1984 and 1990 and 270 controls. Cases aged less than 20 years with a primary brain tumour were identified through the Cancer Surveillance System, a population-based registry in Washington State. The response to participate was 74.3%. Controls were recruited by a two-step random digit dialling procedure. Computer-generated random telephone numbers were tried up to nine times to identify suitable residences (eg other than businesses). For children initially identified in this way, a stratified selection procedure was then used and 270 controls, 78.7% of those eligible, were included. Fewer case mothers had received college degrees than control mothers. Case mothers were also more likely to be non-white, although non-whites accounted for only about 7% of all those studied.

42 Personal interviews gave a 'partial residence history' after which a questionnaire was sent to participating mothers for a history including every home in which the child lived during the three-year period up to the date leading to their inclusion in the study and during the mother's pregnancy. The history included the type of heating sources and electrical appliances used. It was not feasible for power lines to be characterised for all the homes in which a child lived so the hypothesis was that the three-year period represented a late or promotional effect of magnetic field exposure. Histories were provided by 73.7% of mothers of cases and by 77.0% of mothers of controls. Data on ethnicity, mother's education, passive smoking and other characteristics were also collected. External power distribution systems for homes at the date of reference were characterised by drawing scaled maps of all power components within 130 feet (40 m). Wertheimer-Leeper codes were assigned by computer algorithm and were available for 89.3% of homes of the children involved. The homes of about three-quarters of those who did not participate were also mapped. The risk of brain tumour did not rise with increasing exposure using the five-level Wertheimer-Leeper code. Analyses by 'dichotomised' exposure (high versus low), by gender or age at diagnosis, by histological type and confined to the small numbers who lived in only one home did not reveal any noticeably (let alone significantly) increased risks. Wire codes for study participants and eligible non-participants were similar and inclusion of data for non-participants made virtually no difference to the relative risks.

STUDIES OF CANCER IN ADULTS

Netherlands study

43 This was a retrospective cohort study subject to several limitations (Schreiber *et al.* 1993). Analysis was based on the 3549 individuals, apparently of all ages and therefore containing many if not a majority of older subjects, resident in the urban quarter of Limmel in Maastricht between 1956 and 1981 for at least five years and followed until the end of 1987. Their mortality was compared with expected rates in the national population of the Netherlands. Electricity transmission in the Limmel area consists of two overhead power lines and one transformer substation. The cohort was divided into two exposure groups according to distance between the residence and the power lines of the transformer substation. The higher exposure group were those any part of whose houses were within 100 m of the substation or on either side of the power lines. The low exposure group were those living in the other houses in the defined area. Results were presented as standardised mortality ratios (SMR). The tabulated results are not divided according to findings on men and women separately, while the text refers to an increased SMR for laryngeal cancer in men and for brain cancer and Hodgkin's disease in women, the last based on two cases. The authors acknowledged the study's limitations. Their results do not indicate an effect of electromagnetic field exposure on cancer mortality but, in view of the limitations, it also cannot be taken to have provided evidence against the hypothesis. The study is not included in Table 5.1.

Swedish study

44 In defining its population and assessing magnetic field exposure, this nested case-control study (Feychting and Ahlbom, 1994) used the same general methods as the study of children already described. Some 40 000 people were identified in the power line corridors 300 m on either side of any of the 220 and 400 kV power lines in Sweden between 1960 and 1985. As the cases were diagnosed over a 26-year period, the average load on each line was obtained for individual years from 1958 to 1985. Cumulative exposure was defined as the sum of the exposure for each of the 15 years preceding diagnosis, expressed in microtesla years. When results were assessed as the calculated field for the year closest to diagnosis, the relative risk for acute myeloblastic leukaemia was 1.7 (95% CI 0.8, 3.5) and also for chronic myeloblastic leukaemia (95% CI 0.7, 3.8) for exposure of 0.3 μT or more. For lymphoblastic leukaemia, all leukaemias and for brain tumours, relative risks were all near or below 1.0. There were elevated risks in the highest cumulative exposure category for both acute myeloblastic leukaemia, ie 2.3 (95% CI 1.0, 4.6) and chronic myeloblastic leukaemia, ie 2.1 (95% CI 0.9, 4.7). For acute myeloblastic leukaemia, there may also have been an increased risk in the intermediate exposure category, ie 1.5 (95% CI 0.5, 3.7). Adjustment for age, gender and socio-economic status had no material effect. On redefining the highest exposure category as 3.0 μT years or more, there was still an elevated risk for acute and chronic myeloblastic leukaemia, ie 1.9 and 2.7, respectively. Using spot measurements, relative risks were all close to 1.0 with the exception of a risk of 1.5 (95% CI 0.7, 3.2) for chronic myeloblastic leukaemia and for which the relative risk in terms of proximity to power lines (50 m or less) was also raised, at 2.4 (95% CI 1.0, 5.1).

Finnish study

45 Verkasalo *et al* (1996) investigated the risk of cancer in a nationwide cohort study of Finnish adults aged 20 years or more and living close to high voltage power lines. Cumulative exposure was assessed as the sum of the products of residential magnetic field and length of exposure in years. In general, the methods used were similar to those in the Finnish study of cancer in children, already described (see paragraphs 11 and 12). Exposure was based on estimates of the average annual magnetic field separately for each of the years 1970 to 1989 at all buildings closer than 500 m from 110, 200 and 400 kV overhead power lines in Finland. About 90% of the total length of the Finnish power lines in question was included by the identification method used, which was based on power company records. The current spatial locations of phase conductors in power lines and the shortest distance to the central points of buildings were taken into account. Cumulative exposure was categorised using the predetermined cutoff points of 0.2, 0.4, 1.0 and 2.0 μT years. Those with exposure of less than 0.2 μT years served as an internal reference group in some analyses. The study cohort consisted of all people aged 20 years or more who had lived in a building with a calculated magnetic field of 0.01 μT or more for any period during 1970 to 1989. A total of 383 700 people contributed 2.5 million person years and 11% of the person years were associated with a cumulative exposure of 0.40 μT years or more. As a result of the various record linkages possible, data on dates of birth and death, gender, residential history including moves, and social class as well as on cancer incidence were available. Expected numbers of cancer cases were calculated by multiplying person years in the group

under consideration by the corresponding incidence of cancer in Finland, giving standardised incidence ratios. Incidence rate ratios per 1 μT increase in exposure were also calculated. The cohort apparently experienced 2% less cancer than the general Finnish population. All standardised ratios for specific primary sites were between 0.90 and 1.10 apart from 0.85 for laryngeal cancer (95% CI 0.66, 1.08). The only significant ratio was for lung cancer which, at 0.93 (95% CI 0.87, 0.98), was 7% less in the cohort than in the general population. The risk of colon cancer increased with exposure in women (1.16) but not in men (0.95). There were no associations between exposure and cancers of the stomach, rectum, testis, prostate, kidney, bladder, thyroid or non-melanoma skin cancer. Melanoma was the only cancer for which risk was somewhat increased in the three highest categories of exposure in both sexes but none of the ratios was significant.

Taiwan study

46 Li *et al* (1997) conducted a case-control study of the risk of leukaemia, brain tumours and female breast cancer in relation to 60 Hz magnetic fields in Taiwan. Maps of 31 of the 45 districts concerned were available, although not on the same scales. Power company maps indicated 121 high voltage transmission lines of five types in the study area between 1987 and 1992. Data were available on the distance between wires, height above the ground, average and maximum loads, current phase and resistivity of the ground. Distance of each residence from the nearest line was determined. EMDEX measurements were carried out in 407 residences in 1994 and 1995. Agreement between these measured and calculated fields was expressed as kappa and ranged from 0.64 to 0.82 for residences with high exposures by both methods.

47 The National Cancer Registry of Taiwan initially identified 1135 cases of leukaemia, 705 of brain tumours and 2407 of female breast cancer. Controls were patients with other cancers. Unavailability of maps for determining exposure and other reasons reduced the initial numbers of cases to 870, 577 and 1980 for leukaemia, brain tumours and breast cancer, respectively. An index of urbanisation considered to incorporate age, population density, mobility and socioeconomic conditions was used to reduce possible confounding. No direct information was available as it was a condition of access to the registry that study subjects were not interviewed. According to distance from lines there was a significantly increased odds ratio of 2.0 (95% CI 1.4, 2.9) for leukaemia among those less than 50 m from high voltage transmission lines compared with the reference group of those 100 m or more away. Results for brain tumours and breast cancer were inconsistent and not significant. These results were generally confirmed in the analysis according to magnetic field exposure. There was a trend between exposure and risk only for ALL.

American study

48 Wrensch *et al* (1999) studied 492 adults with glioma newly diagnosed between 1991 and 1994 in the San Francisco Bay area and 462 controls identified through random digit dialling and matched for age, gender and ethnic group. Residential exposure assessment consisted of spot measures with EMDEX meters and wire codes for all other California residences in which participants had lived over the seven years before entry to the study. For longest held residences, the relative risk for high compared with low exposure was 0.9 (95% CI 0.7, 1.3). There was no consistent or significant

association of front door spot measurements with risk. The authors acknowledged that potential exposure misclassification and uncertainty about periods of exposure (together with the results themselves) did not lead to the conclusion of an association between residential electromagnetic field exposure and adult glioma, although the possibility could not be excluded.

APPLIANCE USE

49 Several studies have examined cancer risk in relation to the use of electrical appliances. The 1992 report of the Advisory Group reviewed the studies conducted up to that time (NRPB, 1992). Most of these studies looked at the use of electric over-blankets which, in contrast to under-blankets, generally are kept on during the night. Case–control studies of adult cancers did not show any association between electric blanket use and the risk of leukaemia, testicular cancer or breast cancer. A study of childhood cancers provided a slight suggestion of a raised risk of brain tumours associated with exposure *in utero* from electric blankets (Savitz *et al*, 1990). However, the Advisory Group concluded that both this and a separate study of childhood leukaemia (London *et al*, 1991) were incapable of interpretation, owing to the possibility of bias associated with selection of controls, low interview rates and parental recall of the child's appliance use (NRPB, 1992).

50 Since the 1992 report, several more epidemiological studies of electrical appliance use and cancer have been published, of which some are based on studies reviewed earlier in this chapter. For example, Hatch *et al* (1998) have reported on the association between the use of electrical appliances during pregnancy and childhood ALL based on the study in the USA by Linet *et al* (1997). There was an apparently increased risk in children whose mothers reported use of an electric blanket or mattress pad during pregnancy, the odds ratio for ever having used compared with never having used bedroom appliances being 1.59 (95% CI 1.11, 2.29). In contrast, in the New Zealand study of Dockerty *et al* (1998), the odds ratio of childhood leukaemia for mother's use of electric blankets during pregnancy or the three months before pregnancy was 0.8 (95% CI 0.4, 1.6). The leukaemia odds ratio for use of sewing machines during pregnancy was 0.76 (95% CI 0.59, 0.98) in the study of Hatch *et al* (1998) and 1.2 (95% CI 0.6, 2.4) in the study of Dockerty *et al* (1998). Both studies found some evidence of an increased leukaemia risk associated with children's use of an electric blanket or mattress: Hatch *et al* (1998) reported an odds ratio of 2.75 (95% CI 1.52, 4.98), while Dockerty *et al* (1998) cited an odds ratio of 2.2 (95% CI 0.7, 6.4). Hatch *et al* (1998) found that hair dryers, video machines in arcades and video games connected to a television were also associated with increased risks of childhood ALL, although the patterns of risk according to frequency and duration of use were inconsistent. Risks rose with increasing numbers of hours per day that children spent watching television, but were similar according to different distances from the television. Hatch *et al* (1998) concluded that these and other inconsistencies 'must be considered before ascribing … associations to exposures from magnetic fields'.

51 The risk of childhood brain or central nervous system tumours has been studied in relation to electrical appliance use by Dockerty *et al* (1998) and by Preston-Martin *et al* (1996b). The latter publication used data from the American studies in Los Angeles (Preston-Martin *et al,* 1996a) and Seattle (Gurney *et al,* 1996) that were reviewed earlier in this chapter. Dockerty *et al* (1998) reported some suggestion of a raised risk associated with the mother's use during pregnancy of electric blankets (odds ratio 1.6; 95% CI 0.6, 4.3) and with the child's electric blanket use (odds ratio 1.6; 95% CI 0.4, 7.1). However, Preston-Martin *et al* (1996b) found no association with either the mother's use in pregnancy (odds ratio 0.9; 95% CI 0.6, 1.2) or the child's use of electric blankets (odds ratio 1.0, 95% CI 0.6, 1.7). Preston-Martin *et al* (1996b) obtained similar results for heated water bed use, while the findings of Dockerty *et al* (1998) for this and other appliances were imprecise.

52 Lovely *et al* (1994) examined acute non-lymphoblastic leukaemia in adults and personal appliance use, based on data from a case–control study by Severson *et al* (1988) that was reviewed previously by the Advisory Group (NRPB, 1992). The study involved 114 cases from a population-based cancer registry in western Washington state (USA) and 133 controls obtained from the same area by random digit dialling. Prior interest centred on three motor-driven personal appliances (electric razors, hair dryers and massage units), because the peak magnetic fields from their use were higher than from most other domestic appliances. Ever-use of one or more of these appliances was not associated with an increased risk, compared with never-use (odds ratio 0.71; 95% CI 0.41, 1.24), although massage units were more likely to have been used by cases than controls (odds ratio 3.00; 95% CI 1.43, 6.32). Amongst these appliances, there was a significant increasing trend in risk with daily time of use only for electric razors ($p < 0.05$). However, Sussman and Kheifets (1996) pointed out that this association arose only for cases for whom a proxy (rather than the case) reported appliance use. Furthermore, as noted by Lovely *et al* (1994), the number of cases in this study was limited.

53 As regards adult brain tumours, Mutnick and Muscat (1996) have reported preliminary findings from a hospital-based study in the north-eastern USA, based on 328 cases and 284 controls. No statistically significant associations were found with the use of electric blankets (odds ratio 1.1), hair dryers, electric razors, personal computers or other appliances. In a population-based case–control study in Australia, based on 110 cases of glioma, 60 cases of meningioma and 417 controls, Ryan *et al* (1992) cited an odds ratio of 1.48 (95% CI 0.83, 2.63) for glioma and electric blanket use.

54 Gammon *et al* (1998) have conducted a large population-based case-control study of electric blanket use and breast cancer at ages less than 55 years. The 2199 cases were identified from cancer registries in several parts of the USA, while 2009 controls were obtained by random digit dialling in the same areas. There was little or no risk associated with ever having used electric blankets, mattress pads or heated water beds, either at ages less than 45 years (odds ratio 1.01; 95% CI 0.86, 1.18) or at ages 45–54 years (odds ratio 1.12; 95% CI 0.87, 1.43), nor was there an increasing risk with increasing duration of use. A smaller population-based case–control study in the USA of premenopausal breast cancer (Vena *et al,* 1994) reported an odds ratio of 1.43 (95% CI 0.94, 2.17) for electric blanket use throughout the night. However, both in this study and in a combined analysis (Vena *et al,* 1995) of these data and those from an earlier study of postmenopausal breast cancer (Vena *et al,* 1991; reviewed by the Advisory Group in 1992), the risk did not appear to increase with increasing duration of use. Furthermore, in a study of 608 breast cancer cases and 609 hospital and population controls in the USA, Zheng *et al* (2000) obtained an odds ratio of 0.9 (95% CI 0.7, 1.2) for electric blanket use throughout the night. In addition to the above case–control studies, breast cancer and electric blanket use have been examined as part of a large cohort study in America, namely the Nurses' Health Study. Laden *et al* (2000) reported relative risks for ever having used electric blankets of 1.08 (95% CI 0.95, 1.24) and 1.05 (95% CI 0.95, 1.16), based on prospective and retrospective follow-up, respectively; the corresponding numbers of breast cancer cases were 954 and 2426, respectively. After adjusting for known risk factors for the disease, there was little indication of a trend in risk with the number of years of electric blanket use. Finally, in a population-based study of 175 prostate cancer cases and 258 controls in the USA, Zhu *et al* (1999) found an odds ratio of 1.4 (95% CI 0.9, 2.2) for ever having used an electric blanket or heated water bed, but the risk did not appear to increase with increasing duration of use.

MISCELLANEOUS STUDIES

55 Some other studies should be mentioned that do not clearly fall under the headings already considered either because of their particularly small size or for other reasons. Thus, Li *et al* (1998) used what they considered to be a more precise method for assessing exposure in a re-analysis of data on which they had reported previously (Lin *et al*, 1994). They identified 28 cases of leukaemia among 120 696 children aged 14 years or less and reported to the National Cancer Registry in Taiwan between 1987 and 1992. Compared with children living in households more than 100 m away from high voltage transmission lines, those living in households less than 100 m from these lines experienced an increased risk of leukaemia, ie 7 observed cases compared with 2.88 expected giving a standardised incidence ratio of 2.43 (95% CI 0.98, 5.01). This risk was considered particularly noticeable among children aged between 5 and 9 years. However, it would be unwise to attach much importance to results based on such small numbers of cases.

56 Feychting *et al* (1997) conducted a case–control study in Sweden to take account of both residential and occupational exposure in those aged 16 years or more who had lived for at least a year on a property located within 300 m from any of the 220 or 400 kV power lines during 1960 and 1985. There were 325 cases of leukaemia and 223 of central nervous system tumours. Two controls for each case were randomly selected from the study base. For occupational exposure of 0.2 μT or more, the relative risk for leukaemia was 1.7 (95% CI 1.1, 2.7), the increased risk being confined to acute myeloblastic and chronic lymphoblastic leukaemia. For residential exposure of 0.2 μT or more, the relative risk for leukaemia was 1.3 (95% CI 0.8, 2.2) with higher estimates for acute and chronic myeloblastic leukaemia. The relative risk for leukaemia among those highly exposed both at home and at work was 3.7 (95% CI 1.5, 9.4). Relative risks for central nervous system tumours were close to unity.

57 Feychting *et al* (1998) also studied breast cancer, having identified 699 cases in women and 9 in men. For calculated magnetic field levels of 0.2 μT or more, the estimated relative risk was 1.0 (95% CI 0.7, 1.5) for women and 2.1 (95% CI 0.3, 14.1) for men. The relative risk in women less than 50 years of age was 1.8. For women with oestrogen receptor positive cancer the relative risk was 1.6 using an exposure cutoff point of ≥0.1 μT. Neither of these risks was significant. Among oestrogen receptor positive women younger than 50 years at diagnosis, however, the relative risk was 7.4 (95% CI 1.0, 178.1).

58 It has been suggested (Infante-Rivard, 1995) that exposure to electromagnetic fields during pregnancy when mothers work at home using sewing machines, for example, may be associated with a considerable increase in the risk of ALL in childhood, an odds ratio of 5.78 (95% CI 1.27, 26.25) compared with population controls being cited.

COMMENTARY

59 It might be thought that the experience of people heavily exposed at work (Chapter 6) would provide the best test of the general risk of cancer due to exposure to electromagnetic fields, but the difficulty of obtaining accurate, quantitative measures of exposure has discouraged such studies. The study of childhood cancer, particularly of childhood leukaemia, may offer a better test – partly because leukaemia in children is so rare that even small induced risks may stand out, partly because the disease most commonly occurs between 2 and 6 years of age, so that any relevant exposure must have occurred within a short period of the onset of the disease, and partly because so much evidence is now available.

60 A pervasive problem, particularly when the apparent increased risk is relatively small, is the comparability of the cases and controls. In the German (Michaelis *et al.* 1997) and Trans-Canadian (McBride *et al.* 1999) studies the controls were random samples matched for gender and date of birth, selected from relevant populations registers. In the American study (Linet *et al.* 1997) they were less satisfactory, having been derived from a previous nationwide telephone enquiry and biases might have been introduced by the many factors that can influence an individual's willingness to respond to telephone enquiries. In addition, participation was incomplete in all three studies. In both the American (Linet *et al.* 1997) and the Trans-Canadian (McBride *et al.* 1999) studies measurements were made for a higher proportion of affected children than for controls (83% and 63%, and 90% and 76%, respectively). The difference was small in the German (Michaelis *et al.* 1997) study, but it had low measurement rates in both groups (59% and 54%). Judged by British experience, the lower participation rate among the controls is likely to have introduced a material socioeconomic bias which would be reflected in the characteristics of the houses in which the subjects lived (UKCCS, 1999). This was recognised in both of the North American studies and adjustments were made for age, gender, mother's educational level, and family income and for maternal age, maternal education, household income, ethnicity, and number of residences since birth, respectively (Linet *et al.* 1997). These adjustments strengthen confidence in the findings, but when the risk ratios are so small, an element of doubt about the adequacy of the adjustment inevitably remains. While there was a difference in the proportions of all eligible children in the cases and controls in the UKCCS, this was not so evident in those with direct measurements and allowance for any remaining difference did not materially affect the results. The degree of exposure in the UKCCS was low compared with the studies from North America because of differences in the operating characteristics of electricity supply and wiring practices. In the USA and five Canadian provinces, 11.4% and 15.4% of controls, respectively, had exposures higher than 0.2 μT, while in the UKCCS, the proportion was approximately 2%, similar to proportions in Germany and New Zealand. Thus, although the UKCCS included more individuals with electromagnetic field measurements than other studies, it did not have more in high exposure categories than the North American studies. The UKCCS had little power to detect increases in risk at exposures of 0.4 μT or more. It focused on the year before diagnosis and the results are of direct relevance for effects on the promotion or progression (rather than initiation) of malignant disease. While there is a question (see paragraphs 67–70) on the effect of exposures higher than 0.4 μT, for the vast majority of children in the UK there is now considerable evidence that the electromagnetic field levels to which they are exposed do not increase the risk of leukaemia or other malignant disease.

61 Results based on single measures of exposure are likely to have underestimated any risks because of the regression dilution effect. This problem will not have arisen (at any rate so acutely) in studies where exposure has been calculated from multiple measurements over time but its possible effect in others needs to be borne in mind in attempting to reach general conclusions.

OVERVIEWS

62 Reviews of the evidence by government or independent scientific bodies have led to different conclusions at different times. In 1990, a report of a committee of the US Environmental Protection Agency (EPA, 1996) concluded that the field produced by high power electricity cables should be classed as a probable carcinogen – as defined by the International Agency for Research on Cancer (IARC, 1998) – but the report was never approved and was referred back. The US National Research Council (NRC, 1996) concluded that measured fields provided no evidence of a risk, but that living in homes with a high wire configuration was associated with about a 50% excess risk of childhood leukaemia, although this was likely to have been due to confounding with some unknown social factor. Two years later a review by a Working Group organised by the US National Institute of Environmental Health Sciences (NIEHS, 1998) concluded by majority vote of 19 to 9, with 1 abstention, that the fields should themselves be classed as possibly carcinogenic to humans. As already indicated, the Advisory Group thought that the early positive studies were inadequately controlled and that the results to 1992 justified only the formulation of a hypothesis (NRPB, 1992). Two years later the results of studies from Denmark and Sweden, which used unbiased objective data, led the Group to conclude that 'The possibility of a risk exists' (NRPB, 1994).

63 It is now possible to consider the newer studies described together with earlier studies sharing common features. Most have shown an increased risk with higher exposure, which has, however, seldom been statistically significant. Wartenberg (1999) attempted a meta-analysis of 12 studies and obtained an odds ratio for high exposure of 1.3, which was just statistically significant (95% CI 1.01, 69) using a fixed effects model. Angelillo and Villari (1999) carried out their overview on 14 case–control studies and one cohort study. For studies based on wiring configuration codes, the pooled relative risk for childhood leukaemia (all types) was 1.46 (95% CI 1.05, 2.04; p = 0.024) and for exposure according to 24 hour measurements it was 1.59 (95% CI 1.14, 2.22; p = 0.006) using cutoff points that were common to most of the studies. However, lower risks were indicated by the higher quality studies. They concluded that there is now enough evidence against dismissing concerns about electromagnetic fields and childhood leukaemia. By contrast, with a collaborative re-analysis (below), meta-analysis is of doubtful relevance when the quality of the studies has varied greatly as it has in the electromagnetic field studies.

64 In the opinion of the Advisory Group in 1994 (NRPB, 1994) the most reliable data since its 1992 report were initially those obtained in the four Nordic countries and now, so far as results based on direct measures are concerned, such as those from the UKCCS (1999) and the USA (Linet *et al*, 1997) and Trans-Canadian (McBride *et al*, 1999) studies. The Nordic studies (of which there were three when the Advisory Group reported in 1994, since when the Norwegian study has been published) used national registers to identify cases and where they had lived, including all the cases in a defined period within broad corridors containing high power cables. Matched control subjects were selected at random from the same area or drawn from the entire population of the country. Exposure was determined from knowledge of the distance of the house from the nearest cable and the electricity load on the cable while the child lived in its vicinity. However, the studies have the limitation that they do not take account of the effect produced by differential wiring within houses or variation in the use of electricity. This is unlikely to be important when the field produced by proximity to cables is high, but it will be in other situations and there can be little doubt that, in principle, direct measurement of the field should be preferable to the use of surrogate measures, however determined, even though the child does not spend his or her whole time in the house but is also exposed elsewhere.

65 Ten studies have provided some direct measure of exposure, but they cannot usefully be combined as they are of very different quality. Results from the Ontario study (Green *et al*, 1999a,b) are not included because of the drawbacks already mentioned (see paragraph 30). The principal findings of each of the other nine studies are given in Table 5.4. When many different exposure methods were given, data for measurements of average exposure recorded over the longest period have been used. Five studies gave increased risks with high exposure, but none was statistically significant. The first four used only spot measurements and these included the two with risks estimated to be less than 1.0. One of these (Tomenius, 1986) measured the fields only outside the houses. The other (Savitz *et al*, 1988) measured fields inside the house, but they may have been measured many years after the child was discovered to have the disease.

66 In four later studies the measurements were much more complex. In the German study (Michaelis *et al*, 1997), measurements were made over a 24 hour period in the child's bedroom and in the living room in the dwelling in which the child lived longest before the disease was diagnosed. In the American study (Linet *et al*, 1997), a protocol was first developed for assessing the time-weighted average exposure of young children which required a 24 hour measurement in the child's bedroom and a 30 second measurement in the family room, the kitchen, and outdoors within 3 feet of the front door (Kaune *et al*, 1994). For children under five years, attempts were made to measure the fields in all homes in which the child had lived for at least six months and at

TABLE 5.4 Childhood leukaemia and residential magnetic fields: studies with measured exposures

Authors	Total number of cases/controls	High exposure Definition (μT)	Cases/ controls	Relative risk* (95% CI)
Tomenius (1986)	243/212	≥0.3	4/10	0.3 (0.1, 1.2)
Savitz *et al* (1988)	31/191	≥0.2	5/16	1.9 (0.7, 5.6)
London *et al* (1991)	164/144	≥0.27	20/11	1.5 (0.7, 3.3)
Feychting and Ahlbom (1993)	24/344	≥0.2	4/70	0.6 (0.2, 1.8)
Michaelis *et al* (1997)	129/328	≥0.2	4/6	1.5 (0.4, 5.5)
Linet *et al* (1997)				
unmatched analysis	624/615	≥0.2	83/70	1.2 (0.9, 1.8)
matched analysis	463/463	≥0.2	58/44	1.5 (0.9, 2.6)
McBride *et al* (1999)	297/329	≥0.2	49/42	1.4 (0.8, 2.3)
Dockerty *et al* (1999b)	40/40	≥0.2	5/2	2.5 (0.5, 12.8)
UKCCS (1999)	995/977	≥0.2	21/23	0.9 (0.5, 1.7)†

* High exposure compared to all others, except Linet *et al* (1997) ≥0.2 μT *v* < 0.065 μT.

† The Advisory Group gratefully acknowledges the help of Professor Nick Day and Dr Jane Skinner for providing these details.

least 70% of the child's life had to be covered. For older children, one or two homes were measured provided that the child had lived in them for at least 70% of the five years preceding the date of diagnosis. Time-weighted average summary values were calculated for each eligible home and weighted according to the number of years the child had lived in them. In the Trans-Canadian study (McBride *et al*, 1999), electromagnetic field exposure was measured over 48 hours directly for individuals who carried a meter in a small backpack, if the child was well and living in the same residence as at the diagnosis/reference date, a 24 hour measurement was made in the child's bedroom, and a perimeter field measurement of the house was derived from measurements in several specified points round the house. The relationship between the peripheral measurement, roof wiring, and the 48 hour personal measurement was used to predict exposure at all previous residences, and lifetime average exposures were calculated for each residence. The last two studies permitted an examination of the relationship with dose. That derived from the American data provides some indication of a trend (albeit not statistically significant, p = 0.15), while that from the Trans-Canadian data does not. The measurement methods in the UKCCS (1999) have been described earlier (see paragraphs 18–20). UKCCS includes by far the largest number of cases and controls (2226 pairs) with direct measure of exposure, although these were only carried out for 50% of eligible cases and 40% of first-choice controls and were residence-based rather than based on individual monitoring.

67 Recently, Ahlbom *et al* (2000) have published a collaborative re-analysis of magnetic fields and childhood leukaemia based on nine studies with comparable cases and controls and using direct measurements of exposure, either with long magnetic field measurements (24 to 48 hours) (Canada, Germany, New Zealand, the UK and the USA) as the primary measure or, for studies without these long measurements, calculated fields (Denmark, Finland, Norway and Sweden). Original data were used in the analysis. Wire codes were also analysed. There were 3247 cases, of whom 83% had ALL, and

10 400 controls. The exposure categories were pre-specified. There were 44 cases and 62 controls in the highest exposure category (≥0.4 μT). The main results, shown in Tables 5.5 and 5.6, indicate variation in point estimates between studies no larger than to be expected from random variability. In the measurement studies, the summary relative risk for all types of leukaemia in the highest exposure category was 1.83 (95% CI 1.08, 3.11; p = 0.01). Estimates for the two lower exposure categories are close to unity. In the calculated fields studies, the summary relative risk for the highest exposure group was 2.13 (95% CI 0.93, 4.88; p = 0.04). Table 5.5 also shows the results combining both types of study. Continuous analysis gave a relative risk estimate of 1.15 (95% CI 1.04, 1.27) per 0.2 μT (test for trend p = 0.004). As already indicated, these results are largely due to the contribution of ALL, the results for which are shown in Table 5.6. To test for the robustness of the findings, other cutoff points for the highest exposure were used giving relative risks of 1.59, 2.59 and 1.72 depending on the points used. Adjustment for potential confounding variables made little difference to the results. The relative risk for the highest wire-code category (Trans-Canadian and American studies) was 1.24 (95% CI 0.82, 1.87) so there was little if any evidence for the existence of the so-called 'wire-code paradox', ie the higher risks in earlier studies using indirect markers of exposure than in the more recent studies using direct measurements. The considerable potential for bias in the early studies using wire codes has already been mentioned (see paragraph 1).

68 In summary, this detailed analysis of studies with direct measurements has not found a significant association of electromagnetic field exposure with childhood cancer across all levels of exposure, but does suggest a relative risk estimate of about 2.0 in the 0.8% of children exposed to 0.4 μT or more and also the possibility of a trend in risk with increasing exposure. The increased risk in the higher exposure category is unlikely to be due to random variability but incomplete allowance for confounding variables and selection bias may have accounted for some of it.

69 Greenland *et al* (2000) have also recently carried out an overview of all childhood leukaemias based on twelve studies that supplied original individual data. Of the twelve studies, eight were included by Ahlbom *et al* (2000), but three were earlier studies and one was the study by Coghill *et al* (1996). As far as possible, calculated historical fields or averages of multiple measurements were preferred to spot measurements when there was a choice and the 'target measure' was each child's time-weighted average exposure up to three months before diagnosis. The main result was similar to that of Ahlbom *et al* (2000) in that there was some evidence of increased risk at higher levels of exposure, the cutoff point being 0.3 μT rather than 0.4 μT, with a summary odds ratio for those exposed to more than 0.3 μT being 1.7 (95% CI 1.2, 2.3) compared with exposure to 0–0.1 μT. There was also evidence of increasing risk with increasing exposure at levels above about 0.15 μT. Allowance for confounding variables made little difference to the estimates of risk. For the population of the USA, the population attributable fraction of childhood leukaemia associated with residential exposure may have been 3% (95% CI −2%, 8%). A further similarity with Ahlbom *et al* (2000) was less consistency between wire-code categories and the risk of leukaemia than for magnetic fields. The authors concluded that 'both our categorical and trend analyses indicate that there is some association comparing fields above 0.3 μT to lower exposures' but also that 'the inconclusiveness of our results seems inescapable'.

TABLE 5.5 Total leukaemia: adjusted relative risks (95% confidence interval) by exposure level, reference level: < 0.1 μT (Ahlbom et al, 2000)

	Exposure range (μT)		
Study	0.1– < 0.2	0.2– < 0.4	≥0.4
Measurement studies			
Canada	1.29 (0.84, 1.99)	1.39 (0.78, 2.48)	1.55 (0.65, 3.68)
Germany	1.24 (0.58, 2.64)	1.67 (0.48, 5.83)	2.00 (0.26, 15.17)
New Zealand	0.67 (0.20, 2.20)	4 cases / 0 controls	0 cases / 0 controls
UK	0.84 (0.57, 1.24)	0.98 (0.50, 1.93)	1.00 (0.30, 3.37)
USA	1.11 (0.81, 1.53)	1.01 (0.65, 1.57)	3.44 (1.24, 9.54)
Calculated fields studies			
Denmark	2.68 (0.24, 30.45)	0 cases / 8 controls	2 cases / 0 controls
Finland	0 cases / 19 controls	4.11 (0.48, 35.1)	6.21 (0.68, 56.9)
Norway	1.75 (0.65, 4.72)	1.06 (0.21, 5.22)	0 cases / 10 controls
Sweden	1.75 (0.48, 6.37)	0.57 (0.07, 4.65)	3.74 (1.23, 11.37)
Summary			
Measurement studies	1.05 (0.86, 1.28)	1.14 (0.85, 1.53)	1.83 (1.08, 3.11)
Calculated fields studies	1.58 (0.77, 3.25)	0.79 (0.27, 2.28)	2.13 (0.93, 4.88)
All studies	1.08 (0.89, 1.31)	1.10 (0.83, 1.47)	2.00 (1.28, 3.14)

TABLE 5.6 Acute lymphoblastic leukaemia: adjusted relative risks (95% confidence interval) by exposure level, reference level: < 0.1 μT (Ahlbom et al, 2000)

	Exposure range (μT)		
Study	0.1– < 0.2	0.2– < 0.4	≥0.4
Measurement studies			
Canada	1.33 (0.85, 2.07)	1.44 (0.79, 2.60)	1.65 (0.68, 4.01)
Germany	1.29 (0.58, 2.89)	2.19 (0.62, 7.71)	2.21 (0.29, 16.7)
New Zealand	0.71 (0.21, 2.44)	3 cases / 0 controls	0 cases / 0 controls
UK	0.89 (0.59, 1.34)	0. 87 (0.42, 1.84)	0.88 (0.23, 3.39)
USA	1.11 (0.81, 1.53)	1.01 (0.65, 1.57)	3.44 (1.24, 9.54)
Calculated fields studies			
Denmark	0 cases / 2 controls	0 cases / 8 controls	2 cases / 0 controls
Finland	0 cases / 19 controls	4.31 (0.50, 37.2)	6.79 (0.74, 62.6)
Norway	2.25 (0.78, 6.55)	1.49 (0.30, 7.45)	0 cases / 10 controls
Sweden	0.88 (0.11, 7.19)	0 cases / 20 controls	3.46 (0.84, 14.3)
Summary			
Measurement studies	1.07 (0.87, 1.31)	1.14 (0.84, 1.54)	1.91 (1.11, 3.27)
Calculated fields studies	1.42 (0.58, 3.45)	0.84 (0.25, 2.81)	2.23 (0.88, 5.65)
All studies	1.08 (0.88, 1.32)	1.12 (0.83, 1.50)	2.08 (1.30, 3.34)

70 The nature of any association with increasing exposure is unclear, notably whether there is any such increase, and if there is whether there may be a linear or quadratic relationship. This lack of clarity is augmented by the effect of regression dilution resulting from the absence of accurate exposure measurement at the relevant time before diagnosis. About 430 cases of leukaemia (all types) are registered each year in England and Wales in those aged up to 14 years (ONS, 1999). UKCCS indicates that 0.4%

of children are exposed to 0.4 μT or more and, assuming a doubling of risk at this level, some two cases would occur anyway and a further two cases annually might be attributable to electromagnetic field exposure. If regression dilution were concealing a relative risk of 1.5 for those exposed to between 0.2 and 0.4 μT, then the annual number of attributable cases might be six or seven. These estimates assume that any excess risk is confined to the very small numbers of children exposed to high electromagnetic field levels. If there is a linear exposure–response effect, the attributable numbers could be somewhat larger.

CASE-SPECULAR METHOD

71 An interesting and potentially useful new method (case-specular) has recently been described that may increase confidence in the results of the observational studies on which assessing the evidence about residential exposure to electromagnetic fields and cancer has to depend. Even though many of these studies have made detailed allowance for a number of variables that may introduce confounding (ie variables associated with both exposure and the risk of developing malignant disease, of which socioeconomic group is an example that is often relevant) the possibility still remains that either unidentified confounding variables have not been taken into account or that those that are known or suspected have only been allowed for incompletely. The case-specular method for studying wire codes, magnetic fields and disease was developed to try to overcome this difficulty (Zaffanella *et al*, 1998), and, more recently, the results of using the method have been compared with results from two of the early studies of wire codes and childhood cancers (Ebi *et al*, 1999). In summary, the case-specular method compares wire codes of case residences with codes of hypothetical (specular) residences constructed by switching the location of the case residence across the centre of the street. So the specular residence is a mirror-image of the actual residence reflected across the street ('specular' relating to a mirror or reflection). The specular residence is likely to match the neighbourhood characteristics of the case residence very closely but may have a different wire code. Thus, when, for example, there is an overhead power line on one side of the street, the distance from the line to the case and specular residences will differ by about the width of the street. If wire code is an independent risk factor for cancer, there should be not only a preponderance of case residences in streets where power lines are located but also a preponderance on the side of the street where the power lines are located. If cancer incidence is related to wire code because code is a surrogate for exposures that vary with distance from the line, eg magnetic fields, then there should be a greater number of higher code case residences than higher code specular residences. If, however, cancer incidence is independent of wire code there should be no difference between the two groups. Thus, if the association between wire codes and cancer is the result of the wire code acting as a proxy for neighbourhood characteristics or other local factors such as air pollution, then the wire-code distributions of case and specular residences should not differ.

72 Comparing the method with the results of two early studies of wire codes supported the original findings of these studies (Ebi *et al*, 1999), ie odds ratios of about two for very high current configuration residences and childhood cancers, thus not

supporting suggestions that the associations were due to confounding. However, the possibility remains that selection bias in choosing controls could have influenced the original associations, so that this explanation for their results still cannot be ruled out. Furthermore, Ebi *et al* (1999) found indications of wire-code differences not only between cases and their speculars, but also between controls and their speculars. In one study, the controls tended to have higher wide-code residences than the speculars, whilst the reverse was true for the other study. These data were cited by Greenland (1999) – who co-authored the papers by Zaffanella *et al* (1998) and Ebi *et al* (1999) – in a more general methodological examination of epidemiological studies based on the exposure distribution for a case series. Greenland (1999) noted that discrepancies might be expected to occur between estimates from these studies and the ordinary odds ratio estimates from case–control studies. For example, discrepancies may arise because of possible differences in the degree of exposure misclassification between cases and speculars, because of potential over-matching of cases and speculars, or because of bias if there were a tendency for sources of exposure to be located either near or away from actual (rather than hypothetical) residences. Greenland (1999) emphasised that special assumptions are required to transform the results from analyses of case-specular data into relative risk estimates, and that epidemiologists may require considerable experience with such study designs before their strengths and limitations are appreciated fully.

CONCLUSIONS

73 In most of the individual studies on leukaemia in children, odds ratios or relative risks comparing levels of electromagnetic fields generally more than 0.20 or 0.25 μT with all others or those exposed to low levels have been more than 1.0, while the UKCCS (1999) with data on much the largest number with direct measures of exposure indicated no increased risk, although very few children were exposed to high levels. However, the recent pooled analysis of Ahlbom *et al* (2000) of studies with direct or calculated field measurements indicates a relative risk of nearly 2.0 in those exposed to more than 0.4 μT compared to those exposed to less than 0.1 μT. This excess is unlikely to have been due to chance. However, in the high exposure group in the measured field studies, ie mainly from the American study (Linet *et al*, 1997), but not in the calculated field studies from the Nordic region, selection bias may have contributed to the excess. For both the measured and calculated field studies there is also the possibility that confounding may have contributed. These uncertainties make it difficult to know how much of the observed excess may have been due to a causal effect. As a result of the absence of accurate exposure measurements at the relevant time before diagnosis, any causal component will be underestimated at exposures less than as well as more than 0.4 μT. Data on brain tumours come from some of the studies also investigating leukaemia and from others concerned exclusively with these tumours. Here, there is no evidence of an association. There have been many fewer studies in adults. There is no reason to believe that exposure to electromagnetic fields is involved in the development of leukaemia or brain tumours in adults, although this possibility cannot be excluded.

REFERENCES

Ahlbom A, Day N, Feyehting M, *et al* (2000). A pooled analysis of magnetic fields and childhood leukaemia. *Br J Cancer*, **83**, 692–8.

Angelillo I F and Villari P (1999). Residential exposure to electromagnetic fields and childhood leukaemia: a meta-analysis. *Bulletin of the World Health Organization*, **77**(11), 906–14.

Bianchi N, Crosigni P, Rovelli A, *et al* (2000). Overhead electricity power lines and childhood leukaemia: a registry-based, case-control study. *Tumori*, **86**, 195–8.

Coghill R W, Steward J and Philips A (1996). Extra low frequency electric and magnetic fields in the bedplace of children diagnosed with leukaemia: a case-control study. *Eur J Cancer Prev*, **5**, 153–8.

Dockerty J D, Elwood J M, Skegg D C G, *et al* (1998). Electromagnetic field exposures and childhood cancers in New Zealand. *Cancer Causes Control*, **9**, 299–309.

Dockerty J D, Elwood J M, Skegg D C G, *et al* (1999a). Electromagnetic field exposures and childhood cancers in New Zealand (Correction). *Cancer Causes Control*, **10**, 641.

Dockerty J D, Elwood J M, Skegg D C G, *et al* (1999b). Electromagnetic field exposures and childhood leukaemia in New Zealand. *Lancet*, **354**, 1967–8.

Ebi K L, Zaffanella L E and Greenland S (1999). Application of the case-specular method to two studies of wire codes and childhood cancers. *Epidemiology*, **10**, 398–404.

EPA (1996). Proposed Guidelines for Carcinogen Risk Assessment: Notice. Federal Register 61(79), 17961–18001.

Feychting M and Ahlbom A (1993). Magnetic fields and cancer in children residing near Swedish high-voltage power lines. *Am J Epidemiol*, **138**, 467–81.

Feychting M and Ahlbom A (1994). Magnetic fields, leukemia and central nervous system tumours in Swedish adults residing near high-voltage power lines. *Epidemiology*, **5**, 501–9.

Feychting M, Forrsen U and Floderus B (1997). Occupational and residential magnetic fields exposure and leukaemia and central nervous system tumors. *Epidemiology*, **8**, 384–9.

Feychting M, Forrsen U, Rutqvist L E, *et al* (1998). Magnetic fields and breast cancer in Swedish adults residing near high-voltage power lines. *Epidemiology*, **9**, 392–7.

Gammon M D, Schoenberg J B, Britton J A, *et al* (1998). Electric blanket use and breast cancer risk among younger women. *Am J Epidemiol*, **148**, 556–63.

Green L M, Miller A B, Villeneuve P J, *et al* (1999a). A case-control study of childhood leukaemia in southern Ontario, Canada, and exposure to magnetic fields in residences. *Int J Cancer*, **82**, 161–70.

Green L M, Miller A B, Agnew D A, *et al* (1999b). Childhood leukemia and personal monitoring of residential exposures to electric and magnetic fields in Ontario, Canada. *Cancer Causes Control*, **10**, 233–43.

Greenland S (1999). A unified approach to the analysis of case-distribution (case-only) studies. *Statist Med*, **18**, 1–15.

Greenland S, Sheppard A R, Kaune W T, *et al* (2000). A pooled analysis of magnetic fields, wire codes, and childhood leukemia. *Epidemiology*, **11**, 624–34.

Gurney J G, Mueller B A, Davis S, *et al* (1996). Childhood brain tumor occurrence in relation to residential power line configurations, electric heating sources and electric appliance use. *Am J Epidemiol*, **143**, 120–28.

Hatch E E, Linet M S, Kleinerman R A, *et al* (1998). Association between childhood acute lymphoblastic leukemia and use of electrical appliances during pregnancy and childhood. *Epidemiology*, **9**, 234–45.

Infante-Rivard C (1995). Electromagnetic field exposure during pregnancy and childhood leukaemia. *Lancet*, **346**, 177–8.

IARC (1998). IARC Monographs on the Evaluation of Carcinogenic Risks in Humans: Preamble. Lyon, International Agency for Research on Cancer.

Kaune W T, Darby S D, Gardner S N, *et al* (1994). Development of a protocol for assessing time-weighted average exposures of young children to power-frequency magnetic fields. *Bioelectromagnetics*, **13**, 33–51.

Kleinerman R A, Kaune W T, Hatch E E, *et al* (2000). Are children living near high-voltage power lines at increased risk of acute lymphoblastic leukemia? *Am J Epidemiol*, **151**, 512–15.

Laden F, Neas L M, Tolbert P E, *et al* (2000). Electric blanket use and breast cancer in the Nurses' Health Study. *Am J Epidemiol*, **152**, 41–9.

Li C Y, Thériault G and Lin R S (1997). Residential exposure to 60-hertz magnetic fields and cancers in Taiwan. *Epidemiology*, **8**, 25–30.

Li C Y, Lee W C and Lin RS (1998). Risk of leukemia in children living near high-voltage transmission lines. *J Occup Environ Med*, **40**, 144–7.

Lin R S and Lee W C (1994). Risk of childhood leukemia in areas passed by high power lines. *Rev Environ Health*, **10**, 97–103.

Linet M S, Hatch E E, Kleinerman R A, *et al* (1997). Residential exposure to magnetic fields and acute lymphoblastic leukemia in children. *New Engl J Med*, **337**, 1–7.

London S J, Thomas D C, Bowman J D, *et al* (1991). Exposure to residential electric and magnetic fields and risk of childhood leukemia. *Am J Epidemiol*, **134**, 923–37. (Erratum: *Am J Epidemiol*, **137**, 381, 1993.)

Lovely R H, Bishborn R L, Slavich A L, *et al* (1994). Adult leukemia risk and personal appliance use: a preliminary study. *Am J Epidemiol*, **140**, 510–17.

McBride M L, Gallagher R P, Thériault G *et al* (1999). Power-frequency electric and magnetic fields and risk of childhood leukemia. *Am J Epidemiol*, **149**, 831–42.

Michaelis J, Schüz J, Meinert R, *et al* (1997). Childhood leukemia and electromagnetic fields; results of a population-based case–control study in Germany. *Cancer Causes Control*, **8**, 167–74.

Michaelis J, Schüz J, Meinert R, *et al* (1998). Combined risk estimates for two German population-based case-control studies on residential magnetic fields and childhood acute leukemia. *Epidemiology*, **9**, 92–4.

Mutnick A and Muscat J E (1996). Primary brain cancer in adults and the use of common household appliances: a case–control study. *Rev Environ Health*, **12**, 59–62.

NIEHS (1998). Health effects from exposure to power-line frequency electric and magnetic fields. Research Triangle Park, NC, National Institute of Environmental Health Sciences, NIH Publication No. 98-3981.

NRPB (1992). Electromagnetic fields and the risk of cancer. Report of an Advisory Group on Non-Ionising Radiation. *Doc NRPB*, **3**(1), 1–138.

NRPB (1994). Electromagnetic fields and the risk of cancer: Supplementary Report by the Advisory Group on Non-Ionising Radiation of 12 April 1994. *Doc NRPB*, **5**(2), 77–81.

NRC (1996). Possible effects of exposure to residential electric and magnetic fields. Washington DC, National Research Council, National Academy Press.

ONS (1999). Cancer statistics: registrations. Registrations of cancer diagnosed in 1993, England and Wales. Series MB1, No. 26. London, The Stationery Office.

Olsen J H, Neilson A and Schulgen G (1993). Residence near high voltage facilities and risk of cancer in children. *Br Med J*, **307**, 891–5.

Petridou E, Trichopoulos D, Kravaritis A, *et al* (1997). Electrical power lines and childhood leukaemia: a study from Greece. *Int J Cancer*, **73**, 345–8.

Preston-Martin S, Navidi W, Thomas D, *et al* (1996a). Los Angeles study of residential magnetic fields and childhood brain tumors. *Am J Epidemiol*, **143**, 105–19.

Preston-Martin S, Gurney J G, Pogoda J M, *et al* (1996b). Brain tumor risk in children in relation to use of electric blankets and water bed heaters: results from the United States West Coast childhood brain tumor study. *Am J Epidemiol*, **143**, 1116–22.

Ryan P, Lee M W, North B, *et al* (1992). Risk factors for tumors of the brain and meninges: results from the Adelaide Adult Brain Tumor Study. *Int J Cancer*, **51**, 20–27.

Savitz D A, Wachtal H, Barnes F A, *et al* (1988). Case control study of childhood cancer and exposure to 60 Hz magnetic fields. *Am J Epidemiol*, **128**, 21–38.

Savitz D A, John E M and Kleckner R C (1990). Magnetic field exposure from electric appliances and childhood cancer. *Am J Epidemiol*, **131**, 763–73.

Schreiber G H, Swaen G M, Meijers J M M, *et al* (1993). Cancer mortality and residence near electricity transmission equipment: a retrospective cohort study. *Int J Epidemiol*, **22**, 9–15.

Severson R K, Stevens R G, Kaune W T, *et al* (1988). Acute nonlymphocytic leukemia and residential exposure to power frequency magnetic fields. *Am J Epidemiol*, **128**, 10–20.

Sussman S S and Kheifets L I (1996). Re 'Adult leukemia risk and personal appliance use: a preliminary study' (Letter). *Am J Epidemiol*, **143**, 743–4.

Tomenius L (1986). 50-Hz electromagnetic environment and the incidence of childhood tumors in Stockholm county. *Bioelectromagnetics*, **7**, 191–207.

Tynes T and Haldorsen T (1997). Electromagnetic fields and cancer in children residing near Norwegian high-voltage power lines. *Am J Epidemiol*, **145**, 219–26.

UKCCS (1999). Exposure to power-frequency magnetic fields and the risk of childhood cancer. *Lancet*, **354**, 1925–31.

UKCCS (2000). Childhood cancer and residential proximity to power lines. *Br J Cancer*, **83**, 1573–80.

Vena J E, Graham S, Hellmann R, *et al* (1991). Use of electric blankets and risk of postmenopausal breast cancer. *Am J Epidemiol*, **134**, 180–85.

Vena J E, Freudenheim J L, Marshall J R, *et al* (1994). Risk of premenopausal breast cancer and use of electric blankets. *Am J Epidemiol*, **140**, 974–9.

Vena J E, Freudenheim J L, Marshall J R, *et al* (1995). Re 'Risk of premenopausal breast cancer and use of electric blankets'. The authors' reply (Letter). *Am J Epidemiol*, **142**, 446–7.

Verkasalo P K, Pukkala E, Hongisto M Y, *et al* (1993). Risk of cancer in Finnish children living close to power lines. *Br Med J*, **307**, 895–9.

Verkasalo P K, Pukkala E, Kaprio J *et al* (1996). Magnetic fields of high voltage power lines and risk of cancer in Finnish adults: nationwide cohort study. *Br Med J*, **313**, 1047–51.

Wartenberg D (1999). Residential magnetic fields and childhood leukaemia. *Am J Public Health*, **88**, 1787–94.

Wrensch M, Yost M, Miike R, *et al* (1999). Adult glioma in relation to residential power frequency electromagnetic field exposure in the San Francisco Bay area. *Epidemiology*, **10**, 523–7.

Zaffanella L E, Savitz D A, Greenland S, *et al* (1998). The residential case-specular method to study wire codes, magnetic fields and disease. *Epidemiology*, **9**, 1620.

Zheng T, Holford T R, Mayne S T, *et al* (2000). Exposure to electromagnetic fields from use of electric blankets and other in-home electrical appliances and breast cancer risk. *Am J Epidemiol*, **151**, 1103–11.

Zhu K, Weiss N S, Stanford J L, *et al* (1999). Prostate cancer in relation to the use of electric blanket or heated water bed. *Epidemiology*, **10**, 83–5.

6 Occupational Exposure to Time-varying ELF Electric and Magnetic Fields and Cancer

INTRODUCTION

1 The earlier report of the Advisory Group (NRPB, 1992) noted the large number of studies that had been published in the decade before 1992 on the possible link between occupational exposure to electromagnetic fields and cancer, but was unable to reach any firm conclusion about whether or not any occupational hazard existed. The many investigations had not provided any evidence of a quantitative relationship between risk and level of exposure. The very small excess risk of leukaemia in the total data might be attributed to selection bias in favour of the publication of positive results, while the greater excess of brain cancer might indicate an occupational hazard from some types of electronic work, but the nature of the hazard (if it existed) was not clear. No conclusion could be drawn from the reports of excesses of other types of cancer, but it was thought that the experimental evidence justified further investigation of an occupational hazard of breast cancer in men.

2 Here studies published since that report are reviewed, some of which were referred to by the Advisory Group in brief up-dates in 1993 and 1994 (NRPB, 1993 and 1994). The thrust of these studies has continued to centre on leukaemia and brain cancer, but some have highlighted a possible influence of electromagnetic fields on hormone-dependent organs, especially on tumours of the breast, pituitary, and testis, and a link with lung cancer has also been suggested.

3 Since 1992 there has been a shift from national or regional studies of individuals classified as 'electrical or electronic worker' towards cohort studies of industrial populations in the electricity supply industry and industries that are significant users of electricity such as the railways. Some of these cohorts have been used as a basis for nested case–control studies for tumour sites of interest. No further work has been published on welders other than a study of paternal exposure in childhood brain cancer cases, despite the fact that this occupational group was considered to be particularly exposed to electromagnetic fields.

4 Two important features have been attempts to concentrate on large population bases followed for decades and to characterise exposure to electromagnetic fields by measuring electric and magnetic fields using personal dosemeters (Chapter 2). Such studies mainly emanate from North America and from the Nordic countries in which vital statistical data are of a particularly high quality.

STUDIES LACKING PERSONAL EXPOSURE MEASUREMENTS

5 Several studies of importance have been published. Nine of them are cohorts from Nordic countries identified from national censuses and analysed either as cohorts or as nested case–control studies within the cohort. Publication of 20 years of cancer incidence data by occupational group in the Nordic populations extends reporting from the previous Nordic census-based studies. Five American and one Australian population-based case–control studies have addressed electromagnetic field exposure

for tumour sites of relevance and the Decennial Supplement on Occupational Health published by the Office of Population Censuses and Surveys (OPCS, now the Office for National Statistics) has provided the basis for national occupational mortality and cancer registration studies in the UK (OPCS, 1995).

Nordic countries

6 Norwegian census data on economically active males have been reported from the 1960 and 1970 censuses by Tynes *et al* (1992). A cohort of 37 945 males aged 20–70 years was identified as employed in jobs with some electromagnetic field exposure. Two groups were identified either as active at the 1960 census (Group 1) or as active through both 1960 and the 1970 census (Group 2). A total of 3806 cases of cancer were identified between 1961 and 1985 through the cancer registries. All occupationally active males served as the reference population. Modest elevations in standardised incidence ratios (SIR) were found for leukaemia (all types 108, Group 1; 141, Group 2). Statistically significant elevations were also noted for acute myeloid leukaemia (Group 2, SIR 156), chronic myeloid leukaemia (Group I, SIR 150; Group 2, SIR 197). The highest SIRs for all leukaemias were for radio/TV repairmen, radio and telegraph operators and power line workers ranging from 132 to 318 but based on small numbers of cases. For brain cancer the SIRs were mostly close to unity, with the highest being 220 for nine railway track walkers in Group 2.

7 Tynes *et al* (1996) also studied breast cancer incidence in a cohort of 2619 women who worked at sea as radio or telegraph operators in Norway between 1920 and 1960. Using the national population as comparison, the standardised incidence ratio was 1.5 (95% CI 1.1, 2.0), based on 50 cases during 1961–91. For a sub-cohort of 2132 women for whom individual reproductive histories were available, the relative risk after adjustment for fertility factors was again 1.5. A nested case–control analysis within the full cohort showed statistically significant trends in breast cancer risk with duration of employment and shift work among those aged 50 years or over at diagnosis, based on 21 cases, but no such trends were observed for younger women. Adjustment for fertility factors had little influence on the results for the older age group, although data were available for only six cases. Tynes *et al* suggested that shift work may be associated with exposure to 'light at night' and to radiofrequency (RF) or extremely low frequency (ELF) fields, which in turn may be related to the production of melatonin by the pineal gland. While no personal dosimetry for RF or ELF fields was possible, spot measurements were made in the radio rooms of ships with old-fashioned transmitters. At the operator's desk, RF electric and magnetic field measurements were below the level of detection, while ELF magnetic fields were comparable with those encountered in normal workplaces in Norway.

8 A further Norwegian study examined the incidence of breast cancer in economically active women (as defined at censuses) and found a small excess (12%) that was statistically significant, if they had 1000 hours or more potential exposure to electrically enhanced magnetic fields above background at work, after standardisation for socioeconomic class and age at birth of their first child (Kliukiene *et al*, 1999).

9 Guénel *et al* (1993) used Danish census data on occupation and cancer registrations to follow 2.8 million people aged 20–64 years for the period 1970–87. Of this cohort, 13% (172 000 men and 83 000 women) were classified as intermittently or continuously exposed to ELF magnetic fields and the authors used a threshold of an estimated exposure of 0.3 μT for inclusion in the groups. No statistically significant elevations in odds ratios were found for melanoma, breast cancer or brain tumours, but for all leukaemias odds ratios were significantly elevated for continuously exposed men (1.64) based on 39 cases. By occupational group, statistically significant elevated odds ratios were found for all leukaemias in electrical installation workers (1.95, 16 cases) and for foundry workers/machine moulders (2.90, 9 cases). Drivers of electric trains and power station workers had odds ratios close to unity.

10 Floderus *et al* (1994) studied male railway workers as defined in the 1960 Swedish census. Two groups (namely, engine drivers and conductors) had been followed previously to 1979 by Törnqvist *et al* (1991) and no excess observed of either leukaemia or brain cancer, but Floderus *et al* noted that the number of railway workers had halved since 1960, so they examined the results separately for the two periods 1960–69 and 1970–79 and looked also at other groups of railway workers and at incidence rates for lymphomas and tumours of the breast and pituitary. For both engine drivers and conductors, relative risks compared to those for all men of the same age were slightly increased in the earlier period, but not significantly so (engine drivers: leukaemia 1.6 based on 6 cases, brain cancer 1.1 based on 8 cases; conductors: leukaemia 1.3 based on 7 cases, brain cancer 1.3 based on 16 cases). For the latter period all the relative risks were 1.0 or less. For lymphomas the relative risks for engine drivers and conductors combined were 1.0 in both periods. Three cases of breast cancer were diagnosed in these occupational groups all in the earlier period, giving a 5-fold relative risk and 17 pituitary tumours, spread over both periods, giving a relative risk of approximately 2.4, which was statistically significant.

11 A further report by Alfredsson *et al* (1996) on 7466 Swedish engine drivers and 2272 conductors employed during the period 1976–90 noted an elevated risk for lymphatic leukaemia in drivers 2.3 (95% CI 1.3, 13.2) based on 10 cases. This cohort has a 50% overlap in membership in the Floderus *et al* study.

12 Using the same database as Floderus *et al* (1993), Stenlund and Floderus (1997) reviewed male breast cancer and testicular tumours. No association was found with male breast cancer, but the results for testicular cancer revealed an odds ratio of 3.9 (95% CI 1.4, 11.2) for exposure higher than 0.4 μT in men younger than 40 years, based on 14 cases.

13 Occupations with exposure to magnetic fields were reviewed in a case-control study by Rodvall *et al* (1998) of 84 glioma and 20 meningioma cases occurring in men aged 25–74 years registered as living in a defined area in Central Sweden. There was no statistically significant excess of either tumour by occupational title, or surrogate measurement of magnetic field. The relative risk was 1.9 (95% CI 0.8, 5.0) for glioma in those considered to be exposed to magnetic fields greater than 0.4 μT.

14 Using occupational titles from the Swedish census for residents near overhead power lines, Feychting *et al* (1997) found increased risks for all leukaemias and acute myeloid leukaemia and for brain cancer which were statistically significant for all leukaemias at 1.4 (95% CI 1.0, 2.2) for exposure of 0.13–0.19 μT and 1.7 (95% CI 1.1, 2.7) for 0.2 μT and above. For individuals highly exposed at home and at work the relative risk rose to 3.7 (95% CI 1.5, 9.4).

15 In a major study, Anderson *et al* (1999) have brought together occupational cancer incidence data for the four Nordic countries, Denmark, Finland, Norway and Sweden.

Ten million people aged 20-64 years at the time of the 1970 census were followed for cancer incidence over the succeeding 20 years by matching individuals with individuals recorded in the national cancer registries and one million registrations of cancer identified. Some occupational data from other censuses provide a degree of longitudinal verification of occupational studies. For welders, there were elevated risks of cancer of the lung and pleura in all countries but inconsistent elevations for other sites by country. For electrical workers, no evidence of an association with brain cancer, lymphomas or leukaemias (or breast cancer in either sex) was found.

USA

16 Five case-control studies from the USA on occupationally exposed groups have reviewed specific tumours.

17 Rosenbaum *et al* (1994) identified 71 male breast cancers in eight counties in New York State between 1979 and 1988. Occupational data were obtained from city directories for cases and controls (cancer screening centres population). Odds ratios approximated to unity for those deemed to be occupationally exposed to electromagnetic fields.

18 Using American mortality data for 1985-89, Loomis *et al* (1994) reviewed over half a million women with cancer and a known occupation. These included 28 434 cases of breast cancer. An electrical occupation was identified in 68 cases and 199 controls (odds ratio 1.38). The odds ratio rose to 2.15 when the analysis was restricted to post-menopausal women and was highest for telephone installers and repairers (2.17, 15 cases).

19 Coogan *et al* (1996) reviewed risk factors for 6851 newly diagnosed cases of female breast cancer from four states in the USA. The 9475 controls were chosen from state driving licence lists (under 65 years) and from the state Medicare lists (aged 65–74 years). Occupations were classified according to the likelihood of exposure to magnetic fields. The odds ratio was 1.43 (0.99–2.09) for women of 'high' likelihood of exposure. The odds ratios for 'medium' and 'low' were 1.09 and 1.02, respectively.

20 Grayson (1996) reviewed 880 000 US Air Force personnel and from this population identified 230 brain tumour cases. These were matched to 920 controls. Estimation of exposure to non-ionising electromagnetic fields was made from job title and some data on exposures to radiofrequency and microwave fields above 100 W m^{-2}. The modest elevations in odds ratios (1.28–1.39) suggested an association that was more marked for officers than for enlisted men, with the highest odds ratio of 3.3 (95% CI 1.99, 5.45) for senior officers. There was no association found between brain tumours and ionising radiation exposures based on personal dosimetry.

21 Milham (1997) has reported on occupational mortality in Washington State for 1950 to 1989. Of the twelve electromagnetic field exposed worker occupations, ten had elevated leukaemia proportional mortality ratio (PMRs) and all but one of the occupational groups had elevated rates for acute leukaemia.

Australia

22 In a case-control study from Australia Ryan *et al* (1992) reviewed risk factors for 110 cases of glioma and 60 cases of meningiomas compared with 417 controls. No statistically significant elevated risk ratios were found for electrical occupations but a small subset of female glioma cases had a risk ratio of 4.1 (95% CI 1.3, 13.2) for occupational exposure to cathode ray tubes in visual display equipment but based on 7 cases.

UK

23 The UK decennial supplement on occupational health (OPCS, 1995) reviewed mortality and cancer registrations for England and Wales for over one million men and women aged 20–74 years for the period 1979–80 and 1982–90 (data for 1981 were unreliable due to industrial action) by last known occupation. For mortality, elevated proportional mortality ratios for brain cancer were noted for electrical and electronic engineers (139), electricians (117), radio/TV mechanics (117), other electronic maintenance workers (156) and telephone fitters (149). For leukaemia, elevated PMRs were found for radio/TV mechanics (acute myeloid 149), other electronic maintenance workers (acute myeloid 179, chronic myeloid 242). The ratios for railway workers were unremarkable. Electricians had an elevated PMR of 162 for malignant melanoma. For cancer incidence, the PMRs of 118 (brain) and 224 (acute myeloid leukaemia) for radio/TV mechanics were not statistically significantly elevated. For other electrical workers the PMRs of 293 (acute myeloid leukaemia) and 408 (chronic lymphatic leukaemia) were significantly elevated but based on small numbers. Railway engine drivers had a PMR for acute myeloid leukaemia of 223 based on 9 cases.

24 From the 1 034 759 cancer registrations for the period 1981–87 for men and women noted in the decennial supplement, Fear *et al* (1996) have analysed the 371 890 registrations for which valid occupational information was provided. They grouped 12 job categories identified as electrical occupations amounting to 7531 male cancer registrations. Statistically significantly elevated proportional registration ratios (PRRs) adjusted for age, social class and registry were found for cancers of the pleura (201), bladder (114), brain (115), myeloma (136), all leukaemias (123), and acute myeloid leukaemia (129). A PRR deficit was found for lung cancer. The data for women were based on far fewer deaths: excess PRRs were found for pleura (164), brain (140), and all leukaemias (143), but were statistically significant only for a subset defined as malignant tumours of the brain (202 based on 12 cases).

25 In the light of the Fear *et al* analyses, the OPCS data were regrouped (H Inskip, MRC Environmental Epidemiology Unit, Southampton, personal communication) using the same definition of electrical workers. Table 6.1 lists ratios for tumour sites with more than 100 cases and for male breast cancer for two databases with overlapping time frames (1979–80, 1982–90 and 1981–87), which are arbitrarily restricted to 1980 Classification of Occupations (OPCS) amalgamated into 194 job groups (Appendix 2, OPCS, 1995). Statistically significant elevated risks for *both* datasets were found only for pleura, brain, myeloma and a subset of leukaemia – acute myeloid leukaemia. The pleural mesothelioma excess is readily explained by the extent of exposure to asbestos in sections of the industry decades ago.

26 It was noted that the two datasets used in these analyses overlap and do not provide totally independent evidence.

Summary

27 The studies of workers in electrical and electronic occupations continue to suggest elevated risks for leukaemia – particularly acute myeloid leukaemia and possibly chronic lymphatic leukaemia – although the data suggesting a link between electromagnetic fields and brain cancer are weaker and less consistent. However, the Nordic countries census-based study (Anderson *et al*) does not support these findings and it must carry more weight than the UK census-based data study, as the occupations of

TABLE 6.1 Comparison between proportional mortality ratios (PMRs)[a] with adjusted proportional registration ratios (PRR)[a] for electrical workers[b] aged 20–74 years with their 95% confidence intervals (95% CI)

Cancer	Number	PMR[c]	(95% CI)	Number	PRR[d]	(95% CI)
Oral cavity	141	122	(103, 144)	58	94	(73, 122)
Oesophagus	708	110	(102, 118)	211	113	(98, 129)
Stomach	1350	100	(95, 105)	527	99	(91, 108)
Colon	1208	113	(107, 120)	428	105	(96, 116)
Rectum	744	101	(94, 109)	375	106	(96, 118)
Liver	148	83	(70, 97)	34	69	(49, 96)
Pancreas	799	108	(101, 116)	240	102	(90, 116)
Larynx	103	67	(55, 81)	91	83	(67, 102)
Trachea, bronchus and lung	5627	88	(86, 91)	1993	86	(82, 90)
Pleura	207	167	(145, 191)	115	201	(167, 241)
Melanoma	191	128	(110, 147)	91	119	(97, 146)
Other skin	37	93	(66, 129)	653	110	(102, 119)
Female breast	268	102	(91, 116)	83	89	(72, 112)
Male breast	16	84	(48, 136)	14	129	(71, 217)
Prostate	923	108	(101, 115)	381	102	(93, 113)
Testis	45	81	(59, 108)	139	104	(88, 123)
Bladder	629	106	(98, 115)	481	109	(100, 119)
Kidney (except pelvis)	409	120	(109, 133)	149	106	(91, 125)
Brain	570	115	(106, 125)	204	112	(103, 136)
Non-Hodgkin's lymphoma	446	107	(98, 118)	228	108	(94, 122)
Hodgkin's disease	144	138	(116, 162)	101	113	(93, 137)
Myeloma	271	120	(107, 136)	103	134	(111, 163)
All leukaemia	473	107	(98, 118)	217	124	(109, 142)
Acute lymphatic	40	100	(72, 137)	17	116	(72, 186)
Chronic lymphatic	72	90	(70, 113)	49	114	(86, 151)
Acute myeloid	220	114	(100, 131)	80	128	(103, 160)
Chronic myeloid	91	110	(89, 136)	32	112	(79, 158)
Acute monocytic	11	162	(81, 290)	-	N/A	-
Other	27	97	(64, 142)	-	N/A	-

Notes

(a) PMRs for England and Wales 1979–80, 1982–90; PRR for England 1981–87. Both adjusted for age (5 year age groups), social class (6 classes) and (for PRRs) cancer registry (13 registries).

(b) Electrical workers were defined using the Southampton Occupational Classification job groups 029, 136, 137, 138, 139, 140, 141, 142, 143, 155. 156, 161.
Data were restricted to total deaths (or registrations) of 100 or more with exception of the leukaemia subtypes and male breast cancer.

(c) OPCS data derived to match Fear *et al* (1996) (H Inskip, MRC Environmental Epidemiology Unit, Southampton, personal communication).

(d) Data derived from Fear *et al* (1996).

the men who died or developed cancer in the latter study were categorised by different people at different times from those who categorised them in the census. Breast cancer continues to be implicated in relevant occupational exposures. The finding in one study of a pituitary gland excess and in another of testicular tumour excess is possibly of interest. These more recent population-based studies are of a higher quality than previous reports and some have gone to considerable lengths to assess real workplace exposures and to allow for confounding factors. Nevertheless, data from these types of studies are unlikely to produce definitive answers. There is a need now to concentrate on cohorts of workers in relevant industries with high potential exposures.

STUDIES WITH QUANTITATIVE ESTIMATES OF PERSONAL EXPOSURES

28 Cohorts of specific industrial populations for whom measurements of individuals' exposures have been made are the basis for many recently published studies. Several of the studies involve very large populations with detailed and extensive dose estimations for electromagnetic fields as well as consideration of confounding factors. The main results for leukaemia and brain cancer are summarised in Tables 6.2 and 6.3, respectively.

Nordic countries

29 Tynes *et al* (1994a) reviewed a cohort of 5088 male employees at eight Norwegian hydroelectric power companies employed for at least one year between 1920 and 1985. Records were incomplete before 1950 and follow-up was limited to the period 1953–91. Exposure estimations were carried out on the basis of job history and spot measurements of magnetic fields converted to microtesla year (μT year). There was some attempt to assess confounding factors. Average employment in the cohort lasted 22 years, although 80% of subjects were alive at the end of the study period. During the study period 486 cases of cancer were registered. Standardised incidence ratios (SIR) were identified using Norwegian national data. The SIRs for all major cancer sites were close to unity (for sites of special interest: brain 88, leukaemia 90, melanoma 112). There was no effect of duration of employment for these sites. For job held longest the SIR for malignant melanoma was significantly elevated at 2.08 (11 cases) and these cases probably account for the SIR of 2.24 for exposure greater than 35 μT years. Brain and leukaemia cases showed no trend for exposure. A possible association between combined exposure to polychlorinated biphenyls (PCBs) and electromagnetic fields is postulated by the SIR for malignant melanoma at 2.65.

30 Johansen and Olsen (1998) studied cancer incidence among 32 006 individuals with at least three months employment at one of the 99 utility companies in Denmark. Between 1968 and 1993 a total of 3008 cancers were observed, compared with 2825 expected (SIR 1.06; 95% CI 1.03, 1.10). Increased risks for cancers of the lung and pleural cavity were seen, which were confined mainly to workers in jobs with exposure to asbestos. SIRs for leukaemia (0.92 for males, 0.50 for females) and brain cancer (0.79 for males, 1.33 for females) were consistent with unity. Magnetic field levels were assessed on the basis of 25 different job titles for utility company employees and 19 work areas within this industry, together with 196 measurements made for

TABLE 6.2 Occupational population studies: summary of leukaemia findings

Author	Population	Size	Study period	Number of cases	Risk estimates	Notes
Sahl *et al* (1993)	Californian electrical utility	36 221	1960–88	44	1.07 (OR)	OR for each unit of 25 μT years per mean exposure (OR of 1.1 for 6 cases with mean exposure exceeding 5 μT) – one case excluded by authors*
Tynes *et al* (1994)	Five Norwegian hydroelectric power companies	5 088	1920–91	11	0.95, 0.74, 1.04 (SIR)	SIRs for < 5, 5–35, > 35 μT years, respectively
Savitz and Loomis (1995)	Five US electric power companies	138 905	1950–88	164	1.00, 1.04, 1.13, 0.95, 1.11 (RR)	RRs for < 0.6, 0.6– < 1.2, 1.2– < 2.0, 2.0– < 4.3 and ≥4.3 μT years, respectively
Matanoski *et al* (1993)	AT&T workers	124 cases 372 controls	1975–80	35	2.5 (OR)	OR for exposure above the median of the mean magnetic field exposures to below the (1993) median (chronic lymphatic leukaemia cases and 'exposures' of less than 10 years *NOT* included in this study population)
Thériault *et al* (1994)	Two Canadian and one French electrical utility	223 200	1970–89	140	1.00, 1.54, 1.75 (OR)	ORs for < 3, ≥3, ≥15.7 μT years, respectively. ORs for acute non-lymphatic leukaemia (2.41*), acute myeloid leukaemia (3.15*) for exposure ≥3 μT years
Floderus *et al* (1994)	Swedish railway workers	434 000, 482 000 (person years)	1961–69, 1970–79	33, 48	1.2, 0.9 (RR)	RR of 2.7* for engine drivers (1961–69) for chronic lymphatic leukaemia, based on 4 cases
Tynes *et al* (1994)	Norwegian railway workers	52 cases 259 controls	1958–90	52	1.00, 0.97, 0.56, 1.07 (OR)	ORs for < 0.1, 0.1–310, 310–3600 and 1900–3600 μT years, respectively, adjusted for smoking (16.67 Hz magnetic fields)

Author	Population	Size	Study period	Number of cases	Risk estimates	Notes
Miller *et al* (1996)	Ontario Hydro portion of Savitz *et al* (1997)	1 484 cases 2 179 controls	1970–88	50	2.07, 4.45*, 1.67, 1.56 (OR)	Electric fields 172–344, and ≥345 V m^{-1} years; magnetic fields 3.2–7, and ≥7.1 μT years, respectively. Dose–response rate for interaction of electric fields on magnetic field (ORs adjusted for SES, year of hire and potential occupational confounders)
Armstrong *et al* (1994)	Hydro Quebec and EDF (France) portions of Savitz *et al* (1997)	2 679 cases, 4 026 controls	1970–88 (Quebec) 1978–89 (France)	95	0.69, 0.80 (OR)	ORs for pulsed electromagnetic fields above median and 90th percentile for all subjects, respectively
Baris *et al* (1996)	Hydro Quebec portion of Savitz *et al* (1997)	21 744	1970–88	20	1.21, 0.98, 0.71 (SMR)	Magnetic fields above 0.16 μT; electric fields above 5.76 V m^{-1}; pulsed fields above 23.70 ppm, respectively (blue-collar workers only)
Guenel *et al* (1996)	EDF (France) portion of Savitz *et al* (1997)	1 915 cases 7 568 controls	1978–89	72	0.40, 0.58 (OR)	ORs per 500 V m^{-1} years, based on cumulative arithmetic and geometric means, respectively
Johansen and Olsen (1998)	Danish electrical utility	32 006	1968–93	63	0.88 (SIR)	SIRs for males of 1.0 (< 0.1 μT), 1.0 (0.1–0.29 μT), 0.9 (0.3–0.99 μT) and 1.1 (≥0.1 μT)
Villeneuve *et al* (2000)	Ontario Hydro	50 cases 199 controls	1970–88	50	10.17	20+ years, highest tertile of % time spent above 10 V m^{-1}
					8.23	20+ years, highest tertile of % time spent above 20 V m^{-1}
London *et al* (1994)	Los Angeles county workers	2 355 cases 67 212 controls	1972–90	2 355	1.2 per μT	For all leukaemias and magnetic field exposure. Highest elevation (OR 3.2) for phone line workers and splicers (4 cases)

*$p < 0.05$.

TABLE 6.3 Occupational population studies: summary of brain cancer findings

Author	Population	Size	Study period	Number of cases	Risk estimates	Notes
Sahl *et al* (1993)	Californian electrical utility	36 221	1960–88	31	0.81 (RR)	OR for each unit of 25 μT years of exposure (OR of 0.65 for 3 cases with mean exposure exceeding 5 μT)
Tynes *et al* (1994b)	Five Norwegian hydroelectric power companies	5 088	1920–91	13	1.82, 0.71, 0.44 (SIR)	SIRs for < 5, 5–35, > 35 μT years, respectively
Savitz and Loomis (1995)	Five American electrical power companies	138 905	1950–88	144	1.00, 1.61, 1.47, 1.65, 2.29* (RR)	RRs for < 0.6, 0.6– < 1.2, 1.2 – < 2.0, 2.0 – < 4.3 and ≥4.3 μT years, respectively
Theriault *et al* (1994)	Two Canadian and one French electrical utility	223 200	1970–89	108	1.00, 1.54, 1.95 (OR)	ORs for < 3, ≥3, ≥15.7 μT years, respectively
Floderus *et al* (1994)	Swedish railway workers	434 000, 482,000 (person years)	1961–69, 1970–79	45, 76	0.9, 1.0 (RR)	RR of 12.2 (astrocytoma I-II among engine drivers and conductors aged < 30 years, 1961–69), based on 2 cases
Tynes *et al* (1994)	Norwegian railway workers	39 cases 194 controls	1958–90	39	1.00, 0.81, 0.94, 0.97 (OR)	ORs for < 0.1, 0.1–310, 310–3600 and 1900–3600 μT years, respectively (16.67 Hz magnetic fields)
Miller *et al* (1996)	Ontario Hydro portion of Savitz *et al* (1997)	1 484 cases 2 179 controls	1970–88	24	0.57, 0.99, 1.27, 1.33 (OR)	Electric fields 172–344, and ≥345 V m^{-1} years; magnetic fields 3.2–7, and ≥7.1 μT years, respectively (ORs adjusted for SES, year of first hire and potential occupational confounders)
Armstrong *et al* (1994)	Hydro Quebec and EDF (France) portions of Savitz *et al* (1997)	2 679 cases 4 026 controls	1970–88 (Quebec) 1978–89 (France)	84	0.84, 1.90 (OR)	ORs for pulsed electromagnetic fields above median and 90th percentile for all subjects, respectively
Baris *et al* (1996)	Hydro Quebec portion of Savitz *et al* (1997)	21 744	1970–88	20	1.50, 1.24, 0.36 (SMR)	Magnetic fields above 0.16 μT; electric fields above 5.76 V m^{-1}; pulsed fields above 23.70 ppm, respectively (blue-collar workers only)
Guenel *et al* (1996)	EDF (France) portion of Savitz *et al* (1997)	1 915 cases 7 568 controls	1978–89	69	2.59, 1.32 (OR)	ORs per 500 V m^{-1} years, based on cumulative arithmetic and geometric means, respectively
Harrington *et al* (1997)	UK electrical utility	112 cases 654 controls	1972–91	112	1.04, 0.95, 1.18, 0.95 (OR)	Magnetic fields 5.4–13.4, ≥13.5 μT years (arithmetic means), or 4.1–7.9, ≥8.0 μT years (geometric means), respectively
Johansen and Olsen (1998)	Danish electrical utility	32 006	1968–93	72	0.86 (SIR)	SIRs of central nervous system tumours for males of 0.5 (< 0.1 μT), 0.9 (0.1–0.29 μT), 0.7 (0.3–0.99 μT) and 0.7 (≥0.1 μT); for females of 1.1 (<0.1 μT) and 3.3 (0.1–0.29 μT)

*$p < 0.05$.

employees of six companies. No association was found between estimates of average magnetic fields and the incidence of brain cancer (among males and females), leukaemia in males, or female breast cancer.

31 In 1994 Tynes *et al* (1994b) reviewed the cohort of 13 030 railway workers from their 1992 report. They identified 53 cases of leukaemia and 39 brain cancer cases which were matched with 4 or 5 controls from the cohort. Magnetic field calculations were based on time employed and tonnage transported and converted to microteslas normalised to 1 m above the track. The average annual exposure was 19.7 µT (range 0.88–88) from a 16 kV, 16.66 Hz power source. The study found an odds ratio for leukaemia of 0.70 (adjusted for smoking) and 0.87 for brain tumours in men employed on electric railways. There was no trend for cumulative exposure, lag times of 5 and 15 years nor for exposure windows of 5–25 years and 2–12 years before the tumour diagnosis.

32 Floderus *et al* (1993) studied half the male population of Sweden aged 20–64 years between 1983 and 1987. They identified 426 cases of leukaemia and 424 of brain tumour. Two controls per case were drawn from the 1980 census population. Tracing the study subjects and obtaining postal questionnaire information on work histories reduced the final tally to 250 leukaemia cases and 261 brain tumours. These individuals or proxies were used to obtain 1015 workplace magnetic field measurements on 169 jobs for an average of 6.8 hours per day. Possible confounders such as ionising radiation and benzene exposure were also sought. Odds ratios were elevated for all leukaemias but particularly for chronic lymphatic leukaemia with a dose–response relationship by quintile of exposure [< 0.15 (reference), 0.16–0.19, 0.20–0.28, 0.29–0.40, ≥0.41 µT] for arithmetic mean, median exposures and time above 0.2 µT. No such pattern was found for brain tumours, although there were elevated odds ratios in the two highest quintiles for median exposure and a suggestion of a dose–response for time above 0.20 µT. It is not possible to judge the influence of the low response rate nor the use of proxy measurements on the outcome of this study.

USA

33 Sahl *et al* (1993) reported on 36 221 workers at Southern California Edison who had been employed for at least one year between 1960 and 1988. Follow-up of vital status was virtually complete and detailed occupational histories were available on 80% of cases and 83% of the within-cohort controls. Magnetic field assessments were made for 776 person-shifts of volunteer employees. A total of 3125 deaths were recorded in the study period, but no positive associations were found for occupational exposure to electromagnetic fields and death from leukaemia, brain cancer or lymphoma. Three nested case–control studies were performed on the cohort to examine the possible associations more closely. The cases were matched with 10 within-cohort controls. Odds ratios from the exposure scores for the mean, median, 99th percentile and fractions exceeding 1 and 5 µT were all close to unity. For leukaemia, the fraction exceeding 5 µT had an odds ratio of 1.3, and by job title, 'electricians as usual occupation' had an odds ratio of 1.95 for leukaemia and 1.57 for brain cancer. The 'fraction exceeding' scores are the proportion of magnetic field measurements that are above 1 and 5 µT times the number of years on the job. None of these ratios reached conventional statistical significance and no exposure response trends were noted.

34 An update of this cohort with three further years of follow-up to 1991 with a revised occupational classification and revised reference group found elevated SMRs for lung cancer of 2.3 (95% CI 1.0, 5.0) for field staff, 2.2 (95% CI 1.5, 3.1) for line crew, and 2.4 (95% CI 1.6, 3.6) for power plant workers compared with office staff (Kelsh and Sahl, 1997). Information on other risk factors such as smoking was not available.

35 A study by Savitz and Loomis (1995) of employees of five electrical utility companies in the USA comprises a cohort of 138 905 men with at least six months' work experience between 1950 and 1986. Up to 1988, the cohort accumulated 2.6 million person years and 20 733 deaths, including 164 leukaemia cases and 144 brain cancers. Exposure assessment involved complete work histories (collapsed to 22 occupational categories) and 2842 usable exposure measurements across work shifts. The exposure grouping were collapsed to five groups with arithmetic mean values of 0.12, 0.21, 0.39, 0.62 and 1.27 μT (the lowest three groupings corresponding to quartiles and the upper two being split within the highest quartile). Cumulative exposures were estimated by time interval and grouped for latency. Confounders other than smoking were assessed; smoking-related deaths suggested that smoking would not have a major confounding effect.

36 Leukaemia showed no consistent elevations except for more than 20 years as an electrician (2.5, 6 cases). Analyses by leukaemia subtype are not detailed in the paper, but non-significant elevations for acute myeloid leukaemia (2.0) and chronic lymphatic leukaemia (1.9) were found for electricians. Five years or more work in any exposed occupation showed a non-significant increased risk for chronic lymphatic leukaemia (2.1). No effect of cumulative exposure to magnetic fields was shown for leukaemia. Brain cancer mortality was modestly elevated in relation to duration in exposed jobs (0–5 years 1.0, 5–20 years 1.87, and 20+ years 1.45). Cumulative exposures suggested a risk of 1.07 per μT year and of 1.94 per μT year for the 2–10 year exposure window. There were six deaths from male breast cancer compared with 7.5 expected. None of these men had a cumulative exposure above 2 μT years, based on a 2 year lag (D A Savitz, School of Public Health, University of North Carolina, personal communication).

37 Three further reports on this cohort have been published. The first by Savitz *et al* (1997) concentrated on lung cancer and was in direct response to the findings of Armstrong *et al* (1994) (see paragraph 45) concerning lung cancer risks and pulsed electromagnetic fields. No clear pattern of elevated risk was found for duration of employment in jobs associated with exposure to electromagnetic fields, although the relative risk was elevated in the 10–20 year exposure group (1.31) with a weak trend by duration of exposure for power plant operators. A weak effect was also found for increasing exposure. No direct reading for pulsed electromagnetic fields was available. When exposure to such fields was estimated from the description of the job and analogy with the findings by Armstrong *et al*, no trend in risk was observed with increasing exposure.

38 A second analysis dealt with lymphoma and multiple myeloma (Schroeder and Savitz, 1997). Again some evidence existed for a small positive association between non-Hodgkin's lymphoma (NHL) mortality and duration of employment in any exposed job (relative risk 1.4; 95% CI 0.8, 2.4) but this reached statistical significance only for low grade NHL in the lower two exposure groups: relative risks of 2.6 (95% CI 1.1, 6.3) and 2.7 (95% CI 1.0, 7.1) based on 16 and 11 cases, respectively. Results for cumulative magnetic field exposure showed a small increase in NHL mortality above the reference category (relative risk 1.3–1.8) but no dose-response effect was noted. There was little evidence of any link between exposure to electromagnetic fields and Hodgkin's disease or multiple myeloma. The authors believed a causal link between NHL mortality and exposure to electromagnetic fields was unlikely.

39 A third study concentrating on the influence of exposure to polychlorinated biphenyls (PCBs) noted increasing malignant melanoma rates with exposure category for PCBs (Loomis *et al*, 1997).

40 Matanoski *et al* (1993) had access to a cohort of American Telephone & Telegraph (AT&T) employees, most of whom were retired. Mortality records were available for the period 1975–80. Excluded from the study were employees with less than 10 years' service and deaths from chronic lymphatic leukaemia. Of 177 other leukaemias identified, 124 were available for study. Job information was available in 61% of cases and for at least one of the three controls. Exposure measurements were undertaken on 15–61 individuals in each occupational grouping and lifetime mean exposures were estimated. The cable splicers appeared to have the highest exposures. Workers with mean scores above the median had a non-significant odds ratio for leukaemia of 2.5; for scores above the median peak, the odds ratio was 1.6. Increasing risks were seen with increasing cumulated peak exposures, with the highest odds ratios when 10 and 15 year latent periods were allowed after last exposure, that were marginally significant.

41 London *et al* (1994) identified 2355 cases of leukaemia among Los Angeles county males aged 20–64 years with a known occupation between 1972 and 1990. These were compared with 67 212 cancer controls. Magnetic and electric field exposures from job title were quantified by personal measurements for specific tasks and by estimating the amount of time spent at each task. Exposure measurements were made for eight electrical occupations with 278 workers monitored and 105 controls. Of the electrical workers, 121 had leukaemia. There was a weak association between all leukaemias and magnetic field exposure with an odds ratio of 1.2 per μT. The highest (and statistically significant) elevation was for phone line workers and splicers: 3.2 (4 cases). Adjustment for possible confounding factors did not materially alter the results.

42 A further analysis (Kheifets *et al*, 1997a) has examined this cohort for exposure to electric fields. Modest elevations were found for all leukaemias (odds ratios around 1.2) but for chronic lymphatic leukaemia the odds ratio was 1.88 (95% CI 1.12, 3.17) for medium (10–20 V m^{-1}) exposure. There was no trend with exposure and the authors contend that this study offers little support for the hypothesis that electric field exposure is associated with leukaemia.

Canada–France studies

43 Thériault *et al* (1994) utilised a nested case-control approach to study the combined cohorts of Ontario Hydro (31 543 employees), Hydro Quebec (21 749 employees) and the French company Electricité de France (EDF) (170 000 employees). The large French cohort could be studied only for current employees. The study period was in excess of 20 years to 1988. Controls were taken from within the cohort. Exposure assessments were carried out on 2066 workers for a five-day week with calculations of time-weighted averages and cumulative exposure, and assessments were made of confounding exposures. The analyses by exposure were for below the median exposure (3 μT years), above the median, and above the 90th percentile (15.7 μT years).

44 A total of 31 cancer sites were analysed. The odds ratios for acute myeloid leukaemia were statistically significantly elevated with exposure above the median (2.41) but not above the 90th percentile (2.52). Brain cancer odds ratios were also elevated for both metrics (1.54 and 1.95, respectively) but not to statistical significance. For astrocytoma the odds ratio for exposures above the 90th percentile was significant (12.3, 5 cases). No dose-response relationship was noted. Restricting the analysis to odds ratios for mean exposure above 0.2 μT or above 0.3 μT, elevated ratios were noted for acute myeloid leukaemia (2.25 and 1.91, respectively) and for astrocytoma (4.28 and 1.31, respectively). None was statistically significant. Considerable variation in odds ratios occurred between the utilities. The seven cases of breast cancer were too few for useful analysis, but it was noted that there were equal proportions of cases and controls above the median value for cumulative exposure (B G Armstrong, Faculty of Medicine, McGill University, personal communication). The excess risk for malignant melanoma noted among electrical workers that had been reported previously prompted analysis of the 52 cases in this cohort. No association was found between melanoma and exposure to magnetic fields.

45 Using two of the same cohorts (EDF and Hydro Quebec), Armstrong *et al* (1994) reviewed cancer deaths by exposure to pulsed electromagnetic fields. No relationship was found to previously suspect cancer sites but a dose-response relationship was noted between cumulative pulsed fields and lung cancer at Hydro Quebec rising to 6.67 for the highest exposure group (32 cases). The interpretation of this finding is discussed in paragraph 71.

46 Miller *et al* (1996) have reported a nested case-control study focusing on the 233 registered cancers in the *a priori* sites of interest using the Ontario Hydro part of the Canada-France study of Thériault *et al* (1994) and the measurements of both magnetic and electric fields. Cumulative life exposures indices for jobs condensed into 17 categories in 11 work situations were computed with adjustments for earlier years based on company records. Confounding factors were incorporated into the job exposure matrices.

47 For electric fields, elevated odds ratios were noted for haemopoietic malignancies but not for brain cancers. In particular, the odds ratios for the upper tertile for all leukaemias was 4.45 (95% CI 1.01, 19.7). There was a suggestion of a dose-response, but this was not significant after adjustment for socioeconomic status, year of hire, and potential occupational confounding factors. For magnetic fields, elevated odds ratios were noted for all leukaemias, acute non-lymphatic leukaemia, and chronic lymphatic leukaemia but these fell after adjustment. (All leukaemias fell from 2.04 to 1.67, acute non-lymphatic from 3.04 to 1.93, and chronic lymphatic from 1.22 to 0.49.) The odds ratios were elevated for benign and malignant brain tumours, especially after adjustment, but the elevations were not statistically significant.

48 Analysis for an interactive effect of electric and magnetic fields using an additive model found that each level of magnetic field exposure showed an increased odds ratio for leukaemia by increasing electric field exposure. Conversely within each level of electric field exposure, there was no indication of increasing odds ratio with increasing magnetic field exposure. Treating the exposures as continuous variables resulted in odds ratios of 4.27 (95% CI 1.00, 18.17) for 'high' exposures to electric fields and 'low' exposures to magnetic fields, 4.79 (95% CI 1.03, 22.22) for 'high' exposure to electric field and 'medium' exposure to magnetic fields and 5.53 (95% CI 0.88, 34.63) for 'high' exposure to both.

49 A further analysis of the Ontario Hydro cohort by Villeneuve *et al* (2000) tested associations between adult leukaemia and indices by electric and magnetic fields within a nested case–control study. Whilst no clear associations were noted for magnetic field indices, there was an increased risk of leukaemia for the percentage of time spent above certain electric field thresholds and by duration of employment. For exposures above 10 V m^{-1} for more than 15% of the time and for more than 20 years, the odds ratio of leukaemia was 10.17 (95% CI 1.58, 65.30).

50 Electric field exposures were also examined by Guénel *et al* (1996) for the EDF section of the Canada–France study, comprising 170 000 workers. A case–control study of 1915 cases of cancer and 7568 controls was reviewed using arithmetic mean and geometric mean cumulative exposures based on week-long measurements on 850 EDF workers. No information was obtained about cancers that occurred post-retirement. No association was found for lung cancer, leukaemia, or melanoma. For brain cancer odds ratios of 3.08 (95% CI 1.08, 8.74) were found for exposure above the 90% percentile arithmetic mean (387 V m^{-1}), and of 1.63 (95% CI 0.43, 6.24) for exposure above the geometric mean (≥74 V m^{-1}), both based on a total of 69 cases. Using a five-year latency, the former odds ratio was elevated to 3.69 (95% CI 1.10, 12.43) based on 9 cases (≥343 V m^{-1} arithmetic mean) but no similar effect was seen with latency allowances of 10 or 15 years. Adjusting for magnetic field exposure did not influence the findings but the odds ratio for brain tumours by time-weighted average exposure was 7.18 (95% CI 1.17, 44.22) for 6 cases at ≥13 V m^{-1} for more than 25 years' exposure.

51 A mortality study of the Hydro Quebec portion of the Canada–France power workers study was carried out by Baris *et al* (1996). The 21 744 workers were followed from 1970 to 1988 and occupation was coded as the last job. While some association was found between exposure to magnetic fields and brain cancer and leukaemia, the increases in mortality were modest (brain 1.50, leukaemia 1.21), restricted to blue-collar workers exposed to magnetic fields above background levels, and based on small numbers (7 deaths from brain cancer cases and 6 from leukaemia). Deaths from accidents and violence showed significantly elevated risk ratios for magnetic field exposures (relative risk 2.0; 95% CI 1.37, 2.93) but part of this excess was due to electrocution. The evidence for an association between pulsed electromagnetic field exposure and lung cancer was weak – a finding similar to that of Savitz *et al* (1997) and in contrast to that for the Hydro Quebec and French power workers cohorts (Armstrong *et al*, 1994).

UK

52 A large cohort of 84 018 employees of the former Central Electricity Generating Board has provided the material for a case–control study of brain cancer in the UK (Harrington *et al*, 1997). In this, 112 primary cancers of the brain were matched with 654 controls using 675 work-shift magnetic field measurements made recently for another purpose. No significant elevation of odds ratios was found for cumulative exposures in microtesla years, using either arithmetic or geometric means, nor was there any evidence of trend with exposure and no latency effect.

Pooled analysis of data

53 For associations between electromagnetic fields and adult leukaemia Feychting (1996) considered that no firm conclusions could be drawn even when the analysis was restricted to the more recent, more powerful studies. Kheifets *et al* (1997b), in a more analytical review of heterogeneity and study characteristics, found a small elevation in risk, but with no clear pattern of risk with exposure and suggested that there was evidence of publication bias. In a pooled analysis of the three studies with the most detailed assessment of personal exposure (Sahl *et al*, 1993; Thériault *et al*, 1994; Savitz and Loomis, 1995), Kheifets *et al* (1999) found a relative risk of 1.09 for 10 μT years (95% CI 0.98, 1.21) that was not quite statistically significant.

54 For brain cancer, Kheifets *et al* (1995) undertook a careful meta-analysis of the studies of occupational exposure to electromagnetic fields and drew some interesting conclusions. They considered only six studies had sufficiently valid exposure estimates to warrant comparison. Pooled estimates of exposure show a clear pattern of increasing risk from low to medium to high exposures. Confining the analysis to the three studies (Floderus *et al*, 1993; Matanoski *et al*, 1993; Savitz and Loomis, 1995) that they considered had comparable data for pooling confirmed the excess risk in each exposure group, but with no clear dose-response. The meta-analysis of the broad group of studies showed that the greatest excess (up to 30%) was found in those studies that could identify gliomas from all brain tumours. Finally, the authors noted that case-control studies provided higher relative risks than cohort or incidence based studies. It is important to emphasise here the inherent methodological limitations of the cohort and case-control approach. Cohort studies tend to have less bias but the number, accuracy and type of exposure measurements will influence the validity of the conclusions. Case-control studies are retrospective and tend to be more biased, frequently lacking accurate exposure metrics. Again it is notable that the Nordic four-nation study found no evidence of a risk for electrical workers as a whole.

55 In their later pooled analysis of the three studies with the most detailed assessment of personal exposure (Sahl *et al*, 1993; Thériault *et al*, 1994; Savitz and Loomis, 1995), Kheifets *et al* (1999) found a relative risk of 1.12 for 10 μT years which was not quite statistically significant (95% CI 0.98, 1.28).

Melatonin excretion and occupational exposure to magnetic fields

56 One possible mechanism by which exposure to magnetic fields might affect the risk of cancer, particularly breast cancer, is by reducing the secretion of melatonin which, it has been thought, may have an anti-carcinogenic effect (see Chapter 4, paragraph 58). In studies of exposure of railway workers to 16.7 Hz fields and electrical utility workers to 60 Hz fields, there was some evidence of a lowering of melatonin excretion following exposure (Pfluger and Minder, 1996; Burch *et al*, 1999). However, no clear-cut dose-response relationship was found in any of the studies. Potential confounding factors include shift working schedules, daylight exposure variations, and the timing of exposure in relation to urine sample collection.

Summary

57 Of the studies described, most were of reasonable size and some were extremely large, well-characterised populations with good quality health outcome data, extensive personal monitoring for current electromagnetic field exposure, and appropriate

statistical analysis. Some suggest an association with brain cancer but not others. The associations with leukaemia seem to be stronger for myeloid subtypes than for lymphatic, but in the more powerful studies the risk ratios barely reach conventional statistical significance and/or fail to demonstrate a clear dose-response relationship. The question of causality in relation to occupational exposure to electromagnetic fields and cancer is consequently unresolved.

METHODOLOGICAL ISSUES

58 In the past few years, as more studies of occupational electromagnetic field exposure and human health have been published, so too have been the number of review articles. The failure to establish any clear association between exposure levels and cancer rates has focused attention on the methodological difficulties of the studies. Savitz *et al* (1993) believed that the major problem was in the exposure assessments. Whilst the assumption that 'electrical' workers have higher exposure than non-electrical workers has been confirmed, job titles have proved inadequate as a surrogate for exposure. Time-weighted magnetic field measurements are probably a useful matrix but no clear consensus has been reached on the most appropriate - and valid - exposure measure. The use of different measures (mean, peak, above 0.2 μT, etc) by different authors has hampered comparison between studies.

59 Since that review, the publication of the two most powerful studies (Thériault *et al*, 1994; Savitz and Loomis, 1995) allows some opportunity for discussion of methodological issues. These studies involved different workplace exposures, exposure indices and sampling strategies, as well as health outcome endpoints. It appears that in the electricity supply industry estimating past exposures from current monitoring is less of a problem then would be the case in many other industries such as the chemical and extractive industries. In addition, Baris and Armstrong (1996) reviewed job history data from the Canada-France study and found that using last job as a surrogate for all jobs had a correlation coefficient of 0.8 with good specificity and quite good sensitivity. This was especially true for high exposure jobs which tended to be highly skilled and were frequently the last job.

60 Savitz and Loomis (1995) raised the question of whether further studies of this type were worth pursuing. They suggested that the need was for either studies with unique opportunities for accurate historical reconstruction of exposure or more specific, testable, hypotheses concerning biologically relevant exposure metrics or high quality markers of susceptibility to exposure. However, the major problem of reliable estimates of exposure had yet to be solved and many of the studies did not have wide ranges of exposures with which to estimate dose-response relationships.

DISCUSSION

61 The 1992 Advisory Group report (NRPB, 1992) concluded that the studies to date had not provided any evidence of a quantitative relationship between risk and level of exposure for cancer and extremely low frequency electromagnetic fields. The report noted the 'very small excess risk' of leukaemia and that although the brain cancer excess was 'greater', the nature of the hazard (if it existed) was unclear and did not at that stage indicate an occupational cause. In the intervening years, further studies have been published – many of which are more powerful than the earlier ones and have used more sophisticated exposure estimates. These larger studies have, in general, been well executed and have used appropriate analytical methods. A 1995 review concluded, however, that they had not then resulted in greater clarity (Hardell, 1995).

Leukaemia

62 Further studies of electrical or electronic workers have been published using national census databases or case-control studies for particular tumour sites. Modest elevations for all leukaemias, chronic lymphatic leukaemia, and acute myeloid leukaemia have been noted in some but not all the studies. The results from the pooled Nordic studies are, perhaps, the most powerful (Anderson *et al*, 1999) but those from the UK decennial supplement on occupational health (OPCS, 1995) cannot be easily dismissed. The case-control study of Floderus *et al* (1993) shows a dose-response relationship for chronic lymphatic leukaemia, but the low response rate and the use of proxy measurements are methodological drawbacks. The results highlighting workers in the railway industry are conflicting.

63 Several well-executed, large-scale industry-based cohort studies have reviewed the risks for leukaemia. The studies of Southern Californian Edison workers (Sahl *et al*, 1993) showed some modest elevation for the highest exposure score and for electricians and linesman but none was statistically significantly elevated. The Norwegian power workers study (Tynes *et al*, 1994a) raised the possibility of an excess for malignant melanoma but not for leukaemia, whilst the study of five electrical utilities in the USA (Savitz and Loomis, 1995) suggested a modestly elevated excess risk for acute myeloid and chronic lymphatic leukaemia but these risks only reached statistical significance for electricians with at least 20 years' employment. No raised leukaemia risk was seen in the Danish power workers study (Johansen and Olsen, 1998). The study of AT&T workers has a weaker dataset for both exposure assessment and work history and, curiously, excluded chronic lymphatic leukaemia from the diseases studied (Matanoski *et al*, 1993). Nevertheless, it was only in the highest exposure group of cable splicers that a small increase in leukaemia risk was noted. The large-scale Canada-France study found an elevated risk for acute myeloid leukaemia at the highest exposure scores (Thériault *et al*, 1994).

64 The work of Miller *et al* (1996) on electric field measurements and cancer risk has led to several further studies in previously researched populations (Guenel *et al*, 1996; Kheifets *et al*, 1997a). Kheifets *et al* concentrated on leukaemia and occupational job title but failed to show the same level of excess risk found by Miller *et al*. No effect was noted in the EDF portion of the Canada-France cohort (by Guenel *et al*).

65 The earlier Advisory Group report (NRPB, 1992) highlighted the possibility of publication bias in the studies then available for review and it may still be important. In this respect, it is notable that the Nordic four-nation study found no evidence of leukaemia in the total population of electrical workers (Anderson *et al*, 1999). Excess risks where they occur are, in general, modest, seldom reach statistical significance, are not accompanied by a consistent dose-response relationship, and are inconsistent with respect to the cell type principally affected, being sometimes for acute myeloid leukaemia and at others for chronic lymphatic leukaemia.

Brain cancer

66 Conflicting results have also been reported for brain cancer risk. Tynes *et al* (1992) found an excess within the cohort for railway workers but this was not corroborated in the nested case-control study. Guenel *et al* (1993) found no excess, whilst Floderus *et al* (1993) found modest elevations which were largely confined to the younger engine drivers. Methodological shortcomings mentioned in paragraph 54 may be important issues in interpreting this result. A similar restriction of the excess to younger electrical workers was found by Fear *et al* (1996).

67 In the industry-based cohort studies, with electric and magnetic field measurements the probably negative result from Southern Californian Edison (Sahl and Kelsh, 1993) is contrasted with a modest association with exposure from the study of five electrical utilities in the USA (Savitz and Loomis, 1995). The strongest evidence of an association is found in the Canada–France study (Thériault *et al*, 1994), but statistical significance is reached only at the highest exposure groupings but with little evidence of a dose-response relationship. The Harrington *et al* (1997) study of UK electricity generation and transmission workers found no association, but the exposure estimates were based on a small group of surrogate workers, as was the case in the study of Danish utility workers (Johansen and Olsen, 1998). By contrast, the Miller *et al* (1996) study of Ontario Hydro workers and the Guenel *et al* (1996) study of electric field exposure in the EDF population did note an excess at the highest exposures.

Other tumour sites

68 Breast cancer and malignant melanoma were becoming tumours of interest at the time of the earlier Advisory Group report. The investigations published since 1991 have produced conflicting results in studies of electrical and electronic workers but suggested a possible link with telephone and telegraph operators at sea (Tynes *et al*, 1996).

69 There are few reliable data on male breast cancer in relation to detailed individual assessments of occupational exposure. Those that are available do not suggest an association, although they involve only small numbers of cases. While the studies of female breast cancer are based on larger numbers, the absence of comparable exposure information makes it difficult to draw conclusions from them; overall the published studies do not appear to indicate an association.

70 For malignant melanoma, there is evidence of an elevated risk in the jobs held longest in the Norwegian power companies study (Tynes *et al*, 1994a) and this risk rose further when electromagnetic exposure was combined with other workplace exposures especially polychlorinated biphenyls (PCB). The powerful Canada–France study (Thériault *et al*, 1994) did not find an association with exposure to magnetic fields and the EDF portion of the cohort showed no association with electric fields (Guenel *et al*, 1996). The cohort of five electrical utilities in the USA, when analysed for exposure to PCBs, showed a trend for malignant melanoma with increasing exposure (Loomis *et al*, 1997).

71 One study which showed a dose-response relationship between occupational exposure and a risk of cancer was that of Armstrong *et al* (1994) concerning lung cancer and pulsed electromagnetic fields. Such associations can, however, occur readily when multiple cancer sites are examined and the excess could well be spurious, as the overall mortality from lung cancer was below the national rate. The association was weaker in

the recent cohort study of the Hydro Quebec portion of the study population (Baris *et al*, 1996) and in the nested case-control studies of the Ontario Hydro (Miller *et al*, 1996) and the EDF portions (Guenel *et al*, 1996). The Savitz *et al* (1997) paper on the five electrical utilities in the USA did find a modest effect and the reworking of the Southern Californian Edison cohort (Kelsh and Sahl, 1997) now reveals elevated SMRs only for lung cancer. The case for linking lung cancer to electric or magnetic field exposure is, at present, not proven.

72 A new finding is the possibility that pituitary gland tumours may be in excess in populations exposed to electromagnetic fields. Found in one study, this was part of a follow-up to an earlier report (Sahl *et al*, 1993) and may be a chance finding.

73 An association between non-Hodgkin's lymphoma and magnetic field exposure was found in the cohort of five electrical utilities in the USA (Schroeder and Savitz, 1997) but not in the Canada–France study (Thériault *et al*, 1994) and was probably a chance finding.

CONCLUSIONS

74 The most recent studies of occupational exposure to electromagnetic fields and the risk of cancer are, in the main, methodologically sound and some of them have considerable statistical power, but it is still not possible to be sure whether there is a positive association between such exposure and the risk of disease. Excess rates, where they exist, are generally modest and largely restricted to the two cancers that were previously noted: that is, leukaemia and cancer of the brain. Evidence about the particular cell type of leukaemia associated with exposure is conflicting, but is most often said to be the acute myeloid type. No risk of brain cancer and leukaemia has been established with any confidence.

REFERENCES

Alfredsson L, Hammar N and Karlehagen S (1996). Cancer incidence among male railway engine drivers and conductors in Sweden, 1976–90. *Cancer Causes Control*, **7**, 377–81.

Anderson A, Barlow L, Engeland A, *et al* (1999). Work related cancer in the Nordic countries. *Scand J Work Environ Health*, **25** (Suppl 2), 54–8.

Armstrong B, Thériault G, Guenel P, *et al* (1994). Association between exposure to pulsed electromagnetic fields and cancer in electric utility workers in Quebec, Canada and France. *Am J Epidemiol*, **140**, 805–20.

Baris D and Armstrong B G (1996). Exposure to magnetic fields estimated from last job held in an electrical utility in Ontario, Canada: a validation study. *Occup Environ Med*, **53**, 334–8.

Baris D, Armstrong B G, Deadman J, *et al* (1996). A mortality study of electrical utility workers in Quebec. *Occup Environ Med*, **53**, 25–31.

Burch J B, Reif J S, Yost M G, *et al* (1999). Reduced excretion of a melatonin metabolic in workers exposed to 60 Hz magnetic fields. *Am J Epidemiol*, **150**, 27–36.

Coogan P F, Clapp R W, Newcomb P A, *et al* (1996). Occupational exposure to 60-Hz magnetic fields and risk of breast cancer in women. *Epidemiology*, **7**, 459–64.

Feychting M (1996). Occupational exposure to electromagnetic fields and adult leukaemia: a review of the epidemiologic evidence. *Radiat Environ Biophys*, **35**, 237–42.

Feychting M, Forssen U and Floderus B (1997). Occupational and residential magnetic field exposure and leukaemia and central nervous system tumours. *Epidemiology*, **8**, 384–9.

Fear N T, Roman E, Carpenter L M, *et al* (1996). Cancer in electrical workers: an analysis of cancer registrations in England, 1981–87. *Br J Cancer*, **73**, 935–9.

Floderus B, Persson T, Stenlund C, *et al* (1993). Occupational exposure to electromagnetic fields in relation to leukaemia and brain tumours: a case control study in Sweden. *Cancer Causes Control*, **4**, 465–76.

Floderus B, Tornqvist S and Stenlund C (1994). Incidence of selected cancers in Swedish railway workers, 1961–79. *Cancer Causes Control*, **5**, 189–94.

Grayson J K (1996). Radiation exposure, socioeconomic status and brain tumour risk in the US Air Force: a nested case control study. *Am J Epidemiol*, **143**, 480–86.

Guenel P, Raskmark P, Andersen J B, *et al* (1993). Incidence of cancer in persons with occupational exposure to electromagnetic fields in Denmark. *Br J Indust Med*, **50**, 758–64.

Guenel P, Nicolau J, Imberon E, *et al* (1996). Exposure to 50 Hz electric field and incidence of leukaemia, brain tumours, and other cancers among French electric utility workers. *Am J Epidemiol*, **144**, 1107–21.

Hardell L, Holmberg B, Malker H, *et al* (1995). Exposure to extremely low frequency electromagnetic fields and the risk of malignant diseases – an evaluation of epidemiological and experimental findings. *Eur J Cancer Prev*, **4** (Suppl 1), 3–107.

Harrington J M, McBride D I, Sorahan T, *et al* (1997). Occupational exposure to magnetic fields in relation to mortality from brain cancer among electricity generation and transmission workers. *Occup Environ Med*, **54**, 7–13.

Johansen C and Olsen J H (1998). Risk of cancer among Danish utility workers – a nationwide cohort study. *Am J Epidemiol*, **147**, 548–55.

Kelsh M A and Sahl J D (1997). Mortality among a cohort of electric utility workers 1960–91. *Am J Indust Med*, **31**, 534–44.

Kheifets L I, Afifi A A, Buffler P A, *et al* (1995). Occupational electric and magnetic field exposure and brain cancer: a meta-analysis. *J Occup Environ Med*, **37**, 1327–41.

Kheifets L I, London S J and Peters J M (1997a). Leukaemia risk and occupational electric field exposure in Los Angeles County, California. *Am J Epidemiol*, **146**, 87–90.

Kheifets L I, Afifi A A, Buffler P A, *et al* (1997b). Occupational electric and magnetic field exposure and leukaemia. A meta-analysis. *J Occup Environ Med*, **39**, 1074–90.

Kheifets L I, Gilbert E S, Sussman S S, *et al* (1999). Comparative analysis of the studies of magnetic fields and cancer in electric utility workers: studies from France, Canada and the United States. *Occup Environ Med*, **56**, 567–74.

Kliukiene J, Tynes T, Martinsen J I, *et al* (1999). Incidence of breast cancer in a Norwegian cohort of women with potential workplace exposure to 50 Hz magnetic fields. *Am J Indust Med*, **36**, 147–54.

London S J, Bowman J D, Sobel E, *et al* (1994). Exposure to magnetic fields among electrical workers in relation to leukaemia risk in Los Angeles County. *Am J Indust Med*, **26**, 47–60.

Loomis D P, Savitz D A and Ananth C V (1994). Breast cancer mortality among female electrical workers in the United States. *JNCI*, **86**, 921–5.

Loomis D, Browning S R, Schenck A P, *et al* (1997). Cancer mortality among electric utility workers exposed to polychlorinated biphenyls. *Occup Environ Med*, **54**, 720–28.

Matanoski G M, Elliott E A, Breysse P N, *et al* (1993). Leukaemia in telephone linesmen. *Am J Epidemiol*, **137**, 609–19.

Milham S (1997). Occupational mortality in Washington State, 1950–89. Washington DC, NIOSH, US Department of Health and Human Service.

Miller A B, To T, Agnew D A, *et al* (1996). Leukaemia following occupational exposure to 60-Hz electric and magnetic fields among Ontario electric utility workers. *Am J Epidemiol*, **144**, 150–60.

NRPB (1992). Electromagnetic fields and the risk of cancer. Report of an Advisory Group on Non-ionising Radiation. *Doc NRPB*, **3**(1), 1–138.

NRPB (1993). Electromagnetic fields and the risk of cancer. Summary of the views of the Advisory Group on Non-ionising Radiation on epidemiological studies published since the 1992 report. *Doc NRPB*, **4**(5), 65–9.

NRPB (1994). Electromagnetic fields and the risk of cancer. Supplementary Report by the Advisory Group on Non-ionising Radiation of 12 April 1994. *Doc NRPB*, **5**(2), 78–81.

OPCS (1995). Occupational Health. Decennial Supplement (F Drever, Ed). London, HMSO, Series DS No 10.

Pfluger D H and Minder C E (1996). Effects of exposure to 16.7 Hz magnetic fields on urinary 6-hydroxymelatonin excretion of Sevis railway workers. *J Pineal Res*, **21**, 91–100.

Rodvall Y, Ahlbom A, Stenlund C, *et al* (1998). Occupational exposure to magnetic fields and brain tumours in Central Sweden. *Eur J Epidemiol*, **14**, 563–9.

Rosenbaum P F, Vena J E, Zielezny M A, *et al* (1994). Occupational exposure associated with male breast cancer. *Am J Epidemiol*, **139**, 30–36.

Ryan P, Lee M W, North J B, *et al* (1992). Risk factors for tumours of the brain and meninges: results from the Adelaide Adult Brain Tumour Study. *Int J Cancer*, **51**, 20–27.

Sahl J D, Kelsh M A and Greenland S (1993). Cohort and nest case-control studies of hematopoeitic cancer and brain cancer among electric utility workers. *Epidemiology*, **4**, 104–14.

Savitz D A and Loomis D P (1995). Magnetic field exposure in relation to leukaemia and brain cancer mortality among electric utility workers. *Am J Epidemiol*, **141**, 123–34.

Savitz D A, Pearce N and Poole C (1993). Update on methodological issues in the epidemiology of electromagnetic fields and cancer. *Epidemiol Rev*, **15**, 558–66.

Savitz D A, Dufort V, Armstrong B, *et al* (1997). Lung cancer in relation to employment in the electrical industry and exposure to magnetic fields. *Occup Environ Med*, **54**, 396–402.

Schroeder J C and Savitz D A (1997). Lymphoma and multiple myeloma mortality in relation to magnetic field exposure among electric utility workers. *Am J Indust Med*, **32**, 392–402.

Stenlund C and Floderus B (1997). Occupational exposure to magnetic fields in relation to male breast cancer and testicular cancer: a Swedish case control study. *Cancer Causes Control*, **8**, 184–91.

Thériault G, Goldberg M, Miller A B, *et al* (1994). Cancer risks associated with occupational exposure to magnetic fields among electric utility workers in Ontario and Quebec, Canada and France: 1970–89. *Am J Epidemiol*, **139**, 550–72.

Törnqvist S, Knave B, Ahlbom A, *et al* (1991). Incidence of leukaemia and brain tumors in some 'electrical occupations'. *Br J Ind Med*, **48**, 597–603.

Tynes T, Andersen A and Langmark F (1992). Incidence of cancer in Norwegian workers potentially exposed to electromagnetic fields. *Am J Epidemiol*, **136**, 81–8.

Tynes T, Reitan J B and Andersen A (1994a). Incidence of cancer among workers in Norwegian hydro electric power companies. *Scand J Work Environ Health*, **20**, 339–44.

Tynes T, Jynge H and Vistnes A I (1994b). Leukaemia and brain tumours in Norwegian railway workers, a nested case control study. *Am J Epidemiol*, **139**, 645–53.

Tynes T, Hanevik M, Anderson A, *et al* (1996). Incidence of breast cancer in Norwegian female radio and telegraph operators. *Cancer Causes Control*, **7**, 197–204.

Villeneuve P J, Agnew D A, Miller A B, *et al* (2000). Leukaemia in electric utility workers: the evaluation of alternative indices of exposure to 60 Hz electric and magnetic fields. *Am J Indust Med*, **37**, 607–17.

7 Conclusions

1 The Advisory Group provides in this report a comprehensive review of experimental and epidemiological studies relevant to an assessment of the possible risk of cancer resulting from exposures to power frequency (extremely low frequency, ELF) electromagnetic fields (EMFs) that have been published since its first report in 1992. It is not concerned with exposures to high frequencies nor with other potential effects of exposure to power frequencies. The possibility of an association between neurological diseases, such as Alzheimer's disease, and magnetic field exposure is being considered separately. The report summarises the extent of exposure to power frequency electromagnetic fields at home and at work and reviews recent epidemiological investigations of cancer incidence in humans. It also reviews recently published cellular, animal and human volunteer studies.

EXPOSURE ASSESSMENT

2 Studies reviewed in the earlier report by the Advisory Group suffered from a lack of measurement-based exposure assessments. Since then, considerable advances have been made in methods for assessing exposure, both in the case of experimental studies and in epidemiological investigations. Instrumentation allowing personal exposure to be measured has become widely available and has been used in many of the more recently published studies. This has provided a substantially improved basis for many of the epidemiological studies reviewed by the Group.

CELLULAR STUDIES

3 At the cellular level, there is no clear evidence that exposure to power frequency electromagnetic fields at levels that are likely to be encountered can affect biological processes. Studies are often contradictory and there is a lack of confirmation of positive results from different laboratories using the same experimental conditions. There is no convincing evidence that exposure to such fields is directly genotoxic nor that it can bring about the transformation of cells in culture and it is therefore unlikely to initiate carcinogenesis.

4 The most suggestive evidence of an effect of exposure to power frequency magnetic fields on biological systems comes from three different areas:

(a) possible enhancement of genetic change caused by known genotoxic agents,
(b) effects on intracellular signalling, especially calcium flux,
(c) effects on specific gene expression.

5 Those results that are claimed to demonstrate a positive effect of exposure to power frequency magnetic fields tend to show only small changes, the biological consequences of which are not clear.

6 Many of the positive effects reported involve exposure to time-averaged fields greater than 100 μT which are unlikely to be encountered in a domestic situation where typical exposures generally fall in the range between 10 and 200 nT. It is usual to test carcinogens at levels well above those normally encountered in order to demonstrate their potential to have an effect, on the assumption of a linear dose–response relationship without threshold. However, such an assumption may not be justified with non-genotoxic agents and risk assessment is most usefully focused on realistic exposure levels. Furthermore, the induced current density may be radically different *in vivo* as compared with that for cells in culture.

ANIMAL AND VOLUNTEER STUDIES

7 Overall, no convincing evidence was seen from a review of a large number of animal studies to support the hypothesis that exposure to power frequency electromagnetic fields increases the risk of cancer.

8 Rodents, particularly mice, have been used extensively in studies of adult leukaemogenesis; there is, however, currently no natural animal model of the most common form of childhood leukaemia, acute lymphoblastic leukaemia. Most studies report a lack of effect of power frequency magnetic fields on leukaemia or lymphoma in rodents, mostly mice. These include several recent large-scale studies of spontaneous tumour incidence in normal and transgenic mice, and of radiation-induced lymphoma and leukaemia in mice. The transgenic mice used in two of the studies mentioned above develop a disease with some similarities to childhood acute lymphoblastic leukaemia. Further studies found no effect on the progression of transplanted leukaemia cells in mice or rats.

9 Rat mammary carcinomas represent a standard laboratory animal model in the study of human breast cancer. Three recent large-scale studies of rats found that lifetime magnetic field exposure had no effect on the incidence of spontaneous mammary tumours. The evidence concerning electromagnetic field effects on chemically induced mammary tumours is more equivocal. Two early studies suggested that exposure to power frequency magnetic fields increased the incidence or growth of chemically induced mammary tumours in female rats but two more recent studies have not corroborated these findings.

10 Whilst there is no natural animal model of spontaneous brain tumour, a recent large-scale study reported a lack of effect of exposure to power frequency magnetic fields on chemically induced nervous system tumours in female rats. In addition, the low incidence of brain cancers in three recent large-scale rat studies was not elevated by magnetic field exposure. With regard to studies of other tumours, particularly chemically induced skin tumours, the evidence is almost uniformly negative.

11 The possibility that the hormone melatonin acts as a natural tumour suppressor is controversial. Nevertheless, a number of studies have investigated the ability of power frequency electromagnetic fields to alter endogenous circadian melatonin rhythms. Most evidence from human volunteer studies suggests that melatonin rhythms are not delayed or suppressed by exposure to power frequency magnetic fields, although one

recent study provided preliminary data indicating that exposure prior to the night-time rise in serum melatonin may have had this effect in a sensitive subgroup of the study population. In addition, the evidence for an effect of exposure to power frequency magnetic fields on melatonin levels and on melatonin-dependent reproductive status in seasonally breeding animals is largely negative. The evidence concerning power frequency electromagnetic field induced suppression of rat pineal and/or serum melatonin levels is equivocal and the physiological relevance of any effect (if any is produced) remains unclear.

12 There is no consistent evidence of any inhibitory effect of power frequency magnetic field exposure on those aspects of immune system function relevant to tumour suppression that have been examined. In addition, two studies were unable to correlate possible electromagnetic field induced changes in tumour incidence with significant changes in immune function.

RESIDENTIAL EXPOSURE

13 Recent large and well-conducted studies have provided better evidence than was available in the past on the relationship between power frequency magnetic field exposure and the risk of cancer. Taken in conjunction they suggest that relatively heavy average exposures of 0.4 μT or more are associated with a doubling of the risk of leukaemia in children under 15 years of age. The evidence is, however, not conclusive. In those studies in which measurements were made, the extent to which the more heavily exposed children were representative is in doubt, while in those in Nordic countries in which representativeness is assured, the fields were estimated and the results based on such small numbers that the findings could have been due to chance. In the UK, very few children (perhaps 4 in 1000) are exposed to 0.4 μT or more and a study in the UK, with much the largest number of direct measurements of exposure, found no evidence of risk at lower levels. Nevertheless, the possibility remains that high and prolonged time-weighted average exposure to power frequency magnetic fields can increase the risk of leukaemia in children. Data on brain tumours come from some of the studies also investigating leukaemia and from others concerned exclusively with these tumours. They provide no comparable evidence of an association. There have been many fewer studies in adults. There is no reason to believe that residential exposure to electromagnetic fields is involved in the development of leukaemia or brain tumours in adults.

OCCUPATIONAL EXPOSURE

14 Study of populations exposed occupationally to electromagnetic fields can include groups exposed generally at much higher levels than members of the public. They may therefore have a greater potential to detect any adverse health effects. Although recently published studies of occupational exposure to electromagnetic fields and the risk of cancer are, in the main, methodologically sound, and some of them have considerable statistical power, causal relationships between such exposure and an increase in tumour incidence at any site are not established. The excesses, where they exist, are generally modest and are largely restricted to the two cancers that were noted in the 1992 report of the Advisory Group – that is, leukaemia and cancer of the brain. Conflicting evidence exists for the particular cell types of leukaemia associated with the greatest risk but acute myeloid leukaemia is the most cited. The evidence of any risk for brain cancer is conflicting, even that from the most powerful of the studies.

GENERAL CONCLUSION

15 Laboratory experiments have provided no good evidence that extremely low frequency electromagnetic fields are capable of producing cancer, nor do human epidemiological studies suggest that they cause cancer in general. There is, however, some epidemiological evidence that prolonged exposure to higher levels of power frequency magnetic fields is associated with a small risk of leukaemia in children. In practice, such levels of exposure are seldom encountered by the general public in the UK. In the absence of clear evidence of a carcinogenic effect in adults, or of a plausible explanation from experiments on animals or isolated cells, the epidemiological evidence is currently not strong enough to justify a firm conclusion that such fields cause leukaemia in children. Unless, however, further research indicates that the finding is due to chance or some currently unrecognised artefact, the possibility remains that intense and prolonged exposures to magnetic fields can increase the risk of leukaemia in children.

8 Recommendations for Research

1 The Advisory Group recognises that the scientific evidence suggesting that exposure to power frequency electromagnetic fields poses an increased risk of cancer is very weak. Virtually all of the cellular, animal and human laboratory evidence provides no support for an increased risk of cancer incidence following such exposure to power frequencies, although sporadic positive findings have been reported. In addition, the epidemiological evidence is, at best, weak. Nevertheless, considering the ubiquitous nature of power frequency electromagnetic field exposure and the concern about possible adverse health effects, the Advisory Group considers that the following areas of research merit further investigation.

EXPERIMENTAL STUDIES

2 Further biophysical studies might suggest conditions of exposure more liable to affect carcinogenic processes. Particular attention should be given to weak magnetic field effects on biochemical processes involving radical pair intermediates. Consideration should also be given to the possibility that exposure parameters such as the higher frequencies associated with switching transients might be more biologically relevant than experimental data based only on the time-weighted average exposure. Additional dosimetric studies are required using improved tissue conductivity data in order to quantify more accurately the magnitude and distribution of induced current in the body. Consideration needs also to be given to the possible effects that might result from the dispersal of corona ions and the way any such effect might be assessed.

3 At the cellular level, further studies should be carried out of possible enhancement of genetic change caused by known genotoxic agents, effects on intracellular signalling and effects on specific gene expression. These studies should focus, where possible or appropriate, on the replication of studies that have previously suggested positive results.

4 For animal carcinogenesis studies, future work should be based on carefully designed, hypothesis-driven investigations. Such hypotheses may be derived from consideration of mechanistic investigations at the cellular level and epidemiological investigations. With regard to the epidemiological observations concerning possible increased risks of childhood acute lymphoblastic leukaemia, the absence of a natural animal model has imposed significant restrictions on experimentation. However, there are various transgenic mouse models of leukaemia which develop a disease having some similarities to childhood acute lymphoblastic leukaemia which may prove useful in future studies. It would in addition be valuable to study possible power frequency effects on the cellular structure and development of the prenatal and neonatal haemopoietic system and any implications for cellular differentiation and clonal growth. There is no strong epidemiological or experimental evidence concerning increased risks of brain or mammary tumours and therefore there is less imperative for further study. However, a recently developed model of spontaneous medulloblastoma in *Ptch*-knockout mice and, more particularly, a mouse model of astrocytomas, a leading

cause of brain cancer in humans, may prove useful in the investigation of electromagnetic field effects on spontaneous brain tumour incidence. In addition, further investigation should resolve present uncertainties concerning possible electromagnetic field effects on chemically induced mammary tumours.

5 With regard to possible effects on circulating melatonin levels, there is further scope for longer term volunteer studies in the laboratory and volunteer or observational studies in the workplace. However, careful consideration must be given to individual variability in melatonin fluctuation in addition to differences in lifestyle, night-time light exposure and other possible confounding factors.

6 Whilst the evidence concerning possible electromagnetic field effects on the immune system is mostly negative, the effects on tumour rejection *per se* have not been investigated and further study should be carried out using classical tumour rejection models.

EPIDEMIOLOGICAL STUDIES

Residential studies

7 Residential studies published to date have mostly been difficult to interpret because of the potential for the control data to be biased. Further work is required to investigate the extent to which the methods of control selection that have been used could have affected the frequency with which relatively high exposures were recorded.

8 Nothing would seem to be gained by further study of more cases of childhood leukaemia in relation to exposure to extremely low frequency electromagnetic fields in the UK, as the number likely to have been exposed to fields of the strength that may cause a material increase in risk (namely fields of 0.4 μT or more) is too small to provide any useful information. There are, however, parts of the European Union, notably Denmark and Sweden, where such exposures are more common and, moreover, where unbiased evidence can be obtained through the use of national registers. It is, therefore, to be hoped that the European Union will fund an extension of the studies that have been reported from the Nordic countries, which alone might provide clear evidence of the existence of a risk (if one does in fact exist). If parts of the world can be identified where yet greater exposures to children occur frequently, and where good quality epidemiological studies are practical, then study of leukaemia risk in relation to electromagnetic field exposures in those places would be valuable.

9 If relatively high residential magnetic fields do not produce a risk directly, it is possible that they might do so in association with some specific (or near specific) alteration in the cell's DNA. It might therefore be helpful to compare the characteristics of the DNA in cases of acute lymphoblastic leukaemia that occurred after exposure to such fields with the DNA in the general run of the disease. Because there would be so few relevant cases in the UK, the research would be worthwhile only with international collaboration.

Occupational studies

10 Although occupational studies based on job title suggest a consistent link to excess risks of leukaemia and possible brain tumours, occupational cohort studies have not

confirmed this association and are at best equivocal. The more recent cohort studies using better exposure characterisation for magnetic and electric fields either have not shown an association with leukaemia or brain cancer, or the association has been weak. Better quality exposure assessment is needed, preferably with detailed personal records of exposure in large well-characterised cohorts. In addition to cumulative exposure assessments, consideration should be given to the use of metrics such as rate of change of exposure, exposure peaks, duration of exposure above predefined exposure levels and rapid changes in exposure (transients). The paucity of good quality exposure data hampers progress and research within industry is required to correct this deficiency, define the most heavily exposed groups and quantify their exposure. In future cohort studies of exposed workers, note should be taken of the individual's residential history and, when residence had been near a high power transmission line, measurements of exposure at home should also be included.

Appendix

INCIDENCE OF NEOPLASIA IN LIFE-TIME ANIMAL STUDIES

TABLE A1 Tumour incidence in male and female Fischer (F344) rats exposed to 50 Hz magnetic fields for two years (Yasui et al, 1997)

	Exposure conditions					
	Male			Female		
	Sham	500 μT	5 mT	Sham	500 μT	5 mT
Number of animals						
Per group	48	48	48	48	48	48
With primary neoplasia	48	48	48	37	38	42
With benign neoplasia	48	48	47	33	36	33
With malignant neoplasia	16	14	11	14	14	14
Tumour incidence						
Mammary gland fibroadenoma	3	3	6	8	6	6
Mammary gland adenoma	2	0	1	2	4	2
Mammary gland adenocarcinoma	0	0	0	0	2	0
Mononuclear cell leukaemia	5	4	4	8	6	7
Malignant lymphoma	0	0	0	0	1	1
Testes interstitial cell tumour	47	48	47	-	-	-
Endometrial stromal polyp	-	-	-	8	10	11
Preputial/clitoral gland adenoma	4	3	6	7	5	5
Preputial/clitoral adenocarcinoma	1	2	1	1	1	0
Pituitary gland adenoma	6	5	5	18	15	10
Thyroid C-cell adenoma	7	10	5	4	5	4
Adrenal pheochromocytoma	2	5	7	2	3	2
Pancreas islet cell adenoma	0	2	4	1	0	0
Mesothelioma (abdominal cavity)	6	1	3	0	0	0
Subcutaneous tissue fibroma	2	5	9*	0	0	1

* $p < 0.05$ (Fisher's exact method).

Note These data are for tumours where the average incidence is more than one per group; for mammary gland adenocarcinoma and malignant lymphoma.

TABLE A2 Tumour incidence in female Fischer (F344) rats exposed to 60 Hz magnetic fields for two years (Mandeville et al. 1997)

	Exposure conditions					
	Cage control	Sham	2 μT	20 μT	200 μT	2000 μT
Number of animals						
Per group	50	50	50	50	50	50
With primary neoplasms	45	46	42	43	43	41
With benign neoplasms	40	44	39	40	43	37
With malignant neoplasia	12	10	9	13	7	12
Tumour incidence						
Mammary gland fibroadenoma	14	24	22	19	19	17
Mammary gland adenocarcinoma	1	2	3	2	1	3
Mononuclear cell leukaemia	8	5	4	9	3	5
Endometrial uterine polyp	6	6	4	7	6	2
Clitoral gland adenoma	3	4	4	3	10	6
Clitoral gland carcinoma	0	4	2	3	1	0
Pituitary gland adenoma	31	29	20	20	21	22
Thyroid C-cell adenoma	5	4	4	1	2	3
Adrenal gland pheochromocytoma	0	3	2	0	0	0
Pancreas islet cell adenoma	1	1	1	0	4	2
Subcutaneous tissue lipoma	0	1	0	0	2	0
Subcutaneous tissue fibrosarcoma	0	0	1	1	0	1
Lung adenoma	2	1	0	0	1	0

Note The types of neoplasms that occurred only once in the study were not listed.

TABLE A3 Tumour incidence in male Fischer (F344) rats exposed to 60 Hz magnetic fields for two years (NTP, 1999a)

	Exposure conditions				
	Sham	2 μT	200 μT	1 mT (cont)	1 mT (intermitt)
Number of animals					
Per group	100	100	100	100	100
With primary neoplasms	100	98	98	100	98
With benign neoplasms	99	97	97	98	94
With malignant neoplasia	65	59	61	65	58
Tumour incidence (%) (survival-adjusted neoplasm rate)					
Mammary gland fibroadenoma	7	7.4	13.1	11	9.5
Mammary gland fibroadenoma or carcinoma	7	8.6	13.1	11	9.5
Mononuclear cell leukaemia	53.1	50	52	56.2	39.7*
Testes adenoma	95.1	94.8	94.4	95.8	93.8
Preputial gland adenoma	15	10.8	11.6	15.8	11.8
Preputial gland carcinoma	0	0	5.9*	0	2.4
Pituitary gland adenoma	38.8	42.9	33.5	40.4	46
Pituitary gland adenoma or carcinoma	38.8	44	35.8	40.4	49.2
Thyroid C-cell adenoma	17.2	30.0*	30.5*	27.4	21.5
Thyroid C-cell carcinoma	1.2	8.5*	4.8	2.5	5.9
Adrenal medulla benign pheochromocytoma	27.8	28.3	24.5	27.8	39.9
Adrenal medulla benign or malignant pheochromocytoma	30.1	29.6	24.5	27.8	42.2
Pancreas islet adenoma	3.5	3.7	7.2	3.7	2.4
Pancreas islet adenoma or carcinoma	4.7	6.2	7.2	5	5.9
Subcutaneous tissue: fibroma	13.9	9.8	10.6	15.9	14.2
Subcutaneous tissue: fibroma, fibrosarcoma, sarcoma	15	12.1	13	19.2	16.5
Keratoacanthoma, squamous cell papilloma or carcinoma	12.7	8.6	14.2	16	11.7
Malignant mesothelioma	4.6	7.2	5.9	7.2	4.7
Lung (alveolar/bronchiolar) adenoma	3.5	6.1	6	4.9	0
Lung (alveolar/bronchiolar) adenoma or carcinoma	3.5	8.6	6	6.2	0
All organs: benign neoplasms	99.8	99.4	99.4	99.5	96.7
All organs: malignant neoplasms	68.1	64.7	65	69.4	60.7
All organs: benign and malignant neoplasms	100	99.7	99.7	100	98.9

*$p < 0.05$; poly-k test.

Note The types of neoplasms that occurred with an incidence of less than 5% in any group were not listed.

TABLE A4 Tumour incidence in female Fischer (F344) rats exposed to 60 Hz magnetic fields for two years (NTP, 1999a)

	Exposure conditions				
	Sham	2 μT	200 μT	1 mT (cont)	1 mT (intermitt)
Number of animals					
Per group	100	100	100	100	100
With primary neoplasms	98	97	95	91	94
With benign neoplasms	92	94	87	85	86
With malignant neoplasia	40	41	38	39	40
Tumour incidence (%) (survival-adjusted neoplasm rate)					
Mammary gland fibroadenoma	62.5	67	59.8	71.8	57.8
Mammary gland carcinoma	2.3	7.8	5.7	2.4	2.4
Mammary gland fibroadenoma, adenoma or carcinoma	64.7	71.7	60.6	72.9	60.8
Mononuclear cell leukaemia	22.7	19.6	26.4	28.8	25.5
Uterus stromal polyp	15.1	12.2	14.6	14.9	14.2
Uterus stromal polyp or sarcoma	15.1	13.3	14.6	14.9	14.2
Clitoral gland adenoma	14.1	17.5	13	19.5	13.5
Pituitary gland adenoma	65.8	62.5	73.4	58.4	68.1
Pituitary gland adenoma or carcinoma	68.8	63.5	77.4	60.6	70.1
Thyroid C-cell adenoma	17.3	22	21.4	23.5	19
Thyroid C-cell carcinoma	5.9	3.4	3.4	3.5	7.1
Adrenal cortex adenoma	7	2.2	3.4	1.2	0*
Adrenal medulla benign pheochromocytoma	8.5	9.5	4.8	2.4	3.7
Adrenal medulla benign or malignant pheochromocytoma	8.5	10.6	6	2.4	6.1
Subcutaneous tissue: fibroma	4.7	5.6	4.6	0	1.2
Subcutaneous tissue: fibroma, fibrosarcoma, sarcoma	6.9	5.6	4.6	2.4	2.4
Lung (alveolar/bronchiolar) adenoma	3.5	5.5	5.7	1.2	0
Lung (alveolar/bronchiolar) adenoma or carcinoma	4.7	5.5	5.7	2.4	0
All organs: benign neoplasms	95.6	96.2	90.8	91.6	91.3
All organs: malignant neoplasms	43.4	43.4	41.3	44.1	44.7
All organs: benign and malignant neoplasms	99.1	97.6	97.6	96.9	96.5

*$p < 0.05$; poly-k test.

Note The types of neoplasms that occurred with an incidence of less than 5% in any group were not listed.

TABLE A5 Tumour incidence in male B6C3F1 mice exposed to 60 Hz magnetic fields for two years (NTP, 1999a)

	Exposure conditions				
	Sham	2 μT	200 μT	1 mT (cont)	1 mT (intermitt)
Number of animals					
Per group	100	100	100	100	100
With primary neoplasms	71	81	72	74	76
With benign neoplasms	54	50	54	47	52
With malignant neoplasia	40	49	45	49	48
Tumour incidence (%) (survival-adjusted neoplasm rate)					
Malignant lymphoma	8.6	7.8	4.3	8	6.6
Haemangiosarcoma	6.4	11	6.4	9.2	5.5
Liver hepatocellular adenoma	32.3	28.9	34	24.4	35.3
Liver hepatocellular carcinoma	19.8	15.3	21.2	17.1	24.4
Liver hepatoblastoma	2.2	2.3	1.1	4.7	5.5
Harderian gland adenoma	13	17.8	16.9	13.9	12
Harderian gland adenoma or carcinoma	13	19.9	16.9	13.9	15.3
Adrenal cortex adenoma	3.3	0	1.1	6.1	0
Lung (alveolar/bronchiolar) adenoma	28	12.5*	9.6*	18	17.9
Lung (alveolar/bronchiolar) carcinoma	8.6	12.4	12.8	11.5	11.2
All organs: benign neoplasms	57.7	54.8	56.5	51.3	55.9
All organs: malignant neoplasms	41.3	50.3	46.1	51.4	49.7
All organs: benign and malignant neoplasms	73	82.2	73.3	76.5	77.9

*$p < 0.05$; poly-k test.

Note The types of neoplasms that occurred with an incidence of less than 5% in any group were not listed.

TABLE A6 Tumour incidence in female B6C3F1 mice exposed to 60 Hz magnetic fields for two years (NTP, 1999a)

	Exposure conditions				
	Sham	2 μT	200 μT	1 mT (cont)	1 mT (intermitt)
Number of animals					
Per group	100	100	100	100	100
With primary neoplasms	78	80	72	71	68
With benign neoplasms	52	49	54	49	44
With malignant neoplasia	55	58	38	38	44
Tumour incidence (%) (survival-adjusted neoplasm rate)					
Malignant lymphoma	34.7	33.5	24	28.3	21.7*
Haemangiosarcoma	2.2	3.3	1.1	5.5	3.3
Histocytic sarcoma	2.2	2.2	2.2	0	6.5
Liver hepatocellular adenoma	19	11.3	22	20.1	14.3
Liver hepatocellular carcinoma	6.7	5.6	7.7	6.6	6.6
Harderian gland adenoma	11	8.8	15.3	13.4	14.4
Harderian gland adenoma or carcinoma	13.2	8.8	15.3	13.4	14.4
Pituitary gland adenoma	21.9	20.1	24.1	25.8	18.7
Pancreas islet adenoma	2.4	0	8	2.3	3.5
Subcutaneous tissue: sarcoma	4.4	5.4	2.2	3.3	4.4
Subcutaneous tissue: fibrosarcoma or sarcoma	4.4	5.4	2.2	3.3	5.4
Lung (alveolar/bronchiolar) adenoma	10.2	6.6	0*	5.6	6.6
Lung (alveolar/bronchiolar) carcinoma	2.3	6.6	2.2	2.2	1.1
All organs: benign neoplasms	56.2	52.2	58.6	54.1	48
All organs: malignant neoplasms	57.6	59.6	41.1*	42.5*	69.7
All organs: benign and malignant neoplasms	81	81.2	75.8	74.9	69.7*

*$p < 0.05$; poly-k test.

Note The types of neoplasms that occurred with an incidence of less than 5% in any group were not listed.

TABLE A7 Magnetic field effects on gamma radiation induced haemopoietic neoplasm incidence in female C57BL/6 mice (Babbitt et al, 2000)

		Haemopoietic neoplasm number and frequency (%)							
Treatment group	Number of mice per group	Lymphoblastic lymphoma	Lymphocytic lymphoma	Combined FCC, IB and PC lymphomas*	Unidentified lymphomas	Combined lymphomas	Granulocytic leukaemias	Histiocytic sarcomas	Combined haemopoietic neoplasms
Mice exposed to ambient magnetic fields									
0 mT/0 Gy	190	1 (0.5)	2 (1.0)	57 (30.0)	6 (3.2)	66 (34.7)	0 (0.0)	42 (22.1)	107 (56.3)
0 mT/3.0 Gy	190	7 (3.7)	5 (2.6)	59 (31.0)	6 (3.2)	77 (40.5)	3 (1.6)	36 (18.9)	115 (60.5)
0 mT/4.0 Gy	190	9 (4.7)	7 (3.7)	54 (28.4)	2 (1.0)	72 (37.9)	0 (0.0)	36 (18.9)	105 (55.2)
0 mT/5.1 Gy	190	55 (28.9)	4 (2.1)	38 (20.0)	3 (1.6)	100 (52.6)	1 (0.5)	28 (14.7)	129 (67.9)
Mice exposed to a 1.4 mT, 60 Hz magnetic field									
1.4 mT/0 Gy	380	1 (0.3)	7 (1.8)	119 (31.3)	13 (3.4)	140 (36.8)	2 (0.5)	90 (23.7)	225 (59.2)
1.4 mT/3.0 Gy	380	7 (1.8)	11 (2.9)	101 (26.6)	11 (2.9)	130 (34.2)	0 (0.0)	74 (19.5)	202 (53.2)
1.4 mT/4.0 Gy	380	24 (6.3)	12 (3.2)	108 (28.4)	12 (3.1)	156 (41.0)	0 (0.0)	73 (19.2)	228 (60.0)
1.4 mT/ 5.1 Gy	380	80 (21.0) †	8 (2.1)	77 (20.3)	12 (3.2)	177 (46.6)	1 (0.3)	52 (13.7)	227 (59.7)

* Folicular centre cell (FCC), immunoblastic (IB), and plasma cell (PC) lymphomas.
† Significantly reduced compared to the 0 mT/5.1 Gy group.

TABLE A8 Magnetic field effects on DMBA-induced mammary tumours in Sprague-Dawley rats (NTP, 1999b)

Study	Exposure conditions										
	13 weeks; 20 mg DMBA				26 weeks; 10 mg DMBA				13 weeks; 8 mg DMBA		
	Sham	100 μT; 50 Hz	500 μT; 50 Hz	100 μT; 60 Hz	Sham	100 μT; 50 Hz	500 μT; 50 Hz	100 μT; 60 Hz	Sham	100 μT; 50 Hz	500 μT; 50 Hz
Number of animals											
Per group	100	100	100	100	100	100	100	100	100	100	100
Tumour incidence (%) (survival-adjusted neoplasm rate)											
Mammary fibroadenoma	–	–	–	–	75	80.3	76	69.7	–	–	–
Mammary fibroadenoma or adenoma	5.1	3.2	1	2	75.6	80.3	76	69.7	–	–	–
Mammary carcinoma	92.7	88.6	96.7	96	96.8	90.8	95.9	86.6*	43	48	38
Mammary adenoma or carcinoma	93.7	88.6	96.7	96	96.8	90.8	95.9	86.6*	43	48	38
Mammary fibroadenoma, adenoma or carcinoma	93.7	88.6	96.7	96	97.8	98.9	97.9	92.7	–	–	–

*$p < 0.05$; poly-k test.

Glossary

EPIDEMIOLOGICAL TERMS

Bias any process at any stage of inference which tends to produce results or conclusions that differ systematically from the truth.

Case-control study an investigation into the extent to which a group of persons with a specific disease (the cases) and comparable persons who do not have the disease (the controls) differ with respect to exposure to putative risk factors.

Chi-square (χ^2) statistic a statistic to test for any association between disease risk and a measure of exposure. For a case-control study, this is based on the classification of cases and controls by level of exposure. To test for any association, the statistic should be compared with the χ^2 distribution on the appropriate number of degrees of freedom.

Cohort study an investigation involving the identification of a group of individuals (the cohort) about whom certain exposure information is collected, and the ascertainment of occurrence of diseases at later times. For each individual, information on prior exposure can be related to subsequent disease experience.

Confidence interval (CI) an interval calculated from data when making inferences about an unknown parameter. In hypothetical repetitions of the study, the interval will include the parameter in question on a specified percentage of occasions (eg 90% for a 90% confidence interval).

Confounder a factor that is correlated with the exposure of interest and, independently, is related to the disease under investigation.

Degrees of freedom (df) the number of independent comparisons that can be made between the members of a sample. This important concept in statistical testing cannot be defined briefly. It refers to the number of independent contributions to a sampling distribution (such as χ^2, t and F distributions). In a contingency table it is one less than the number of row categories multiplied by one less than the number of column categories.

Discordant pair a pairing of a diseased case and a matched control for which the case and the control differ in their exposure to a given factor.

Matched odds ratio the odds ratio *(see below)* calculated on the basis of the comparison of cases and controls that are matched with respect to potential confounding factors.

Odds ratio the ratio of the odds of disease occurrence in a group with exposure to a factor to that in an unexposed group: within each group, the odds are the ratio of the numbers of diseased and non-diseased individuals.

One-sided test a test for a difference in only one direction (eg a test for an increased - but not a decreased - risk in an exposed group relative to a comparison group).

Probability value the probability that a test statistic would be as extreme as or more extreme than observed if the null hypothesis were true. The letter p, followed by the abbreviation ns (not significant) or by the symbol < (less than) and a decimal notation such as 0.01, 0.05, is a statement of the probability that the difference observed could have occurred by chance under the null hypothesis.

Proportional mortality ratio (PMR) the ratio of the fraction of deaths due to a particular cause in a cohort to the corresponding fraction in a general population, adjusted with respect to age (and sex if relevant) on the basis of the distribution of deaths from all causes in the cohort. PMR is often expressed as a percentage, ie a PMR of 100 indicates that proportionate mortality is the same in the cohort and the general population.

Proportional registration ratio (PRR) analogous to the proportional mortality ratio (PMR) but based on cancer registrations rather than deaths.

Relative risk the ratio of the disease rate in the group under study to that in a comparison group, with adjustment for confounding factors such as age, if necessary. For rare diseases, the relative risk is similar to the odds ratio *(see above)*.

Significance level the probability of obtaining a result at least as extreme as that observed in the absence of a raised risk. A result that would arise less than one in twenty times in the absence of an underlying effect is often referred to as being 'statistically significant'.

Standardised incidence ratio (SIR) the ratio (x 100) of the number of incident cancers in a group to the number expected in the general population with the same mixture of ages and sexes and interval of follow-up. Therefore an SIR of 100 signifies no raised risk, an SIR of more than 100 signifies a raised risk.

Standardised mortality ratio (SMR) the ratio of the observed number of deaths from a given cause in a cohort to that expected on the basis of both mortality rates for a general population and the age (and, if relevant, sex) distribution of person-years for the cohort. It is often expressed as a percentage, ie an SMR of 100 indicates that the age-adjusted mortality rate is the same in the cohort and the general population.

Statistical power the probability that, with a specified degree of confidence, an under-lying effect of a given magnitude will be detected in a study.

Synergism combined effect of two or more interacting agents that is greater than the addition of the single agent effects with known dose–effect relationships.

TERMS ASSOCIATED WITH ELECTROMAGNETIC FIELDS

Dielectric a class of materials that act as electric insulators.

Dosimetry measurement of the absorbed dose or dose rate by an object in a radiofrequency field.

Electric field strength (E) the force on a stationary unit positive charge at a point in an electric field. The magnitude of the electric field vector (unit $V\ m^{-1}$).

Harmonics multiples of the fundamental frequency used for a particular source, eg 50 Hz harmonics are 100 Hz, 150 Hz, 200 Hz, etc.

Helmholtz coils arrangement of two current carrying coils to produce a uniform magnetic field distribution between the coils.

Hertz (Hz) one cycle per second.

Impedance (of free space) the ratio of electric to magnetic field strength of an electromagnetic wave. In free space the value is 377 Ω.

Permeability (μ) the quantity which, when multiplied by the magnetic field strength, gives the magnetic flux density. It indicates the degree of magnetisation in a medium when a magnetic field is applied.

Permittivity (ε) the quantity which, when multiplied by the electric field strength, gives the electric flux density. It indicates the degree of electric polarisation in a medium when an electric field is applied.

Power (flux) density (S) the power crossing unit area normal to the direction of wave propagation.

Root mean square (RMS) certain electrical effects are proportional to the square root of the mean value of the square of a periodic function; this is known as the effective value or root mean square value.

Wavelength (λ) the distance between two successive points of a periodic wave in the direction of propagation, in which the oscillation has the same phase.

Documents of the NRPB

Further information on these and other NRPB publications is available on the NRPB website (www.nrpb.org.uk).

VOLUME 1 (1990)

No. 1 Radiological Protection Act 1970

Directions by the Health Ministers under the Radiological Protection Act 1970

Statement by NRPB: limitation of human exposure to radon in homes

Human exposure to radon in homes: recommendations for the practical application of the Board's Statement

No. 2 Gut transfer factors: values proposed by a Nuclear Energy Agency Expert Group for radionuclides ingested by members of the public

Gut transfer factors: values for plutonium and americium in shellfish and best estimates for actinides in food

No. 3 Patient dose reduction in diagnostic radiology (Joint report with the Royal College of Radiologists)

No. 4 Statement by NRPB: principles for the protection of the public and workers in the event of accidental releases of radioactive materials into the environment and other radiological emergencies

Emergency reference levels of dose for early countermeasures to protect the public: recommendations for the practical application of the Board's Statement

Radon affected areas: Cornwall and Devon

VOLUME 2 (1991)

No. 1 Statement by NRPB: principles for the protection of patients and volunteers during clinical magnetic resonance diagnostic procedures

Limits on patient and volunteer exposure during clinical magnetic resonance diagnostic procedures: recommendations for the practical application of the Board's Statement

VOLUME 3 (1992)

No. 1 Electromagnetic fields and the risk of cancer (Report of an Advisory Group on Non-ionising Radiation)

No. 2 Statement by NRPB: approval of consumer goods containing radioactive substances

Criteria of acceptability relating to the approval of consumer goods containing radioactive substances

Radiological protection standards: ionisation chamber smoke detectors; radiological time measurements instruments; tritium light sources; compasses containing gaseous tritium light sources; thoriated gas mantles

No. 3 Statement by NRPB: radiological protection objectives for the land-based disposal of solid radioactive wastes

Radiological protection objectives for the land-based disposal of solid radioactive wastes: recommendations for the practical application of the Board's Statement

No. 4 Protection of the patient in x-ray computed tomography

Radon affected areas: Derbyshire, Northamptonshire and Somerset

VOLUME 4 (1993)

No. 1 Statement by NRPB: 1990 recommendations of ICRP

1990 recommendations of ICRP: recommendations for the practical application of the Board's Statement

No. 2 Occupational exposure: guidance on the 1990 recommendations of ICRP

Public exposure: guidance on the 1990 recommendations of ICRP

Medical exposure: guidance on the 1990 recommendations of ICRP

Values of unit collective dose for use in the 1990s

No. 3 Dose quantities for protection against external radiations: guidance on the 1990 recommendations of ICRP

No. 4 Statement by NRPB: diagnostic medical exposures to ionising radiations during pregnancy

Diagnostic medical exposures: exposure to ionising radiation of pregnant women – biological basis of the Board's Statement

Estimates of late radiation risks to the UK population

No. 5 Statement by NRPB: restrictions on human exposure to static and time varying electromagnetic fields and radiation

Restrictions on human exposure to static and time varying electromagnetic fields and radiation: scientific basis and recommendations for the implementation of the Board's Statement

Electromagnetic fields and the risk of cancer (Summary of the views of the Advisory Group on Non-ionising Radiation on epidemiological studies published since its 1992 report)

No. 6 Radon affected areas: Scotland and Northern Ireland